INTERNATIONAL APPROACHES TO RAPE

Edited by Nicole Westmarland and
Geetanjali Gangoli

D1614970

First published in Great Britain in 2012 by

The Policy Press
University of Bristol
Fourth Floor
Beacon House
Queen's Road
Bristol BS8 1QU
UK
t: +44 (0)117 331 4054
f: +44 (0)117 331 4093
tpp-info@bristol.ac.uk
www.policypress.co.uk

North American office:
The Policy Press
c/o The University of Chicago Press
1427 East 60th Street
Chicago, IL 60637, USA
t: +1 773 702 7700
f: +1 773-702-9756
e:sales@press.uchicago.edu
www.press.uchicago.edu

British Library Cataloguing in Publication Data
A catalogue record for this book is available from the British Library.

Library of Congress Cataloging-in-Publication Data
A catalog record for this book has been requested.

ISBN 978 1 84742 621 5 paperback

Cover design by Qube Design Associates, Bristol.
Front cover: image kindly supplied by iStockphoto.
Printed and bound in Great Britain by
Marston Book Services Ltd, Oxfordshire
The Policy Press uses environmentally responsible print partners.

We dedicate this book to our babies,
all born during the editing of this book:
Aman Frederick Gangoli-Rew,
Rukhmini Lily Gangoli-Rew
and Oscar Milo Westmarland-Morrison.
We hope their generation will be a more peaceful one.

Contents

Notes on contributors

Nadia Aghtaie is an active member of the Violence Against Women Research Group and is currently finishing her PhD at the School for Policy Studies at the University of Bristol, UK. She is conducting comparative research on gender-based violence in Iran and the UK. Prior to this, she conducted empirical research and worked on the Criminal and Civil Codes of Iran in relation to domestic violence and the impact of misinterpretation of Shari'a law on women's lives. She is interested in women's rights globally and in Iran and Afghanistan in particular. She has presented her work at several international conferences. She lectures on childhood studies and social policy at the University of Bristol.

Sandy Brindley is the National Coordinator for Rape Crisis Scotland. She holds an MPhil in women's studies from the University of Glasgow. She has been involved in the Rape Crisis movement in Scotland for the past 15 years, at both a local and a national level. She has been involved in the advisory groups for a number of major legal reviews, including the Scottish Law Commission's review of the law on sexual offences, and the Crown Office's review of the investigation and prosecution of rape and other sexual offences. She was heavily involved in the development of Rape Crisis Scotland's public awareness campaign, This is Not an Invitation to Rape Me.

Michele Burman is Professor of Criminology at the University of Glasgow where she is also Co-Director of the Scottish Centre for Crime and Justice Research and Co-Convener of the International Centre for Gender and Women's Studies. She holds a PhD from the University of Edinburgh on legal constructions of female sexuality in sexual offence trials. She has long-standing research interests in gender-based violence, female offenders, youth crime and youth violence, and gender crime and justice, particularly the criminal justice response to rape and sexual violence.

Patricia Easteal is a socio-legal academic, author and advocate at the University of Canberra, Australia. She received a PhD in legal anthropology from the University of Pittsburgh. She investigates the substance and practice of the law; specifically, how criminal law, family law, discrimination law, employment law and immigration law are affected by cultural context. She has published 14 books and over 120 academic journal articles and chapters with a primary focus on access to justice for women, particularly victims of domestic violence, sexual assault and discrimination.

Geetanjali Gangoli works at the Centre for the Study of Gender and Violence, School for Policy Studies, University of Bristol, UK. She has previously taught at the University of Delhi, and has been a Sir Ratan Tata Visiting Fellow at the London School of Economics and Political Science and a research fellow at the International Centre for the Study of Violence, University of Sunderland. She has published in the areas of domestic violence and young people, prostitution and trafficking, feminisms and law, forced marriage, domestic violence, and perpetrators of domestic violence. She edits the journal *Policy & Politics*, published by The Policy Press.

Lee Lakeman is a collective member at Vancouver Rape Relief and Women's Shelter and is Regional Representative for the Canadian Association of Sexual Assault Centres. As author of *Obsession with Intent: Male Violence Against Women*, she documented front-line anti-rape work, including 100 cases of sexual assault. She has previously chaired Against Male Violence for the National Action Committee on the Status of Women, and the World March of Women, and is author of the alternate report on violence to the Convention for the Elimination of All Forms of Discrimination Against Women. In 2008, with her collective, she hosted Flesh Mapping: Vancouver Markets Pacific Women (an exploration of trafficking and prostitution in Vancouver and its effect on the women of the Pacific Rim) and Policing Violence Against Women (a feminist international gathering to advance civilian oversight of police).

Lynn Hecht Schafran is an attorney based in the US and since 1981 has been Director of the National Judicial Education Program to Promote Equality for Women and Men in the Courts, a project of Legal Momentum in cooperation with the National Association of Women Judges (www.legalmomentum.org/our-work/njep). She designs and presents programmes for national, state and federal judicial colleges and advises the state supreme court task forces on gender bias in the courts that emerged in response to these programmes. She is co-author of a two-day model judicial education curriculum, Understanding Sexual Violence: The Judicial Response to Stranger and Nonstranger Rape and Sexual Assault, used by judges and multidisciplinary audiences across the US, as well as a DVD version and an adaptation for prosecutors.

She is co-author of a web course/resource, Intimate Partner Sexual Abuse: Adjudicating this Hidden Dimension of Domestic Violence Cases (www.njep-ipsacourse.org).

Lisa Vetten has worked in the field of violence against women since 1991 and is currently employed as a senior researcher and policy analyst by the Tshwaranang Legal Advocacy Centre in South Africa. She has also worked in an advisory capacity with a number of government departments around the development of policy and law in this area. On the basis of her research experience, she regularly testifies on behalf of both the prosecution and defence on different aspects of violence against women.

Jillian Weinberger is a writer living in Brooklyn, New York. She has worked at the Russell Sage Foundation, a social science research institute, and the National Judicial Education Program to Promote Equality for Women and Men in the Courts at Legal Momentum. She is currently a contributing writer for the *Ms. Magazine* blog and the online journal *Conducive Chronicle*, among other publications. She holds a BA in American studies from Wesleyan University.

Nicole Westmarland is a lecturer in criminal justice at Durham University, UK. She holds a MA in women's studies and a PhD in social policy and social work from the University of York. She is a feminist academic activist, and is heavily involved in the Rape Crisis movement. Between 2003 and 2009 she was chair of Rape Crisis England and Wales (the national Rape Crisis network). She has been on the board of Tyneside Rape Crisis since 2001. This is her second edited collection with Geetanjali in the International Approaches series.

Qihua Ye is an associate professor at the School of Philosophy, Zhongnan University of Economics and Law, China. She holds a PhD and a Master's from the University of Bristol and the University of Newcastle, respectively. She is a member of the Violence against Women Research Group at the University of Bristol. She is currently researching and teaching gender and violence, and violence against women, as well as social research methods. Her interests include social policy, law, family, gender, violence, psychology, linguistics, physical and mental health, and emotions. She has published more than 10 articles in relation to family, gender and violence in Chinese academic journals.

ONE

Introduction: approaches to rape

Nicole Westmarland and Geetanjali Gangoli

It is a depressing reality that rape still remains internationally prevalent in the 21st century. Despite many advances in gender equality, male violence against women continues at a level described by the World Health Organization as pandemic: internationally, at least one in three women have been beaten or coerced into sex, or have experienced other abuse in her lifetime (www.who.int). Rape, however it is defined, falls under the wider umbrella term of 'sexual violence', which also includes acts such as flashing, sexual harassment, forcing someone to watch pornography, sexual bullying and other forms of non-consensual sexual contact. This book focuses, in the main, on the specific act of rape[1].

The book gives an overview of the socio-legal and political approaches taken in relation to rape across nine countries worldwide. It is written at a time in which many governments have begun to take rape more seriously than in the past and have started to implement wide-ranging reforms. This is therefore an ideal time to describe what that range of reforms has been, and to assess the degree to which they have been successful. In this introductory chapter, we briefly introduce ourselves and the chapters that follow, while pulling out some of the themes that cut across the chapters.

Situated knowledges: our approaches to rape

In our previous book in this series, *International Approaches to Prostitution*, we felt that it was important to reflect on our personal socio-political understandings of prostitution. Clearly, rape does not divide the feminist world to anywhere near the same degree as prostitution does. However, since we often read books and try and work out what perspective the author or authors are 'coming from', we felt it would be beneficial to continue our previous book's use of personal reflection boxes. What follows is a brief overview, written from our individual perspectives, which explains our interest and background as it relates to rape.

Box 1.1: Personal reflection – Nicole Westmarland

When I was a child I remember being interested in animal rights and the anti-vivisection movement. I think I signed up to some campaign that had been advertised in one of those teenage magazines you read before you're a teenager to pretend to be more grown up than you actually are. It wasn't until my teenage years that I began to realise that human beings, particularly women and girls, are also treated badly. It wasn't until later still, at university as a (perhaps only slightly) mature student, that I began to learn about feminism and realised that the bad things that happen to women and girls are not about 'them' and their behaviours or personalities, but are embedded in patriarchal society. Some would perhaps argue that the term 'patriarchy' is now outdated and too broad a concept to use in modern society, but I still use it, since I have not yet found a term that better describes the systematic and structural inequalities faced by women and girls worldwide.

I made my first explorations into feminist anti-rape movements when I was in my mid-twenties. I joined Tyneside Rape Crisis in 2001 as a volunteer on its management committee, and an emerging national group called the Truth About Rape campaign soon after. A few years later, in 2003, the national Rape Crisis Federation (the umbrella membership body for Rape Crisis Centres across England and Wales) got into difficulties and had to close quickly. A small group of women of women from a few individual Rape Crisis Centres, including myself, met in London to decide what should be done. We drew up a plan of action, and I agreed to chair the new group (which we temporarily named the Rape Crisis Coordination Group). This group went from strength to strength, and became what is now Rape Crisis (England and Wales), with a strong board, national paid workers and a dedicated membership. It operates a 'bottom-up', regional model (where regional representatives are elected to sit as the national board members) and has been very successful in a number of ways, including turning around the rapid decline in the number of Rape Crisis Centres in England and Wales.

In the five years I chaired Rape Crisis England and Wales (2004-09), I continued my academic teaching and research, including finishing my PhD in 2005 on rape and human rights. I feel that I have really had the best of both worlds in terms of my education, although I would have to admit that the Rape Crisis work is far more difficult, challenging, frustrating and complicated (not to mention sheer hard work) than my academic work. But it is also the most empowering. I strongly believe that rape and other forms of violence against women are not inevitable parts of life that must be tolerated – I believe that they can and will be ended, and hope that I can continue to play a role in the struggle to move towards a world without rape.

Box 1.2: Personal reflection – Geetanjali Gangoli

Growing up in India, I was very much aware of the different ways in which women and men are treated, and even before I reached adolescence, I became aware of the sexualisation of women's bodies by men. My first memory of being groped on a bus in New Delhi was when I was only ten years old, and I can still remember the shock and, yes, the shame I suffered as a result. I felt too ashamed to tell my mother about it, and it was only later that I realised that sexual assault in the public sphere was seen by most women and girls as a 'normal' experience. I also noted, as I grew up, the ways in which sexual assault and rape were portrayed in the media as sex, and often presented in titillating ways. Instinctively as an adolescent I felt that this was wrong, but found it difficult to articulate why.

As a young university student, I joined a left-wing political party's women's group, and later a more middle-class feminist collective. While I learnt much about women's oppression in the first group, I felt frustrated by what I believed was a lack of feminist politics. By this time, I had read many of the western feminist classics like Simone de Beauvoir's *The Second Sex*, Marilyn French's *The Women's Room* and Susan Brownmiller's *Against my Will*. I found that the left-wing women's group did not prioritise sexual oppression, and saw gender-based violence as subsidiary to class struggle. While I did and still do acknowledge the role of class in perpetuating gender inequality, I also felt (again instinctively) that sexuality or sexual violence were key elements that needed to be unpacked and understood to challenge patriarchy and class oppression.

Within the feminist collective, I felt much more 'at home'. We had discussion groups and consciousness-raising groups on different aspects of women's oppression – work, housework, relationships – and it still strikes me as remarkable that in most of these discussions, our experiences and views of sexual violence permeated the discussions. In the late 1990s, I also worked for a year with a working-class women's group with strong feminist politics in New Delhi, and again the issue of sexual violence seemed to be crucial to women's experiences of oppression. So it seemed to me that irrespective of class, sexual violence was a key issue, although obviously class (and other forms of social identity such as ethnicity, religion and so on) played a pivotal role in mediating these experiences. So working-class women who reported sexual violence to the police were less likely to be believed than middle-class women, although both groups were likely to suffer shame when they experienced sexual violence.

Once I moved to the UK in 1999, I was interested to note that here, too, feminist groups prioritised sexual violence within women's experiences of violence, and that the media was responsible both for sexualising women's bodies and treating rape as titillation. Like Nicole, I believe that none of this is inevitable – anywhere in the world – and we need to fight this. A world without rape and sexual violence may sound idyllic, but we can achieve it.

Structure of the book

The chapters in this book are not sequential and can be read in any order or dipped into as required. As with our prostitution book, we have asked the chapter authors to stick as near as possible to a predefined structure in order to allow readers to find and/or compare sections of interest easily.

The chapters are organised alphabetically by country, starting with Australia and ending with the US. Chapter Two, on Australia, is written by academic Patricia Easteal. She describes a series of government and community programmes, including the Australian Government's National Plan to Reduce Violence against Women (launched in 2009). However, she argues that although reforms have been made, they will continue to be limited in their effectiveness until the reality of rape is better understood. Lee Lakeman, one of the collective members at Vancouver Rape Relief and Women's Shelter, is in an ideal position to assess the current situation in Canada, and she does so in Chapter Three. She describes a number of key cases and reviews, but explains that change has been severely hampered by formal rather than substantial understandings of equality. China is a country that we were particularly keen to include, since little is known about how rape is dealt with there. Qihua Ye, in Chapter Four, explains that although rape is considered to be one of the most serious crimes, both the definition of rape, and the law concerning which acts constitute rape, are unclear. Nicole Westmarland describes the situation in England and Wales in Chapter Five, and critically evaluates the legal and policy reforms introduced under New Labour between 1997 and 2010. She explains that while a range of new laws and policies have been developed, practice and funding have not developed at the same rate.

In Chapter Six, Geetanjali Gangoli explains how rape law in India has been used to control women's sexuality. However, feminist activists have had some success in demanding change, leading to significant amendments in 1980 and a newly proposed sexual assault bill that is currently before parliament. Academic Nadia Aghtaie describes the situation in Iran in Chapter Seven. She explains that rape is classed as adultery with force and duress, in the category of sex outside marriage. Since a conviction needs male witnesses under the law, this means that rape in Iran is particularly difficult to prove. Academic Michele

Burman and Rape Crisis Coordinator Sandy Brindley joined together to describe law and policy in Scotland in Chapter Eight[2]. They explain that Scotland is at the forefront of international opinion in recognising that rape is a form of gender-based violence and embedding policy within this framework. However, Scotland has a very low conviction rate and progressive changes to rape law were made later here than in some other countries. Burman and Brindley conclude that many of the policy changes made have not been consistently adopted into practice, and that new legislation alone is not a sufficient response to rape. In 2007, sexual offences legislation was overhauled in South Africa, a process that is explained by Lisa Vetten, who works in an advocacy centre, in Chapter Nine. Vetten concludes that despite new policies and interventions, there is no joined-up approach, and health and policing responses remain inconsistent and unsympathetic. Chapter Ten focuses on the US, and is authored by attorney and Director of the National Judicial Education Program to Promote Equality for Women and Men in the Courts, Lynn Hecht Schafran, and writer Jillian Weinberger. They point to a range of improvements that have been implemented, but highlight a range of ongoing problems that have undermined the effectiveness of such improvements.

Why these countries?

In our previous book we featured countries from Europe and Asia, a task that proved somewhat difficult due to the geographical and sociological breadth of the two continents. In giving the current book a worldwide focus, the decisions were even more difficult and there are inevitably more omissions than there are inclusions. The factors that we used to guide our decisions when selecting countries were a wide geographical spread and the availability of authors who were not purely academic but had links with wider anti-rape movements, and who could write in the English language. While some of the chapters cover countries that have undergone recent reforms, and have thus been addressed in other literature (such as England and Wales, Australia and South Africa), we were particularly keen to include chapters on countries where little has been written in the English language on the issue of rape (for example, China and Iran).

Admittedly, there are some countries we would have liked to feature but were unable to for various reasons. It is seems particularly regrettable that we were unable to include a chapter on the Democratic Republic of Congo (DRC). An international campaign, called Stop Raping our Greatest Resource: Power to Women and Girls of Democratic

Republic of Congo, (www.stoprapeindrc.org) has been established in the DRC to raise awareness about rape and work towards improving the situation for women and girls. The campaign website reports that five million people have died as a result of the violence in the DRC, the number of women and girls who have been raped since the conflict began runs to hundreds of thousands, and in South Kivu, eastern DRC, an estimated 40 women are raped every day. Nearly 50% of sexual violence survivors are children. Health workers report increases in the incidence and severity of sexual violence in the eastern DRC, with gang rape, sexual slavery, the mutilation of women's genitalia and the killing of rape victims all commonplace (Wakabi, 2008).

Rape and other forms of sexual violence happen to all women, all over the world. No group of women is immune from the acts or fear of sexual violence. However, it must be recognised that women living through war and conflict are particularly vulnerable to extreme forms of sexual violence. While rape may be condoned in many areas of the world, it is often actively promoted in war and conflict zones. It is essential that the international community responds to sexual violence within war and conflict situations and that it does not get overlooked as 'not our problem', 'too difficult to think about' or 'too far away to help with'. Until all women are free, none will be free.

We now move on to look at some of the themes that cut across the countries included in this book.

Honour, shame and stigma

Shame and stigma are major reasons why women are silenced by rape. As argued elsewhere (Chantler and Gangoli, forthcoming), shame is often attributed to particular cultures and communities, primarily South Asian or Muslim cultures. However, there is much research that has found shame to be experienced outside of South Asian and Muslim cultures, for example, among adult survivors of child sexual abuse (Feiring et al, 2002), people living in abusive family environments (Hoglund and Nicholas, 1995) and women who have experienced a range of forms of sexual violence (Kelly, 1988). There is also literature on how certain stigmatised members of society, including prostitutes, can feel a sense of shame due to their occupation (see Pheterson, 1990; Tomura, 2009). Women's bodies in the context of war and conflict are frequently read as repositories of community honour that can be violated by sexual abuse (Sangari and Vaid, 1989), but shame can also be experienced individually by women who have experienced sexual violence (Gangoli et al, 2006). Women's experiences following rape may depend on their position in society. In India, for example, middle-class, married or 'virtuous' and virginal women are more likely to be believed than working-class or minority women, or those who transgress sexual norms. However, to some extent, this is also true of countries such as England and Wales and Scotland, for example for women who have consumed alcohol prior to the rape or who are judged by society to dress 'provocatively'. Hence, shame is much more widespread than is commonly articulated in western contexts. Acknowledging this helps to prevent shame being perceived as a marker only of cultural others.

In India, China and Iran, the concept of shame is associated with any form of sexual activity outside marriage and raped women are often seen as being 'spoilt'. There are variations in this across these countries; for example, in India and China, the spread of globalisation may have weakened sexual stigma in the case of pre-marital sex, especially in middle-class and urban circles, but rape is still seen as stigmatising the woman and frequently her family. In Iran, ideals of virginity, a lack of tolerance for non-marital sex and the existence of the moral police make it difficult for women experiencing rape to speak out.

Globalisation

As noted above, the impact of globalisation in some contexts has contributed to a shift in sexual mores. In India and China, for example, marriages are now delayed, especially in urban centres, and there is more acceptance of sex outside marriage. Globalisation has also led to an increase in the sexualisation and commodification of women's bodies, and the rise of the internet has led to increased access to pornography (Knight, 2006; Gangoli, 2007; Altman, 2008). Certainly, some judgements in India refer to the growing commodification of women's bodies and confusion about gender roles as potential contributors to sexual violence (see Chapter Six). While this is somewhat problematic, as it tends to make excuses for men's sexual violence, there is some connection between globalisation and the increased sexualisation and commodification of women's bodies. For example, China has witnessed an increase in reported rape cases since the adoption of economic reforms in the late 1970s.

Globalisation has also increased wealth disparities between the rich and the poor in countries like India, China and Iran, and this contributes to 'class envy'. As noted above, in these countries women's bodies are seen as repositories of class and community honour, and there have been an increase in the number of sexual attacks on middle-class women by working-class men in India (Anand, 2008) and China. In addition, the increase in wealth and disposable income has also led to women being 'compensated' for rape financially. In Chapter Four, Ye explains how there have been cases where money is used to settle rape claims privately rather than through the legal process.

Impunity for rape

Even in countries with developed sexual offences legislation and strong women's movements, impunity for rape continues. Rape conviction rates remain low in England and Wales in spite of a complete overhaul of sexual offences legislation through the 2003 Sexual Offences Act. Scotland is considered to be a world leader in terms of situating rape law and policy in the context of gender-based violence, yet it also continues to struggle with a low conviction rate and negative societal attitudes towards rape victims. Similarly, in Canada, the strong and active feminist anti-rape movement has not yet been successful in changing the attitude and behaviour of Canadian authorities. As Lakeman points out in Chapter Three: 'Women, the most likely victims of violent crime and the least likely to commit such crime, do not and cannot rely on Canadian authorities to criminalise men who enact sexist violence (p 37)'.

In Iran, it is very difficult to prove rape, since male witnesses are required. Further to this, perpetrators can annul the punishment by denying the act after confession or by repenting prior to testimony. This gives men almost complete impunity in the case of rape.

A marital rape exception within rape law allows men to rape their wives with no fear of legal repercussions. Responses to marital rape can offer an insight into the way in which women's sexuality is judged, and the extent to which they are considered the property of their husbands. In Iran, men have an unqualified right over the bodies of their wives. In India, the rape law offers a criminal law exemption in the case of marital rape, except in the case of a minor, although there are now civil provisions available to redress marital rape for adult victims. It was not until 2005 in the US that marital rape exemptions were eliminated across all state, federal and military laws (Schafran et al, 2008).

Rape myths

Rape myths are defined by Burt (1980) as '... prejudicial, stereotyped, or false beliefs about rape, rape victims, and rapists' (p 217). Despite the passage of time since they were first identified as problematic and researched by people like Burt, rape myths continue to prevail in modern society (see, for example Temkin and Krahê, 2008; Brown et al, 2010). Although slightly different terminology is used in each of the chapters ('community attitudes' in Chapter Two on Australia and 'attitudes to rape' in Chapter Five on England and Wales), the fact that false beliefs continue to surround rape, rape victims and rapists is clearly visible throughout the book. It is apparent that every stage of the criminal justice process can be influenced in some way by rape myths. As Lakeman highlights in Chapter Three: 'Neither democracy nor fair trials are possible in the fog of mythology' (p 36). Many of the authors highlight that while these myths and negative attitudes continue, while large parts of society continue to hold on to prejudicial and conflicting stereotypes about women's sexuality, legal changes alone will continue to have limited impact. This ties in closely with the theme of continued problems in practice despite reforms, and in some places complete overhauls, of law and policy.

Recent reforms on paper but problems with practice

Even where sexual offence law and policy has been subject to major revisions to ensure it is appropriate to the 21st century, problems remain. As this book shows, these problems are particularly apparent in Scotland, Australia, Canada, South Africa, the US, and England and Wales.

Problems with rape and the criminal justice system are often dismissed on the grounds of rape being 'a difficult crime to investigate'. However, there are multiple examples in this book of policies existing but simply not being followed, even though adhering to such policies would almost certainly have led to better outcomes for rape victim survivors. In Chapter Nine, Vetten explains how in South Africa during the run-up to the 2010 World Cup the police failed to record some of the rapes that were reported to them in an attempt to reduce the number of documented rapes and therefore portray South Africa as a safe, welcoming country for tourists. Schafran and Weinberger describe a similar incident in the US, in Pennsylvania, where the police deliberately miscoded thousands of rape reports so they did not have to conduct full investigations on them. Moreover, improvements in police investigation procedures created through scientific advances cannot be properly realised if policies are not implemented. For example, Chapters Nine and Ten both describe problems with the analysis of rape evidence kits in South Africa and the US.

The issue of discretion, where laws and policies can be broad and allow for individual interpretation, is also important when considering how policy is translated into practice. Arbitrary discretion leads to the problem highlighted by Vetten in Chapter Nine – the distinction between formal and informal policy. Likewise, in both the US and in England and Wales, judges continue to enjoy a wide margin of discretion in terms of the admittance of sexual history evidence in court. The situation described in Iran, where 'moral police' continue to patrol the streets, is perhaps the ultimate example of discretion in the policing of women's bodies and sexuality.

In addition to continuing legal reform and the translation of policy into practice, what is urgently needed is a change in public perception of rape victims, a shift in police and other key professionals' attitudes and behaviour when investigating rape cases, and an increase in the number of sustainable support services following rape. This may sound like a depressing place to be, with so far left to go despite the vast amount of work already completed. However, we have little choice – we must continue the hard work and learn from and support each other in order to create a world free from sexual violence. We hope that readers of this book will find inspiration from all that has already been achieved across the world and from the strength of the women who stand up and demand change.

Notes

[1] We are very grateful to Lizzy Kirkham and Becca Lawrence, both postgraduates at Durham University, for their assistance in preparing this book. We also owe thanks to an anonymous peer reviewer whose positive suggestions have undoubtedly strengthened the book.

[2] Sadly, Kate Cavanagh, who was originally approached to contribute to this book, died in 2008. Kate was a highly respected academic and activist in the area of violence against women and is very much missed.

References

Altman, D. (2008) 'Aids and the globalisation of sexuality', *Social Identities*, vol 14, no 2, pp 145-60.

Anand, S. (2008) 'Fair sex, fair game', www.tehelka.com/story_main37.asp?filename=Ne090208fair_game.asp

Brown, J., Horvath, M., Kelly, L. and Westmarland, N. (2010) *Has Anything Changed? Results of a Comparative Study (1977-2010) on Opinions on Rape*, London: Government Equalities Office.

Burt, M.R. (1980) 'Cultural myths and support for rape', *Journal of Personality and Social Psychology*, vol 8, pp 217-30.

Chantler, K. and Gangoli, G. (forthcoming) 'Forced marriage: cultural anomaly or violence against women?', in R. Thiara, M. Schroettle and S. Condon (eds) *Violence against Women and Ethnicity: Commonalities and Differences across Europe: A Reader*, Leverkusen: Barbara Budrich Publishers.

Feiring, C., Deblinger, E., Hoch-Espada, A. and Haworth, T. (2002) 'Romantic relationship aggression and attitudes in high school students: the role of gender, grade, and attachment and emotional styles', *Journal of Youth and Adolescence*, vol 21, no 5, pp 373-85.

Gangoli, G. (2007) *Indian Feminisms. Campaigns against Violence and Multiple Patriarchies*, Aldershot: Ashgate.

Gangoli, G., Razak, A. and McCarry, M. (2006) *Forced Marriages and Domestic Violence Among South Asian Communities in North East England*, Bristol: Northern Rock Foundation and University of Bristol.

Hoglund, C.L. and Nicholas, K.B. (1995) 'Shame, guilt and anger in college students exposed to abusive family environments', *Journal of Family Violence*, vol 10, no 2, pp 141-55.

Kelly, L. (1988) *Surviving Sexual Violence*, Minneapolis, MN: University of Minnesota Press.

Knight, N. (2006) 'Reflecting on the paradox of globalisation: China's search for cultural identity and coherence', *China: An International Journal*, vol 4, no 1, pp 1-31.

Pheterson, G. (1990) 'The category "prostitute" in scientific inquiry', *Journal of Sex Research*, vol 27, no 3, pp 397-407.

Sangari, K. and Vaid, S. (1989) *Recasting Women. Essays in Colonial History*, New Delhi: Oxford University Press.

Schafran, L., Lopez-Boy, S. and Davis, M. (2008) 'Making marital rape a crime: a long road traveled, a long way to go', *Connections*, vol 10, no 1, pp 15-21, www.wcsap.org/advocacy/PDF/CONNECTIONS_IPSV.pdf

Temkin, J. and Krahé, B. (2008) *Sexual Assault and the Justice Gap: A Question of Attitude*, Oxford: Hart Publishing.

Tomura, M. (2009) 'A prostitute's lived experience of stigma', *Journal of Phenomenological Psychology*, vol 40, no 1, pp 51-84.

Wakabi, W. (2008) 'Sexual violence increasing in the Democratic Republic of Congo', *The Lancet*, vol 371, no 9606, pp 15-16.

TWO

Sexual assault law in Australia: contextual challenges and changes

Patricia Easteal

The national context in relation to rape

Australia has a strong feminist movement, which has advocated successfully over the past several decades for Commonwealth and state government funding, programmes and policy concerning prevention, victim support, community education and law changes in the area of rape. Since the mid-1980s, the Commonwealth government has had a policy unit – currently the Office for Women[1]. It is currently housed within the Department of Families, Housing, Community Services and Indigenous Affairs. Relevant rape prevention and community education policies normally originate and are implemented through this office and its state and territory counterparts.

In addition, generally packaged as part of Violence Against Women campaigns or strategies, there have been various task forces over the past 25 years spearheading national and local action plans. Most recently, the federal government's 11-member National Council to Reduce Violence Against Women and their Children began its work in 2008. One of the outcomes from this council was the government's Time for Action: The National Plan to Reduce Violence Against Women, launched in 2009. This plan included more money for prevention activities, perpetrator programmes and a national domestic violence and sexual assault telephone and online 24-hour-a-day, seven-day-a-week crisis service.

There have been some Commonwealth initiatives, though, that focus solely on rape. The Australian Centre for the Study of Sexual Assault (ACSSA) was set up a few years ago 'to improve access to current information on sexual assault in order to assist policymakers and others interested in this area to develop evidence-based strategies that respond to, and ultimately reduce, the incidence of sexual assault'[2].

Each state or territory has the equivalent of the Office for Women; New South Wales (NSW), for instance (www.women.nsw.gov.au), has a Violence Prevention Coordination Unit and oversees state/territory initiatives for women. Each jurisdiction funds its own sexual assault victim services[3]. Further, within each state since 1976, a number of Reclaim the Night Marches are organised each October. This is just one of a number of community education, prevention and victim solidarity activities that take place in Australia.

Given all of these government and community programmes, one might imagine that in Australia there is a promising context for equitable rape laws and just trials for rapists in which victim witnesses would not be re-traumatised. However, as this chapter describes, despite all of the campaigns and resources available for survivors, there does seem to be a resistance to changing attitudes about rape, which affects the criminal justice response.

Australia remains a male-dominated society. Men have a relative lack of responsibility in relation to domestic work and childcare; they tend to identify with the breadwinner role and are more concerned with increasing their incomes and their upward mobility. This pay differential and differences in power between the sexes have a knock-on effect in terms of the gendered division of labour in the home and vertical and horizontal segmentation in paid employment (Easteal, 2010). As women leave paid work for months or years, this in turn perpetuates the salary differential between the sexes. The gendered pay gap and public–private dichotomy perpetuate the devaluation of women and male dominance '... like a steady torrent of patriarchal rain upon the values, roles and structures of the society that in turn impact on the law' (Easteal, 2001, p 12).

It is within such a context that mythology about rape, male sexuality and female sexuality flourish; a continuum emerges with 'authentic rape' or 'real rape' (stranger, injures, physical force, report immediately) at one end and 'not quite legitimate assault' (partner, non-physical coercion, delay in reporting, victim 'provocation') at the other end. Thus, in a survey examining community attitudes about violence against women, Taylor and Mouzos (2006) found that despite some positive changes over the previous decade, negative attitudes and stereotypes towards violence against women persist. In another study, 98 % of participants considered the victim's dress, behaviour, chastity, alcohol consumption and prior acquaintance with the perpetrator as relevant in determining the seriousness of any particular offence (Clark, 2007).

Accordingly, the evidence of victims of rape is assumed to be intrinsically unreliable, and it is a common (mis)perception that '...

women are prone to fabricate allegations of sexual offences out of jealousy, spite, regret, or even "for no reason at all" and that such allegations are "very easy to fabricate but extremely difficult to refute'" (VLRC, 2001, p 155).

There is a gradation of credibility based on the attributes of the victim, with some victims seen as more unreliable than others. Those seen as extra incredible include victims who allege they were sexually assaulted as children (Taylor, 2004), partner rape victims (Easteal and Feerick, 2005; Lievore, 2005; Heenan and Murray, 2006), indigenous women (Department for Women, 1998; Easteal, 2001) and victims with a cognitive impairment (Jordan, 2004).

Judges, jurors and legal practitioners are influenced to varying degrees by these community attitudes (Neame and Heenan, 2003; Easteal and Gani, 2005; Taylor and Mouzos, 2006). For instance, in the context of partner rape, some judicial use of phrases like 'little short of rape' and 'special relationship' to describe a violent marriage significantly minimise the nature and effects of rape in an intimate relationship (Easteal, 1998). Such attitudes can translate into ambivalent implementation of rape legislation. For example, although the immunity of husbands from prosecution and a 'license to rape' have been abolished since 1981, partner rape has particularly low reporting, prosecution, and conviction rates (Lievore, 2003; 2005; Easteal and Feerick, 2005; Easteal and Gani, 2005; Heenan and Murray, 2006).

There are many more examples of the limited efficacy of decades of law reform, which was intended to redress injustices towards the victim/witness. Some of these are discussed in this chapter.

Prevalence

About one third (34 %) of Australian women report that they have experienced rape in their lifetime (Mouzos and Makkai, 2004). Nearly one in five women and 5.5 % of men have experienced sexual violence since the age of 15; 80% of women who have experienced rape know the perpetrator (ABS, 2006). A 2007 Australian study of rape and related offences confirmed this fact, and also found that most offences are perpetrated in residential settings (Borzycki, 2007).

Reporting

Only a small proportion of victims report being raped to the police, and where the perpetrator is a current or former partner, the rate of disclosure is even lower. Research suggests that between one in four

(ABS, 2007) and one in six (VLRC, 2004) of those assaulted make a report to the police. Those who fall at the 'genuine rape' end of that covert but omnipresent rape typology are more likely to report; for instance in Queensland, only 5-10% go to the police when the rapist is a current partner compared with 35% of those assaulted by a stranger (Kift, 2003, p 294). Aboriginal (Atkinson, 2001) and non-English speaking (Easteal, 1999) women may also be particularly less likely to report.

Of the minority who do go to the police, some do not do so immediately. Delayed reporting can lead to the disappearance of evidence and, as described later in this chapter, can be used in trial to discredit the witness.

Most Australian jurisdictions do have specialist police units designed to investigate complaints and provide support for complainants. In the Australian Capital Territory (ACT), for example, the Sexual Assault and Child Abuse Team (SACAT) has medical examination rooms with a connecting bathroom, bedroom and interview room and the Adult Sexual Assault team is made up of eight specialist investigators who are required to complete the Sexual Offences Investigation Program conducted by the Australian Federal Police Training College. Officers are trained to treat complainants sensitively as well as being versed in the procedures designed to build a strong case for SACAT functions by referrals from varying agencies. However, they are not members of the initial response team and so those officers first at the call may not be trained in interviewing rape victims. In addition, as a result of confusion about guidelines, not all police officers refer rape complaints to the prosecution (Office of the Director of Public Prosecutions (ACT) and Australian Federal Police, 2005).

Prosecution

Prosecutors review cases to determine if there are 'reasonable prospects of a conviction' in accordance with the Director of Public Prosecutions' prosecution policy. As cases reflecting the 'real' rape stereotype are most likely to result in a conviction, it is these cases that are most likely to proceed to trial at the prosecutor's discretion (Taylor, 2001a; Cripps and Taylor, 2009).

A lack of forensic evidence may be pivotal in the decision to discontinue. Criminal matters require a high standard of proof beyond reasonable doubt and in the absence of corroborating evidence such as forensics, there is little chance of conviction. A reluctance to prosecute results from a lack of such evidence and no physical injuries (Office of the Director of Public Prosecutions (ACT) and Australian Federal Police, 2005).

There is therefore significant attrition at this point: one study, looking at five jurisdictions, found that 38 % of the rape prosecutions overall were dropped; those more likely to proceed involved 'force *and* the victims actively expressed non-consent' (Lievore, 2005, p 5).

Conviction/acquittal

The conviction rate in rape trials is very low with even lower rates for those assaults not conceptualised as 'real' rape (as described earlier in the chapter) (Heath, 2005), which is further evidence of the attrition rate through the criminal justice system (see Fitzgerald, 2006 for NSW statistics). Acquittals occur more frequently than guilty findings and more often than in other serious offences (Taylor, 2007) – in about one quarter of sexual violence matters in higher and lower courts the defendants were acquitted (ABS, 2007). That proportion is misleadingly low:

> If the defendants who pleaded guilty in the ABS higher courts data are removed from the equation, this means that 58 percent of those who pleaded not guilty in the higher courts where a decision was finalised were acquitted in 2005-06, 57 percent in 2004-05 and 61 percent in 2003-04. (Taylor, 2007, p 2)

Low conviction rates no doubt are an indicator that most rape matters have little or no corroborating evidence with the offences occurring in the private domain. Factors such as the location of the assault, the level of physical injury sustained by the victim, admissions of guilt by the accused, the completion or absence of a medical examination and community attitudes towards sexual violence can influence jury decision making and sexual assault trial outcomes (Heenan, 1997). Offences that do culminate in conviction therefore 'reflect only a portion of offences committed' (Clark, 2007, p 20).

Sentencing

In those sexual offence matters decided in higher criminal courts across Australia, 69% of offenders received custodial sentences, 15% received fully suspended sentences and 15% received non-custodial orders (ABS, 2004, p 78). The mean aggregate sentence time for those charged with an aggravated sexual assault was 92.5 months (around seven-and-a-half years), with the expected time to serve being 59.9 months (around five years). The mean aggregate sentence time for all sexual assault and related offences was 59.2 months (just over four-and-a-half years), with the expected time to serve being 38 months (around three years) (ABS, 2004, p 82). These sentences are relatively low considering that the maximum sentence for rape in Victoria is 25 years' imprisonment (1958 Crimes Act, s 38) and that aggravated sexual assault in NSW carries a maximum penalty of 20 years' imprisonment, with a standard 'non-parole' period of ten years (1900 Crimes Act, s 61J).

In 2003, NSW amended s 21A of the 1999 Crimes (Sentencing Procedure) Act, intended as a restatement of common law sentencing principles (Debus, 2002). Judicial discretion is maintained though with no guidance about what impact actions such as violation of trust, prior consensual sex and negation of consent, the victim's wishes and the offender's problems should have on the eventual sentence. Increased awareness of aggravating factors (at least as expressed by judges in their sentencing remarks) arguably is *not* translating into increased sentences or even custodial sentences (Cripps and Taylor, 2009). In fact, looking at local, district and supreme courts, the most common sentence (52.6%) imposed on conviction of sexual assault not involving a child in NSW in 2004 was non-custodial (Fitzgerald, 2006). Thus, of the minority of sexual assaults that do result in a guilty plea or verdict, the sentencing process appears to be further tainted by rape mythology (Lievore, 2005).

Legal framework: theory and practice

In Australia, the six states and two territories have enacted round after round of law reform over the past few decades; a few of the criminal law and evidence law changes are outlined in the section that follows.

The legal definition of rape has broadened with time to include oral, anal and vaginal penetration with any body part or with an object; the exact wording varies across jurisdictions. In fact, that sort of jurisdictional heterogeneity is one of the key issues in Australian rape law. Another is the huge gap between the black letter law of statutes (the theory) and how they are actually applied (the practice).

Consent

Consent is what distinguishes between consensual sex and sexual assault. It is therefore of paramount consideration in every sexual assault trial. The prosecution must prove two elements: the physical – that the woman did not consent (in relation to which a jury in Victoria should now be directed that the fact that a complainant did not say or do anything does not indicate consent); and the mental – that the accused was aware that the complainant was not consenting, or might not be consenting, did not care about consent or had no reasonable grounds to believe in consent, depending on the jurisdiction. Most defence lawyers rely on arguing that there was consent, as it is a dangerous strategy for defence to argue mistaken belief. Thus, the focus of the trial tends to be on the physical element of consent and judges' directions in consent may be verbose and very complex (Easteal and Feerick, 2005).

There is no longer the requirement in any Australian jurisdiction that there be physical resistance in order to demonstrate a lack of consent (Heath, 2005), with Victoria's provisions on the physical element of consent '... regarded as a best-practice approach' (Heath, 2005). However, it is debateable whether it has made prosecutions more effective.

With the 1991 Victoria reforms described by McSherry (1998), judges were required to direct the jury that 'the fact that a person did not say or do anything to indicate free agreement to a sexual act is *normally* enough to show that the act took place without that person's free agreement' (1958 Crimes Act (Vic) s 37(a)), and, under s 37(1)(b), if relevant to the specific facts of the matter, 'that a person is not to be regarded as having freely agreed to a sexual act just because she did not protest or physically resist or sustain physical injury' (these sections were substituted in 2007 by s 37AAA and 37AA as discussed later).

A study of the 1991 changes identified six trials out of 27 in which there was a failure to direct juries that 'saying and doing nothing' ought not to be construed as an indication of consent in circumstances where this direction may have been relevant (Heenan and McKelvie, 1998, p 298). More recent research found too that some judges were not advising jurors about the factors that could vitiate or negate consent and/or were adding commentary to their directions, which was sometimes not in synch with the aims of the sections (VLRC, 2004). An example would be a judge advocating blanket consent or implied consent by advising jurors that consent can be given at a time prior to the act.

The Victorian Law Reform Commission report (VLRC, 2004) not surprisingly recommended further amendments such as deleting the word 'normally' from s 37(1)(a). Accordingly, in 2007, the 1958 Crimes Act (VIC) was amended to further define consent. This round of changes resulted in additional jury directions under sections 37AAA and 37AA. Consequently, Victoria legislation does lead Australia on the physical element issue; however, it falls down in relation to having an objective mental element for rape. It has retained the Morgan (1976 AC 182) approach – requiring proof of a subjective fault element in all cases except where the accused has failed to turn their mind to the question of consent. Consistent with this, jurors are directed to take reasonableness into account to determine whether the accused was aware that the complainant was not consenting or might not have been consenting. NSW, on the other hand, has added an 'objective fault test'. If the prosecution proves there was no consent (physical element), all it has to prove under s 61HA(3)(c) of the 1900 Crimes Act is that the defendant had no reasonable grounds for a belief in consent.

In many of the other code states, rape is an offence of strict liability. All the prosecution has to prove is sexual intercourse without consent. It is then left to the defence to argue that the accused made an honest and reasonable mistake as to consent; reasonableness in this context would require that the accused had turned his mind to the issue, usually by taking steps to ascertain consent, and had some basis for his belief.

Corroboration and delay in reporting

Until about 30 years ago, judges in Australia had to warn juries not to convict on the uncorroborated evidence of complainants who were regarded as especially unreliable as a class of witness. Women (and children) testifying about sexual assault were, and still are, regarded by (some) judges as belonging to that category. One justification for judges needing to warn jurors about rape victims' credibility has been if there is delay in reporting.

A real mixed bag of laws across jurisdictions abolished any requirement to warn about the dangers of convicting an accused of a sexual offence on the uncorroborated testimony of the victim. Then two High Court cases diluted the effectiveness of these reforms. First, in *Longman v R* (1989) 168 CLR 79, the High Court unanimously reversed a conviction on the basis that the trial judge had failed to warn that it was unsafe to convict on the uncorroborated testimony of the complainant. A year earlier, legislation (1906 Evidence Act (WA) s 36BE(1), replaced by s 50 in 1988) had been enacted stating that the judge 'shall not give a warning unless *satisfied that such a warning is justified in all the circumstances*' [emphasis added]. Since Longman, judges generally give a 'Longman warning' in order to avoid appeals (Grey, 2007). Thus, Kathy Mack (1998, p 65) concludes that judges have continued to exercise their discretion to comment on the evidence because of 'social and judicial attitudes, which accept and endorse the myths which were used to justify the older practices of denigrating the credibility of those who testify about sexual assault'.

Second, the majority in the High Court case of *Crofts v R* (1996) 139 ALR 455 held too that the reforms were intended only to abolish the rules, which presumed that women *as a class of witness* were untrustworthy; that they were not intended to create a presumption of reliability for all women who allege rape. Trial judges in individual cases could continue to warn the jury that 'in fairness to the accused' complainants who do not report their sexual abuse at the first 'reasonable' opportunity lack credibility as witnesses, the effect of which is to impugn the credibility of alleged victims of rape (Bronitt, 1998). Indeed, this strategy of discrediting witnesses does continue to be used by defence lawyers despite some jurisdictions having mandatory directions that highlight to the jury that there may be 'good reasons' for delay in making a complaint of sexual assault; for instance in Western Australia under the 1906 Evidence Act, s 36BD.

Since 2006 with s 294(2)(c) of the 1986 Criminal Procedure Act, judges in NSW '(a) must warn the jury that absence of complaint or delay in complaining does not necessarily indicate that the allegation that the offence was committed is false, and (b) must inform the jury that there may be good reasons why a victim of a sexual assault may hesitate in making, or may refrain from making, a complaint about the assault'. Section 294(2)(c) states that judges must not warn the jury that delay in complaining is relevant to the victim's credibility unless there is sufficient evidence to justify such a warning (Donnelly, 2009). 'Sufficient evidence', however, remains open to judicial interpretation.

Analysis of court proceedings in Victoria, showed that the impact of mandatory directions in s 61(1) of the 1958 Crimes Act could be neutralised too by general comments about the significance of prompt as opposed to delayed complaints (Heenan and McKelvie, 1997, pp 70-1). Note, too, that s 61(1)(b) was amended to delete the word 'necessarily' and includes that there may be good reasons why a victim of a sexual assault may delay or hesitate in making a complaint. However, in research of 24 cases taking place after that deletion, judges gave the former warning using the word 'necessarily' in 12 of 14 cases that involved a delay (VLRC, 2004, p 362).

Directions about delayed reporting can also be neutralised by contradicting each other:

> On the one hand, juries are told that there may be good reason for the delay and delay does not necessarily mean that the allegation is false. On the other hand, juries are also told

that they can take the delay into account when determining whether to believe the complainant. The two directions together can be nonsensical. (Boniface, 2005, p 268)

Sexual reputation and history

A 'rape shield' was placed on the admission of evidence relating to 'sexual reputation' in all jurisdictions except the Northern Territory [Sexual Offences (Evidence and Procedure) Act 1983 (NT) s 4(1)] where the trial judge retains discretion to admit such evidence. Every jurisdiction in Australia limits the admissibility of evidence of sexual history or sexual experience, requiring court permission based on stated criteria.

However, this 'rape shield' has been pierced in various ways (Henning and Bronitt 1998: 93). For instance, traditionally in cross examination, the defence has not been limited to questioning the complainant on issues arising from evidence she provided in examination in chief. Instead, under the common law, the only principal limit on the evidence which the defence may adduce has been its relevance. This enabled extensive interrogation into many contentious issues including any previous consensual sex between the victim and the defendant, and between the victim and others. Such questioning is used to imply that there was actually consent or that, because there had been consensual sex in the past, the defendant had the mistaken belief that the woman was consenting.

Not unexpectedly then, evaluation in several Australian jurisdictions shows that such questions are still being admitted, often without reference to relevant legislation (Heath 2005: 13). This results in extensive opportunities for the defence to adduce sexual experience evidence, contrary to the aims of the legislation (Henning and Bronitt 1998: 76,84).

Protection against intrusive questioning has also been limited, since certain evidence about sexual history is admissible with the court's permission. In the ACT for example, the 1991 Evidence (Miscellaneous Provisions) Act allows evidence of sexual activities of the complainant deemed to have 'substantial relevance to the facts in issue' or 'be a proper matter for cross-examination about credit' (s 51, 53). 'Substantial relevance' can be interpreted through social myths about 'real' rape, female sexuality, male sexuality and intimate relationships.

A High Court case may act to further weaken the shield. In a 5-0 ruling, the court in *Bull v The Queen* (2000) held that the trial judge should have allowed the jury to hear evidence of a phone call between the woman and one of the men accused of raping her a couple of hours later, which the defence said showed that, contrary to the evidence of the complainant, there were clear sexual overtones in the invitation extended by her.

Key issues

Policing problems

Poor police practice in rape cases can leave complainants feeling re-victimised. Most of the women interviewed by Easteal and McOrmond-Plummer (2006) who turned to the police did not feel wholly supported. Similarly, the VLRC report (2004) found through its focus group research with several Centres Against Sexual Assault and Victorian police members that there was still room to improve police attitudes and understanding about sexual assault.

Insensitivity may be evidenced by police minimising what has occurred through their choice of words in questions they ask. For example, in an interview with one woman whose ex-boyfriend was charged with 'unlawfully confining a person', 'sexual intercourse without consent' and 'intentional threat to kill', the officer asked, 'How did he come to rape you?'. After she responded that he had forced her legs open, the officer asked, 'How long did he lay on top of you in that position making love to you, fucking you, whatever words you want to use ... raping you?' (Easteal and Feerick, 2005, p 190). Easteal and Feerick (2005) found that such treatment by the police could have an effect on victims' decision about whether to continue legal proceedings.

Another common complaint about police is their lack of relaying information and keeping the complainant informed of progress with the investigation. This includes the lack or inadequacy of explanations given for why charges are not laid (Easteal and McOrmond-Plummer, 2006; NSW Violence Against Women Specialist Unit, 2006).

Prosecution problems

As noted earlier, stereotypes and myths are also acted out in the prosecution process, specifically in decisions to discontinue. Moreover, if there are any differences between what the victim says to police in different interviews and/or at committal, the prosecutor may pre-empt the defence raising these discrepancies at trial by labelling the victim as unreliable and dropping the case. Indeed, prosecutors assess a complainant's credibility, paying attention to consistency and evaluating victims' conformity to 'typical' psychological and emotional reactions to rape (Office of the Director of Public Prosecutions (ACT) and Australian Federal Police).

The complainant may ask for the matter to be discontinued because the prosecution has dissuaded her (sometimes subtly and sometimes directly) that there is little hope of a guilty verdict or because her cross-examination at the committal hearing was prohibitively traumatic (Easteal and Feerick, 2005). Thus not surprisingly, there is some evidence that victims show more willingness to pursue prosecution in the presence of evidentiary factors that increase the prospects of conviction (Kerstetter, 1990) and that criminal justice officials sometimes manipulate victims' choices in line with their assessments of the prospects of conviction (Kerstetter and van Winkle, 1990).

Problems at trial

Those who use the criminal justice system continue to find it traumatising, humiliating and distressing (Taylor, 2004;VLRC, 2004). One of the key issues is that of time. In the Real Rape, Real Pain partner rape survivor sample, one woman waited 18 months for the trial; it was cancelled twice. She ended up feeling frustrated, weary and powerless (Easteal and McOrmond-Plummer, 2006).

A further problem is that the complainant does not have a lawyer or anyone advocating for her in the courtroom. Victim witnesses can become upset in court when facts that they consider to be relevant are not raised. For example, not all judges deem evidence of domestic violence as relevant in partner rape trials (see *R v An* (2000), for instance), and the victim can do nothing (Easteal and Feerick, 2005).

As mentioned earlier, the victim's credibility is often attacked through cross-examination and jury warnings (Lievore, 2003). Barristers may cross-examine certain types of victim (for example, incest survivors, victims of partner rape) in ways designed to destroy their credibility (Taylor, 2007). They may be asked questions to which they can only answer 'Yes' or 'No' but are impossible to answer in that way. The questions may be asked in a non-chronological way, the objective being to confuse and make the victim appear unreliable. Complainants are cross-examined about lying and making false reports and about their motives in reporting sexual assault. In the *Heroines of Fortitude* report (Department for Women (NSW), 1996, p 169), over half the victims (53.7%) were asked whether they had a motive for false reporting. A median of victims were asked five questions on this issue, while 84.3% were asked an average of seven questions focused on lying. The partner/

complainants in the Heenan (2004) study were likely to be asked about previous consensual sex.

Aside from cross-examination issues, as a consequence of law reform followed by pivotal case law such as Longman and Crofts, rape trials generally involve 'a multitude of directions' as enunciated by Wood CJ in the 2002 NSW case of *R v BWT* (2002) (Boniface, 2005, pp 263-4). These many directions may serve as the source of appeals; 55.5 % of conviction appeals were argued about alleged defects in a trial judge's warnings and directions in sexual assault trials (Boniface, 2005, p 263). As Justice McHugh pointed out in *KRM v The Queen* in 2001: '[T]he more directions and warnings juries are given the more likely it is that they will forget or misinterpret some directions or warnings'.

Indeed, a recent study found that the judge's summing-up of evidence was less helpful in sexual assault hearings than in other trials. Jurors in trials with adult/child sexual offences were 1.4 times more likely than jurors in trials dealing with non-sexual offences to report that this judicial discourse did not help them 'at all' in reaching a verdict or only helped 'a little bit' (Trimboli, 2008). In fact, 'a direction instructing jurors that a particular use of evidence is forbidden is likely to fail to the extent that it conflicts with the jury's common sense reasoning' (Boniface, 2005, p 267).

Problems with sentencing

As a consequence of issues canvassed in cross-examination, some judges are apt to take a negative view of the victim's supposed character or sexual history (Taylor, 2001a, 2001b). It is also possible that given myths about 'real' rape, the nature of the tie between victim and offender affects judicial weighting. Analysis of Victorian sexual assault cases (Kennedy et al, 2009) confirms previous studies suggesting that breach of trust is commonly viewed as an aggravating variable in sentencing offenders within parenting-type relationships but not when sentencing partner perpetrators (Warner, 1998; Heenan, 2004; Easteal and Gani, 2005; Krahé et al, 2006; Stewart and Frieberg, 2008). Sentences in those cases remained lower though than where the offender was unknown to the victim and where the rape included physical violence. Mitigating variables, although similar for all categories of defendants, may be given more weight where the defendant is related to the victim (Warner, 2005), which neutralises the consideration of breach of trust (Kennedy et al, 2009), and where the perpetrator and victim are indigenous (Taylor et al, 2009).

Other normative variables form part of judicial heuristics. Easteal and Gani (2005) identify some partner rape cases with histories of domestic violence in which judges looked at offenders' emotional upset at a relationship break-up as a mitigating variable at sentencing. Warner (1998) also discusses other cases of sexual assault by a partner where the offender's emotional state was raised in mitigation. Further, some sentencing judges and appellate courts recognise abusive contexts in which pleas for leniency for a partner defendant by a victim need to be understood. Ironically, given that understanding, other judges seem to be particularly concerned about imprisonment jeopardising the family unit, despite antecedents of violence. Taylor's (2004) work revealed that some judges reject victim impact statements (in part or in whole) and question victim claims of harm, even when such claims are supported by therapeutic evidence

Analysis of sexual offence cases involving indigenous children demonstrates how cultural stereotypes might influence legal reasoning and decision making too (Cripps and Taylor, 2009; Taylor et al, 2009). A Queensland case involving a 10-year-old Aboriginal child is an apposite example of a judge holding the victim culpable for her own rape (a mitigating factor in lessening the offence's seriousness). Similarly, in a Northern Territory trial, the judge declared that the indigenous child in question knew what was 'expected' of her, in terms of submission to an older man under contentious claims of traditional marriage.

The case for more legislative, policy and cultural change

Australian rape laws are based on an 'open-plan' model. This indeterminacy needs to be removed as much as possible to limit judges and jurors from interpreting 'grey' areas through the filtering of false mythology. Accordingly, the VLRC (2004) proposed that judicial instructions be clear and concise, always address delay in prosecution appropriately and eliminate the harshest forms of the warning that state that it may be unsafe or dangerous to convict on uncorroborated evidence. These legal and practice changes would be more directive and allow for less judicial discretion. Further, there is a need in Australia for more consistency between jurisdictions.

The 2009 addition of Section 41 to the Evidence Act (Cth) (NSW) (ACT) (VIC) reduces judicial discretion through legislation, classifying sexual offence witnesses as vulnerable and mandating judges to intervene. Prior to the 2009 addition, courts merely had the discretion to disallow improper questions and the exercise of that discretion was found to be 'patchy and inconsistent' and 'seldom invoked by judges' (ALRC, 2005, 5.96-5.106). How mandatory is mandatory though? Under s 41, unless the judge or prosecutor perceives the question to be improper, the issue of mandated intervention is moot. Despite the legislation providing guidance as to the definition of an improper question – for example, forbidding questions that are 'unduly humiliating', 'put in a manner or tone that is belittling, insulting' or based on 'stereotype' alone (s 41(1)(b)(c) and (d)) – it is the perception of the judge, prosecutor and to a lesser extent the defence lawyer that will be determinative. Their perceptions are informed by a long history of training in adversarial trial dispute resolution and may remain steeped in rape mythology. In other words, their perceptions will often not be the same as those of the complainant who is facing cross-examination.

Even if law reform as described did tighten the loopholes effectively, which is debatable, it is not enough. Culture change has been identified as a necessary accompaniment to any legislative reform (VLRC, 2004). As Kift (2003, p 293) concludes:

> Research … has shown that reform of substantive and procedural law has not necessarily translated into real change for victims and, in many instances, has been subverted by a legal culture that tends to discredit and disbelieve women and children who allege sexual abuse.

There are a number of ways in which this necessary change in culture can be effectuated, including as an offshoot of law reform. For instance, NSW s 275A, the forerunner to s 41, aimed to set a 'new standard for the cross-examination of witnesses in criminal proceedings' thus focusing on the courtroom conduct and culture of barristers and leading to culture change.

Indeed, court processes need to better meet the victims' need for protection from being re-traumatised. This can be legislated as illustrated by the following examples. Note the jurisdictional variation though, which means that if a person is a victim of sexual assault there are some states or territories where their witnessing experience may be relatively easier than in others.

The 2008 Sexual and Violent Offences Legislation Amendment Act (which commenced on 1 June 2009) in Australia's capital aims to achieve this goal in a number of ways. It was 'designed to extract the 'best' evidence possible from witnesses who may otherwise suffer a disadvantage' (Revised Explanatory Statement, 2008).

The Act amended the committal hearing process by allowing a transcript or written statement of an audio or visual recording between police and a witness to be admissible as evidence for a sexual assault victim. It introduced a pre-trial hearing for children and intellectually impaired victims, as well as other sexual assault victims who are likely to 'suffer severe emotional trauma; or be intimidated or distressed'. This latter grey area – that is, deeming some complainants to be particularly vulnerable – may prove to be yet more fertile ground in which myths can flourish.

The Act also includes restrictions on the victim's view of the accused if giving evidence in the courtroom or when giving evidence via closed circuit television (CCTV). Screens or other arrangements are to be made available. Other jurisdictions, such as South Australia (1929 Evidence Act, s 13A) also offer special arrangements for taking evidence including CCTV or a screen, as does Victoria (1958 Evidence Act, s 37B, 37CAA) and the Northern Territory if deemed 'a vulnerable witness' (Evidence Act, s 21A).

In some jurisdictions such as the ACT, South Australia, Victoria, and Queensland, a self-represented accused is no longer permitted to personally cross-examine a witness in a sexual or violent offence proceeding if that witness is a complainant, a similar act witness, a child witness for the prosecution, or a witness for the prosecution who has a mental or physical disability that affects their ability to give evidence. In Western Australia (1906 Evidence Act, s 25A(1)(a)), the self-represented accused can cross-examine, but the judge can order this to be done with the accused in one room and the complainant in another.

Under the new legislation in the ACT, sexual assault complainants are entitled to have a person of their choice with them for emotional support while giving evidence. The 2001 Evidence (Children and Special Witnesses) Act (Tasmania) (s 4.4 (1)) enables children to have a support person when giving evidence. The Northern Territory Evidence Act names children as vulnerable (s 21D) but no support person is mentioned; however, in relation to other categories of vulnerable witnesses (s 21B – sexual abuse or serious violent offences) under s 21A(2)(c), a friend or relative can provide support to the vulnerable witness. This is also the case in South Australia if the witness is considered to be vulnerable.

Towards a better understanding of rape

In addition to tightening laws and amending courtroom process, judges and jurors do need to be better equipped to understand the reality of rape. This can be achieved in a number of ways, such as further training of court personnel. Targeted training may work the best. One way of such targeting could be via specialist court lists. The Criminal Justice Sexual Offences Taskforce (2006) reviewed the requirements of a specialist court for NSW and concluded that a case management system should be implemented that involved specialist judges and prosecutors. The Victoria Law Reform Commission (VLRC, 2004) similarly recommends a specialist list. Perhaps, with appropriate education, provisions like s 41 could make a difference, as this does give judges who wish to use it a mandate to control proceedings more closely, particularly in a specialist jurisdiction.

Aside from training for specialist judges, cultural attitudes need to be changed to minimise the chance of selecting jurors who adhere to false myths. A fairly recent study (VicHealth, 2006) found that 40% of Australians sampled believed rape resulted from men's inability to control their need for sex, while some continue 'to believe men are uncontrollable sexual beasts and women are liars and temptresses'. Smaller proportions in 2006 believed that 'women who are raped often ask for it' (6% compared with 15% in 1995) but 15% still believe 'women often say no to sex when they mean yes', about the same proportion as in 1995. So although there has been some improvement – no doubt due in part to government community education programmes – there remains a need for more outreach and education programming. This has been dramatically illustrated by the frequency of public iteration of myths concerning 2009 revelations about high-profile rugby players and non-consensual group sex.

In April 2009, the then Australian Prime Minister announced funding for another public information campaign targeted at men and boys to highlight the attitudes and behaviours that play a role in violence against women, stating that '… our national resolve must be zero tolerance. Zero tolerance when it comes to violence against women and violence against children' (Rudd, 2009).

The commitment is there. However, it is vital that any education campaign or further legal reform is underpinned with the victims' reality and not with a silencing of their voices or with misperception about certain issues, which only perpetuates rape mythology.

Notes

[1] See www.fahcsia.gov.au/sa/women/overview/Pages/default.aspx

[2] See www.aifs.gov.au/acssa clearinghouse database to learn more about the training, research and other programming currently available in Australia.

³ For a list, see www.livingwell.org.au/Counsellingandsupport/Australiawide
sexualassaultservices.aspx

Further reading

Easteal, P. (1998) *Balancing the Scales: Rape, Law Reform and Australian Culture*, Sydney: Federation Press.

Heath, M. (2010) 'Criminal law: rape', in P. Easteal (ed) *Women and the Law in Australia*, Sydney: LexisNexis.

Taylor, C. (2004) *Court Licensed Abuse*, New York, NY: Peter Lang.

Atkinson, J. (2001) 'Violence against Aboriginal women: reconstitution of community law – the way forward', *Indigenous Law Bulletin,* vol 5, no 11, www.austlii.edu.au/au/journals/ILB/2001/62.html

ABS (Australian Bureau of Statistics) (2004) *Sexual Assault in Australia: A Statistical Overview*, ABS Cat No 4523.0, www.ausstats.abs.gov.au/Ausstats/subscriber.nsf/0/C41F8B2864D42333CA256F070079CBD4/$File/45230_2004.pdf

ABS (2006) *Personal Safety Survey*, ABS Cat No 4906.0, www.abs.gov.au/AUSSTATS/abs@.nsf/DetailsPage/4906.02005 (Reissue)?OpenDocument, www.ausstats.abs.gov.au/ausstats/subscriber.nsf/0/056A404DAA576AE6CA2571D00080E985/$File/49060_2005%20(reissue).pdf

ABS (2007) *Criminal Courts Australia 2005-06*, ABS Cat No 4513.0, Canberra: ABS, www.ausstats.abs.gov.au/ausstats/subscriber.nsf/0/BE01F559C5AE0804CA2572AB001F0271/$File/45130)2005-06.pdf

ALRC Report 102, NSWLRC Report 112, VLRC (2005) *Final Report Uniform Evidence Law*, www.austlii.edu.au/au/other/alrc/publications/reports/102/10.html#Heading126

Boniface, D. (2005) 'The common sense of jurors vs the wisdom of the law', *UNSW Law Journal*, vol 28, no 1, p 261.

Borzycki, M. (2007) 'Pilot study on sexual assault and related offences in the ACT: stage 3', *AIC: Research and Public Policy Series*, no 79, pp viii–ix.

Bronitt, S. (1998) 'The rules of recent complaint: rape myths and the legal construction of the "reasonable" rape victim', in P. Easteal (ed) *Balancing the Scales: Rape, Law Reform and Australian Culture*, Sydney: Federation Press.

Clark, H. (2007) *Judging Rape: Public Attitudes and Sentencing*, ACSSA Newsletter, www.aifs.gov.au/acssa/pubs/newsletter/n14pdf/n14_5.pdf

Criminal Justice Sexual Offences Taskforce (2006) 'Responding to sexual assault: the way forward', NSW Attorney General's Department, www.lawlink.nsw.gov.au/lawlink/clrd/ll_clrd.nsf/pages/CLRD.pdf

Cripps, K. and Taylor, C. (2009) 'White man's law, traditional law, bullshit law: customary marriage revisited', *Journal of Colonialism and Law*, vol 10, pp 59-72.

The Honourable RJ Debus (2002) Attorney General, Second Reading Speech, Crimes (Sentencing Procedure) Amendment (Standard Minimum Sentencing) Act 2002, *NSW Parliamentary Debates* (Hansard), Legislative Assembly 23 Oct 2002, 5815.

Department for Women (NSW) (1996) *Heroines of Fortitude: The Experiences of Women in Court as Victims of Sexual Assault*, Canberra: Pirie Printers.

Donnelly, H. (2009) 'Delay and the credibility of complainants in sexual assault proceedings', Judicial Commission of NSW www.judcom.nsw.gov.au/publications/benchbks/sexual_assault/donnelly-delay_and_credibility_of_complainants.html

Easteal, P. (1998) 'Rape in marriage: has the license lapsed?', in P. Easteal (ed) *Balancing the Scales: Rape, Law Reform and Australian Culture*, Sydney: Federation Press.

Easteal, P. (1999) 'Reaching out to survivors in the ACT: culturally or linguistically diverse, disabled, and older', *Women Against Violence: An Australian Feminist Journal*, vol 6, pp 56-9.

Easteal, P. (2001) *Less Than Equal: Women and the Australian Legal System*, Chatswood: Butterworths.

Easteal, P. (2010) 'Setting the stage: the "iceberg" jigsaw puzzle', in P. Easteal (ed) *Women and the Law in Australia*, Sydney: LexisNexis.

Easteal, P. and Feerick, C. (2005) 'Sexual assault by male partners: is the license still valid?', *Flinders Journal of Law Reform*, vol 8, no 2, pp 185-207.

Easteal, P. and Gani, M. (2005) 'Sexual assault by male partners: a study of sentencing factors', *Southern Cross University Law Review*, vol 9, pp 39-72.

Eastel, P. and McOrmond-Plummer, L. (2006) *Real Rape, Real Pain*, Melbourne: Hybrid Publishers.

Fitzgerald, J. (2006) 'The attrition of sexual offences from the New South Wales criminal justice system', *Crime and Justice Bulletin*, no 92, pp 1-12, www.lawlink.nsw.gov.au/lawlink/bocsar/ll_bocsar.nsf/vwFiles/cjb92.pdf/$file/cjb92.pdf

Grey, A. (2007) 'Not-so-uniform evidence law: reforming Longman warnings' *Current Issues in Justice Administration*, vol 19, no 2, pp 172-82.

Heath, M. (2005) *The Law and Sexual Offences against Adults in Australia* (ACSSA Issues, No 4) Melbourne: Australian Centre for the Study of Sexual Assault, www.aifs.gov.au/acssa/pubs/issue/i4.html

Heenan, M. (1997) 'Sex crimes and the criminal justice system', *Australian Feminist Law Journal*, vol 9, pp 90-5.

Heenan, M. (2004) 'Just "keeping the peace": a reluctance to respond to male partner sexual violence', *Australian Centre for the Study of Sexual Assault*, vol 1, www.lawlink.nsw..gov.au/lawlink/bocsar/11_bocsar.nsf/vwFiles/CJB92.pdf/$file/CJB92.pdf

Heenan, M. and McKelvie, H. (1997) *Evaluation of the Crimes (Rape) Act 1991*, Attorney General's Legislation and Policy Branch, Sydney: Department of Justice.

Heenan, M. and McKelvie, H. (1998) *Rape Law Reform Evaluation Project, Report No 2: The Crimes (Rape) Act 1991: An Evaluation Project*, Melbourne: Department of Justice.

Heenan, M. and Murray, S. (2006) *A Study of Reported Rapes in Victoria 2000-2003*, www.police.vic.gov.au/retrievemedia.asp?Media_ID=19462

Henning, T. and Bronitt, S. (1998) 'Rape victims on trial: regulating the use and abuse of sexual history evidence', in P. Easteal (ed) *Balancing the Scales: Rape, Law Reform and Australian Culture*, Sydney: Federation Press.

Jordon, J. (2004) *The Word of a Woman: Police, Rape and Belief*, Basingstoke: Palgrave Macmillan.

Kennedy, J., Easteal P., and Taylor, C. (2009) *Rape Mythology and the Criminal Justice System: A Pilot Study of Sexual Assault Sentencing in Victoria*, Melbourne: ACSSA Aware.

Kerstetter, W. (1990) 'Gateway to justice: police and prosecutorial response to sexual assaults against women', *Criminology*, vol 81, no 2, pp 267-313.

Kerstetter, W. and van Winkle, B. (1990) 'Who decides? A study of the victim's decision to prosecute in rape cases', *Criminal Justice and Behaviour*, vol 17, no 3, pp 268-83.

Kift, S. (2003). 'A legal process or a justice system? Sex offences in Queensland: still seeking justice', *Alternative Law Journal*, vol 28, no 6, pp 292-310.

Krahé, B., Temkin, J. and Bieneck, S. (2006) 'Schema-driven information processing in judgements about rape', *Applied Cognitive Psychology*, vol 21, no 5, pp 601-19.

Lievore, D. (2003) *Intimate Partner Sexual Assault: The Impact of Competing Demands on Victims' Decisions to Seek Criminal Justice Solutions*, Canberra: Australian Institute of Criminology, www.aic.gov.au/conferences/other/lievore_denise/2003-02-AIFS.html

Lievore, D. (2005) 'Prosecutorial decisions in adult sexual assault cases', *Trends & Issues in Crime and Criminal Justice*, no 291, pp 1-6, www.aic.gov.au/publications/tandi2/tandi291t.html

Mack, K. (1998) '"You should scrutinise her evidence with great care": corroboration of women's testimony about sexual assault', in P. Easteal (ed) *Balancing the Scales: Rape, Law Reform and Australian Culture*, Sydney: Federation Press.

McSherry, B. (1998) 'Constructing lack of consent', in P. Easteal (ed) *Balancing the Scales: Rape, Law Reform and Australian Culture*, Sydney: Federation Press.

Mouzos, J. and Makkai, T. (2004) *Women's Experiences of Male Violence: Findings from the Australian Component of the International Violence Against Women Survey, IVAWS*, Research and Public Policy Series No 56, Canberra: Australian Institute of Criminology.

Neame, A. and Heenan, M. (2003) *What Lies Behind the Hidden Figure of Sexual Assault?*, AIFS Briefing 1, Melbourne: Australian Institute of Family Studies, www.aifs.gov.au/acssa/pubs/briefing/acssa_briefing1.pdf

NSW Violence Against Women Specialist Unit (2006) 'Improving service and criminal justice responses to victims of sexual assault', Sydney: Department of Community Services.

Office of the Director of Public Prosecutions (ACT) and Australian Federal Police (2005) *Responding to Sexual Assault: The Challenge of Change (Sexual Assault Response Program Report)*, Canberra: Director of Public Prosecutions, www.dpp.act.gov.au/pdf/DPP%20SARP%20report%20(11Feb05).pdf

Revised Explanatory Statement, Sexual and Violent Offences Legislation Amendment Bill 2008 (ACT) 2, www.legislation.act.gov.au/b/db_32859/RelatedMaterials/explanatory_statements.asp

Rudd, K. (2009) Address to the National Council to Reduce Violence Against Women and Children, www.pm.gov.au/media/Speech/2009/speech_0959.cfm

Stewart, F. and Freiberg, A. (2008) *Provocation in Sentencing*, Melbourne: Sentencing Advisory Council.

Taylor, C. (2001a) 'The legal construction of victim/survivors in parent-child intrafamilial sexual abuse trials in the Victorian County Court of Australia in 1995', *Women Against Violence*, vol 10, pp 57-9.

Taylor, C. (2001b) 'A name by any other word does not necessarily make it merely another rose', in Mills, A. and Smith, J. (eds) *Utter Silence: Voicing the Unspeakable*, London: Peter Lang.

Taylor, C. (2004) *Court Licensed Abuse*, New York, NY: Peter Lang.

Taylor, N. (2007) 'Juror attitudes and biases in sexual assault cases', *Trends & Issues in Crime and Criminal Justice*, no 344, pp 1-6, www.aic.gov. au/publications/tandi2/tandi344t.html

Taylor, N. and Mouzos, J. (2006) *Community Attitudes to Violence Against Women Survey: A Full Technical Report*, Canberra: Australian Institute of Criminology, www.aic.gov.au/publications/reports/2006-11-violenceAgainstWomen.pdf

Taylor, S.C., Cripps, K. and Davies, M. (2009) 'A necessary rebuke: the Arakun case', *Indigenous Law Journal*, vol 10, pp 59-72.

Trimboli, L. (2008) 'Juror understanding of judicial instructions in criminal trials', *Crime and Justice Bulletin No. 119,* New South Wales: New South Wales Bureau of Crime Statistics and Research.

VicHealth (2006) *Two Steps Forward, One Step Back: Community Attitudes to Violence Against Women: Progress and Challenges in Creating Safe and Healthy Environments for Victorian Women*, Victoria: VicHealth, www.vichealth.vic.gov.au/~/media/ResourceCentre/PublicationsandResources/Letter/VicHealth_Letter_28.ashx

VLRC (Victorian Law Reform Commission) (2001) *Sexual Offences: Law and Procedure*, Discussion Paper (8.135), Victoria: VLRC, www.lawreform.vic.gov.au/wps/wcm/connect/Law+Reform/Home/Completed+Projects/Sexual+Offences/LAWREFORM+-+Sexual+Offences+-+Discussion+Paper

VLRC (2004) *The Sexual Offences: Final Report*, Victoria: VLRC, www.lawreform.vic.gov.au/wps/wcm/connect/Law+Reform/Home/Completed+Projects/Sexual+Offences/LAWREFORM+-+Sexual+Offences+-+Final+Report

Warner, K. (1998) 'Sentencing for rape', in P. Easteal (ed) *Balancing the Scales: Rape, Law Reform and Australian Culture*, Sydney: Federation Press.

Warner, K. (2005) 'Sexual offending: victim, gender and sentencing dilemmas', in D. Chappell and P. Wilson (eds) *Issues in Australian Crime and Criminal Justice*, Chatswood: LexisNexis Butterworths, p 243.

THREE

Ending rape: the responsibility of the Canadian state

Lee Lakeman

The Canadian context: 'Our home on native land'

Hillary Angel Wilson and Cherisse Houle: both were Aboriginal women and both were murdered and dumped outside Winnipeg, Manitoba in 2008. It was rumoured that the young Winnipeg women endured rape by a group of men in return for food and crack cocaine. These separate incidents of racialised sexual violence connect many others in Canada. Sensational cases in British Columbia convicted sexual predators Robert Pickton, Donald Michel Bakker, Andrew William Evans, Judge David Ramsey and Bishop Hubert O'Conner. In September 2009, the Manitoba Attorney General announced a provincial task force to examine the 75 unsolved cases of missing and murdered Aboriginal women. While this sounds like a positive development, in fact it is another police-controlled local task force that is likely neither to engage those women who demanded the change, nor question the Canadian federal government on its unattended responsibility to prevent or at least effectively police and prosecute violence against women.

In the wake of the attacks described above, debates raged about the relative impact of incest in grooming girls for sexist abuse, including prostitution; of Aboriginal women's poverty pressing women into unsafe, unwise relationships and situations; of men's claim to sex on demand and sex for money; of colonialist and sexist practices and attitudes within state institutions from which women seek help; of the unrelenting rates of sexual violence by men of all 'races' against women, in particular against Aboriginal women. Male violence against Aboriginal women has the attention and sympathy of the public, if not media and policy makers. In 2010, this organises and mediates public response to rape in Canada.

For all women and girls, sexist violence remains both a cause and a consequence of unequal social, economic, civil and political power in relation to men. The 1995 Federal Action Plan for Gender Equality following the Beijing United Nations Conference emphasised the interconnections between equality and gender, as well as other personal characteristics, conceding that all must be addressed to correct the systemic nature of inequality. Despite this long-standing official recognition, the Canadian legal/political responses to violence against women are built on patriarchal underpinnings and continue to be implicated in the continuing oppression of women and particular groups of women. Feminists demanded a full public inquiry:

> Poverty and economic dependence, combined with racism and indifference from legal authorities, make Aboriginal women and girls easy prey for violent men, and endemic violence is difficult for them to escape. The Native Women's Association of Canada has now documented 520 cases of missing and murdered women; more than half of those women and girls have been murdered or gone missing since 2000. (Feminist Alliance for International Action, 2010, p 1)

When it comes to addressing inequities Canada must account for a continuing colonial history but also for its rejection of the post-war achievements of social and economic programmes that provide for women members. The loss of social programmes wears heavily on women exercising freedom, especially those trying to avoid, recover from or escape violence (Young et al, 2007).

A clear picture of violence against women in Canada is ellusive. Sexist myths persist:

> Myths help men individually and as a class to rationalize their sexual abuses or to distinguish their own 'natural' sexual aggression or ordinary sexual opportunism from the really culpable and injurious kind practised by those aberrant, truly violent, genuinely scary men the criminal law is meant to isolate and jail. (McIntyre et al, 2000, p 74)

Neither democracy nor fair trials are possible in the fog of mythology. Claire L'Heureux-Dube, former Justice of the Supreme Court of Canada, listed examples of myths and stereotypes recognised by the Supreme Court of Canada that have warped the law's treatment of sexual assault claimants:

- The rapist is always a stranger.
- Women are less reliable and credible as witnesses if they have had prior sexual relations.
- Women will always struggle to defend their honour.
- Women are more likely to have consented to sexual advances if they have had sexual relations in the past.
- Women are 'more emotional' than men, so unless they become hysterical nothing can have happened.
- Women mean 'yes' even if they say 'no'.
- Women deserve to be raped on account of their conduct, dress and demeanour.
- Women fantasise about rape and therefore fabricate reports of sexual activity even though nothing has happened. (L'Heureux-Dube, 2001)

Women, the most likely victims of violent crime and the least likely to commit such crime, do not and cannot rely on Canadian authorities to criminalise men who enact sexist violence. Sexual assault is the most under-reported violent crime in the Canadian General Social Survey on Victimization. Some studies estimate that 78% of sexual assault crimes are never reported to police (Kong et al, 2003). Non-government feminist organisations, including the Canadian Association of Sexual Assault Centres (CASAC), note even lower police reporting rates in their published national research (Lakeman, 2005). Despite efforts to improve justice system responses to sexual assault, the low reporting rate is only declining; only 8% of sexual assaults were reported to police in 2004, a significant drop compared with previous years (Gannon and Mihorean, 2004).

The women's movement has created access to free, 24-hour 'aftercare' programmes in most urban communities. Such services assist individual women in reporting assaults or in accessing medical or psycho-social aid. Many are still women-controlled, autonomous centres of information and advocacy, embodying the desired future in non-hierarchical structures, democratic decision making, inclusive membership policies and affirmative action strategies, all focused on advances for women. Vancouver Rape Relief and Women's Shelter and Toronto Multi-Cultural Women against Rape, both established in 1973, connect individual responses to rape and campaign for particular reforms and more systemic social change (Rebick, 2005).

The Canadian Criminal Code lists no specific offence of rape, wife assault or violence against women (this is discussed in more detail below). But in the 1990s, under the guidance of researchers like Holly Johnson, Statistics Canada began to chart the prevalence of sexual assault among women. It bypassed inadequate police sources and interviewed women directly about their experiences of violence. The methodology of the national Violence against Women Survey (VAWS) of 1993 incorporated a broad range of questions on sexual harassment, sexual assault and intimate partner violence.

> The most detailed information on sexual assault is available from the 1993 national VAWS. At that time, 39% of Canadian adult women reported having had at least one experience of sexual assault since the age of 16. The definition of sexual assault in this survey included violent sexual attacks and unwanted sexual touching, both of which are consistent with Criminal Code definitions of sexual assault. (Johnson, 2006, p 24)

According to Statistics Canada's crime victimisation survey, which interviews women anonymously, an estimated 460,000 Canadian women were victims of sexual assault in 2004 and just 8% reported the crime to the police (Gannon and Mihorean, 2004). According to Johnson (2006, 2011), victimisation surveys suggest that less than 10% of sexual assaults are reported to the police. Police data significantly underestimates incidences of sexual assault. This underestimation is confirmed by the number of women who call on member centres of CASAC. At least one in four women in Canada experience criminal predatory sexual behaviour during their lifetimes. Most rape and criminal sexual assault goes unreported to authorities and those that are reported rarely result in arrests, let alone criminal convictions.

Canada has a 40-year herstory of public policy review and policy initiatives claiming to address the prevalence and nature of violence against women. CASAC piloted research with the Winnipeg Rape Incidence Survey Project (Brickman et al, 1980), and with *99 Federal Steps Toward an End to Violence Against Women* (Lakeman, 1990), which united the broader women's movement in the National Action Committee on the Status of Women behind the anti-violence wing. In 2003, with *Canada's Promises to Keep: The Charter and Violence Against Women* (Lakeman, 2004), CASAC again researched and recommended policy in an effort to confront rapists, ease and document the experience of women, theorise the relationships between violence and women's oppression and unite efforts to lobby the federal government for comprehensive reform.

CASAC centres report that women are raped most often by men in their homes and families, including by fathers, husbands and brothers

---

and by men in positions of public trust such as teachers, coaches or caregivers to the disabled. Other men often reported to CASAC are dates, casual acquaintances and co-workers – those with easy access and some familiarity. Men reported to CASAC centres also target those women forced or daring to occupy more public space: young women out of the home or at university; women in the streets or in parking lots at night, for example shift-working nurses or factory workers; women in bars and restaurants or public parks; and those drawing attention as public figures. CASAC claims that the tangle of laws, policies and procedures of the Canadian state surrounding such violations does too little to interfere with acts of sexual and sexist violence, ignoring and compounding the depressed legal economic and social status of women in relation to men.

According to CASAC Rape Crisis centres, it is now more common than in previous decades for police to attend incidents when called and conduct investigations. Nevertheless, most criminal cases are still lost at the first level of police response. The immunity from criminal prosecution enjoyed by men committing rape and sexual assault within marriage was removed during the 1980s law reforms that challenged the view that the marriage contract implied consent. Despite this and the addition of the criminal harassment or anti-stalking law, most physical and sexual criminal assaults on wives and ex-wives reported to transition houses, Rape Crisis centres and police go unprosecuted. Furthermore, front-line CASAC workers and centres have uncovered incidents of police using polygraphs and threats to lay criminal mischief charges against victims in unproven or unprovable complaints of rape and sexual assault. Women are often discouraged from complaining by such threats (Lakeman, 2005).

Jane Doe was the unnamed fifth rape victim of a Toronto sexual predator dubbed 'the Balcony Rapist'. In 1987, she launched an 11-year legal battle against the Toronto police, complaining that they used her 'as bait' in their investigation and failed to protect her. She maintains that the arrest and prosecution of the rapist resulted from feminist organising and not from police actions. She won the case, first establishing the legal right for citizens to sue the police (Doe, 2003). Law professor Elizabeth Sheehy gathered together front-line activists from the Ottawa Sexual Support Centre, the Montreal Rape Crisis Centre (*le mouvement contre the viol and l'incest*) and Vancouver Rape Relief and Women's Shelter, researcher Holly Johnson and academics and survivors including Jane Doe for a conference at the University of Ottawa Law School. In considering the decade since that Jane Doe case victory, participants at the Sexual Assault Law, Practice and Activism in a Post-Jane Doe Era conference, on 6 March 2009, had little positive to say about changes in police and court responses to rape in Canada.

Among other developments, the promotion of forensic evidence kits and advances in the use of DNA evidence had meshed with the social confusion generated by TV detective shows. Together they had created the illusion that DNA evidence is key to a good legal case. Most cases of rape do not hang on or solve the problem of identity of the attacker; he is usually known. Rather, they hang on the question of consent. DNA cannot prove nor disprove consent. Nevertheless, authorities presume that cases that do not involve DNA have a lesser chance of conviction. When they are instructed by their political masters to cut costs and to proceed only with 'a likely chance of conviction', these cases are less desirable to prosecute.

The increase in the age of sexual consent in Canada along with increased police attention to internet child pornography have only minimally reduced the immunity of offending men, particularly since these measures have little impact on incestuous rape. Many are concerned about two current legal cases in favour of total decriminalisation of the sex trade, as this has the potential to lead to the legalisation of paid rape (Benedet and Hoogstraten, 2008). There is little accurate media coverage of the issues, the public debates, the nature of consent, the veracity of women complaining, the relationship between rape and prostitution, and the responsibility of the state to interfere with and condemn violence against women. The commercial media demonisation of the few rapists caught and convicted has a detrimental effect on the perception of 'everyday rape' and sexual assault cases as reported to feminist centres and help centres. Sexual assaults by men in the family, coaches, teachers, priests and other men known to women, especially those rapes conducted with coercion, stealth or abuse of trust rather than with life-threatening brutality, fade from public concern – or as Whoopi Goldberg claimed of the Roman Polanski rape of an adolescent girl, 'not rape-rape'. In that same commercial media, the hyper-sexualisation of girls is largely still unrestrained by law or policy.

The legislative framework: good bones?

In Canada the law covering rape before 1981 refused to recognize rape in marriage, let men off if they 'honestly believed' they had consented to intercourse and allowed defence attorneys to question a victim on her sexual history, in a widespread belief that women who were sexually active were probably 'asking for it'. (Rebick, 2005, p 70)

Rape is the responsibility of the men who commit it. But those in power collude by rendering women vulnerable to attack, by failing to protect women from men and by inadequately responding to the injustices committed against women, both individually and collectively.

Canada is a signatory to the United Nations Universal Declaration of Human Rights, the United Nations Convention on the Elimination of All Forms of Discrimination against Women, (CEDAW), including the optional protocol – the 1993 Declaration on the Elimination of Violence Against Women, the Palermo Protocol (signed in 2000 by Canada) – and the 1995 Beijing Platform for Action. In addition, feminists won a 'rights' framework for women in the Charter of Rights and Freedoms in the repatriated constitution of 1982. Canadian jurists and politicians are obliged to 'read together' domestic and international law and policy, making the best of both available to women in Canada.

A substantive approach to equality consistent with international language and concepts requires the government to take necessary action to assure equal outcomes. Government-planned de-gendering or mainstreaming of law is now understood as a formal equality approach. In a restrictive interpretation of the new Charter of Rights and Freedoms, the government proposed to treat men and women exactly the same regardless of pre-existing inequality. The 'mainstreaming' of women's issues continues to have a detrimental effect on the women it is intended to protect.

In 1983, parliament repealed the Criminal Code category of rape and created three new categories to the offence of assault to signify sexual violence as a serious personal injury causing significant but various harm to the victim. Level I sexual assault (s 246.1) is a hybrid offence with a possible punishment of up to six months in jail or a $2,000 fine, and up to 10 years in jail if the Crown proceeds by indictment; level II sexual assault with a weapon includes threats to a third party and bodily harm, punishable by up to 14 years in prison; and level III aggravated sexual assault (s 246.3) is punishable by up to life in prison. There is little evidence to support women's hopes for greater criminal justice response to rape with these reforms. In fact, there is evidence that the police have adapted by increasingly classifying reported sexual assaults as level I assaults.

The corroboration requirement (physical evidence or third-party testimony) and the doctrine of recent complaint were formally removed and limits were placed on the ability of defence lawyers to ask questions about the sexual history of the complainant, which became referred to as the 'rape shield provision'. The legislation was later amended in 1987 to allow for only the restricted production and disclosure of the complainant's private records (such as medical or school records) to the accused at the discretion of the judge, to protect the right of the accused to a full defence to the charge of sexual assault. These amendments to the Criminal Code were met with staunch opposition from the Canadian Bar Association as well as civil liberties associations, which argued that judicial restriction on the accused's access to the complainant's private records and the prevention of the use of evidence regarding the complainant's sexual history were a violation of the accused constitutional right to a full answer and defence. In 1991, in *R v Seaboyer and Gayme*, the Supreme Court of Canada ruled the rape shield provision to be unconstitutional.

That Supreme Court ruling coincided with the appointment of the first female Justice Minister, Kim Campbell of the Conservative Party, and her debut at a 1991 national conference on Women, Law and the Administration of Justice. This consultation, along with a deluge of mail from the public, supported feminist lobbying for a new rape shield law. In 1992, CASAC played a key role in gathering feminists together to support the drafting of Bill C-49, a comprehensive amendment to the rape shield provision that moved towards fair trials by limiting the defence of mistaken consent by requiring the accused to substantiate his claim of belief in consent. The amendment specified the conditions under which no consent can be obtained, such as intoxication or diminished capacity of the complainant, or the perpetrator being in a position of trust and authority. The new law sought to refocus criminal trials so as to move away from discrediting the conduct of complainants and towards questioning the behaviour of the accused. It challenged the presumption of women's agreement to sex, and demanded that men seek and obtain agreement.

Defence lawyers continued to challenge the constitutionality of Bill C-49, often circumventing s 276 (restriction of sexual history evidence) using s 278 (provision and disclosure of confidential records) especially in cases involving vulnerable complainants (such as adolescent girls, racialised girls and women, those with histories of mental illness or those who had sought the services of a Rape Crisis centre or counsellor), and in cases of historical sexual assault.

In *R v O'Connor* (1999), the Supreme Court of Canada ruled in a case of historical sexual assaults at a residential school by a Catholic bishop. The bishop was principal of the school, and was accused of sexual assault against young Aboriginal women who had been his students and employees. The complainants' records and privileged communications such as school employment, medical and therapeutic records were demanded by the defence and were to be disclosed. The charges against the accused bishop were stayed, as the Crown could not produce the records for the defence. (Many documents were lost or destroyed, left blowing in the wind in buildings abandoned with the assimilation policy of residential schools in the decades since the young women's confinement there.)

In consultations led by CASAC involving a broad list of equality-seeking groups, the Canadian government passed Bill C-46 in May 1997 to constrain the use of disclosure requests. Feminists sought total protection of women's private records, but were only assured closer scrutiny of communication documents sought by the defence for the purposes of discrediting the complainant.

The complainants, with interventions by Aboriginal women and other feminists, forced the bishop, Hubert O'Connor, back into court and held him legally responsible, but were undermined again when O'Connor was diverted from any further prosecution and from incarceration to a community 'sentencing circle'. Aboriginal women and feminists protested on the lawn of the British Columbia provincial legislature.

Access (for the defence bar and the defendants) to complainant women's private records, including diaries, and medical, employment and counselling records, has been limited by law. This has helped to reduce the practice of the defence bar to use such records to 'whack the complainant' in cross-examination in court and to reduce threats to complainants of media exposure of such private information, which could scare women away in advance of planned court appearances as witnesses and complainants. However, the amendment to limit access was constitutionally challenged as vitiating the accused's right to a full defence (*R v Mills*, 1999), but the Supreme Court of Canada upheld s 278 (restricted provision of third-party records) and ruled that restricted access to private records was not unconstitutional but did require judges to test the necessity of the records against the interests of justice for the accused and the complainant's right to privacy.

In 1999, a judge lashed out at feminists in his lower court in *R v Ewanchuk*. His ruling held that the perpetrator was entitled to the defence of implied consent – although no such defence existed in law – because of the young complainant's dress and conduct during a job interview. In its decision, the Supreme Court of Canada overturned the lower court's acquittal of the accused, threw out the defence of implied consent and expressed a feminist analysis of sexual violence as a matter of equality, as it is an offence against human dignity and a violation of human rights:

> The question of implied consent should not have arisen. This error does not arise from the findings of fact but from mythical assumptions. Complainants should be able to rely on a system free of such myths and stereotypes, and a judiciary whose impartiality is not compromised by these biased assumptions. It denies women's sexual autonomy and implies that women are in a state of constant consent to sexual activity. (L'Heureux-Dube and Gonthier, in *R v Ewanchuk*, para 7)

However, in 2006, the federal government removed 'equality' from the criteria for any non-government work being funded through the Status of Women Ministry. This was a final step in dismantling the machinery of state intended to monitor and advance the equality of citizenship of women in Canada. In 1960s and 1970s, the Canadian government had established mechanisms for advancing women's interests: a Status of Women Ministry with funds to disperse to non-governmental women's groups, a research arm, an arm's length Canadian Advisory Committee on the Status of Women and an internal policy division to press for equality in all government initiatives, including the budget. All have been cut. Women are not equally represented in any parliament of Canada, or on the Supreme Court, or in any mechanism of governance. Women in Canada have not achieved equal pay or equal wealth and still do more than their share of caring for the sick, the young and the old.

In December 2009, women gathered at the University of Quebec at Montreal to mark the 20th anniversary of the most widespread public expression of Canadian women's uprising against women's inequality and violence against women. It was their hope to revitalise the movement by reconsidering its herstory. In 1989, Marc Lepine entered the école polytechnique, the engineering school where he had been refused a student place, with a gun in his hand. Separating the women from the men, and carrying a note declaring his hatred of feminists, he killed 13 students and one worker – all female – and then himself. Women took to the streets to assert their analysis, grief and outrage, not only at Lepine, but also at the mainstream media and government officials who in many cases refused to recognise the political motivation and significance of the event. In general, only the women involved in the uprising saw the Montreal Massacre, as it became known, as indicative of a world in need of change and sexist violence as preventing that change.

In almost every town and city across Canada, thousands of women took to the squares and the streets, and talked to the cameras to articulate their view of the continuum of Lepine's murderous misogyny and the pervasive culture created by men's assaults, rapes and murders. Virtually every college-aged girl had been educated either by direct contact with the feminist anti-violence wing of the movement or by its spin-offs. They were the success of the 'conscientisation' or consciousness-raising efforts of the anti-rape activists of the 1970s and 1980s. Women in the streets cited, as their own, statistics and arguments linking femicide by Lepine to rape and women's inequality in Canada. Those efforts compelled politicians to respond (Lakeman, 1992). On feminists' insistence, parliament designated 6 December an annual day of memorial. Canadian parliamentary hearings of the Justice Committee resulted in both an all-party report called *The War on Women* and the appointment of a Canadian Panel on Violence against Women that documented women's experiences.

Key issues

Canada is signatory to the United Nations Declaration on the Elimination of Violence Against Women, agreeing that all forms of inequality compound women's vulnerability to sexist violence and that violence compounds women's inequality. In this light, it is significant that Canada did not sign the Declaration the Rights of Indigenous Peoples until 2010, and in 2009 that the United Nations found that the Canadian government had failed to comply with its human rights commitments under CEDAW. The United Nations identified two areas in which human rights violations against women were so pressing that they required immediate action:

- persistent failure to provide adequate social assistance to women and girls living in poverty;
- endemic violence against Aboriginal women and girls.

The CEDAW Committee asked the government to report back on the actions it had taken in these two areas by November 2009. In February, women's groups in British Columbia issued a response to government inaction (www.rapereliefshelter.bc.ca), aptly titled *Nothing to Report*.

Limits on the human rights approach are evident in government inaction but also in the decisions of the Supreme Court of Canada in the last decade. When adjudicating between women's equality rights claimed under the Charter of Rights and Freedoms and government policies, the Supreme Court unnecessarily deferred to government (especially in cases where claims required significant government expenditure) (www.womenscourt.org; McIntyre and Rodgers, 2006; Young et al, 2007; Cohen and Pulkingham, 2009). The Court Challenges Program of Canada (particularly the Equality Panel) did encourage equality-seeking claimants to participate in and initiate court cases challenging federal policy on compliance with equality rights, but funding for this has been withdrawn. A commitment to promoting human rights for women would require massive change. Policy may have shifted but so have mechanisms, including cost-sharing agreements between the provinces and the federal government, the national control of delivery of services in health and welfare, and the structures of law enforcement and administrations (Lakeman, 2005).

The current Conservative-dominated federal government has promoted an ideological 'law and order' approach to both law reform and budgets to address violence against women (tougher sentences, minimum sentences, more funding for police, security and prisons). Matched with financial cuts to all social support services. Simultaneously, it has continued to Balkanise the administration of justice (prosecutorial policy, court house practices and police practices without equality protections). Cuts to provincial budgets, the lack of government responsibility for justice administration and the absence of national leadership on sexist violence have had a particularly detrimental impact on policing, national equality standards and national assistance for women's groups. Regional variations in the number and nature of cases classified as unfounded by the police, as well as reports of police scaring women away from complaining – for example, by threatening to use polygraph tests or bring mischief charges for 'false reports' (Lakeman, 2005) – all point to procedural problems and a need for an equality seeking model and more joined-up federal–provincial approach. Federal criminal justice policy to accommodate budget cuts has diverted cases out of courts and prisons and into provincial 'harm reduction' or 'restorative justice' programmes, with no attached increase of funding to the provinces and no assurances of any positive or even neutral outcome for women. Women's groups have mounted resistance, for instance in Nova Scotia they have campaigned against the policy, resulting in a ban on the application of restorative justice diversions in cases of violence against women in that province.

A substantive approach to women's civil economic social and political rights requires not only expenditure and equality monitoring machinery, but also an active, respectful relationship between the state and the equality-seeking women's movement. CASAC hosted annual consultations over six years with three consecutive justice ministers of two different parties, and despite these being attended by dozens of feminist advocates from across the country, such public consultations are no longer held, defeated by the rhetoric that women, particularly feminists, are a special interest group with no rightful claim to government intervention.

In the 1970s, direct action resulted in the establishment of women-run, women-centred Rape Crisis centres across the country. Feminists not only tended to the women who called the centres but also mobilised hundreds, if not thousands, of young women through training and public education sessions and further direct action measures such as Take Back the Night marches and other anti-violence activities. Such activity continues to aid women's cause.

Early funding for Rape Crisis centres, once awarded from government, was monitored through national equality-seeking mechanisms charged with advancing women. However, with Balkanisation, provincial or local funding tools have begun to replace them with 'victim assistance' models of intervention, answerable to local police, or provincial criminal justice or health ministries rather than equality mechanisms. In British Columbia, the network now consists of 92 police- and 61 community-based victim assistance programmes but no Rape Crisis centre receives operating funds. Many victim centres operate as extensions of the state, under the direction of police, the crown prosecutors' offices, hospitals or mega charities. They are pressed to 'coordinate' at local and national levels with the very arms of the state they were constituted to criticise. These centres, modelled on professional practices in medicine or criminology, and tightly 'coordinated' by state institutions, exhibit no overarching commitment to sex equality and little or no capacity for independent activist research or for women-centred critiques of mainstream institutional responses. Some lack any gender analysis, much less a sex equality practice.

The remaining independent women's anti-rape centres are increasingly expected to stand in for or replace welfare programmes and social services cut from government; that is, to respond to all types of women's needs from mental health support to addiction services and public housing, with inadequate and shrinking resources. Nevertheless, these centres remain the predominant source of information about the social political phenomenon of rape and a main source of advocacy and public education on behalf of individuals and groups of women raped. Front-line research in Rape Crisis centres in the 1970s documented, in the language of the day, that men attack 'within their own class, race and down'. In 2010, few would deny that race and class compound women's vulnerability and men's culpability. Still, government policy fails to ameliorate, much less stop, a continuous herstory of sexually violent attacks including rape against Aboriginal women in colonial fortresses, residential schools, group homes and foster care. These attacks were usually perpetrated by 'settlers' at the edges of reserves, now by male truckers and travellers on the highways between settlements ill served by public transit, and by male curb-crawlers seeking to pay for rape in urban ghettos.

The connection between race/class and sexually violent attacks on women and between lack of government intervention and sexually violent attacks is evident in several recent sensational incidents in Vancouver. Examples include the attacks of the so-called Green River Killer, who prowled the Pacific coast for hitchhikers and street prostitutes, and the murderer and rapist pig farmer Robert Pickton, who targeted addicted women from the poorest urban ghetto population, where Aboriginal women were over-represented and often prostituted. He may well have delivered them as party favours to Hell's Angels motorcycle gang members who frequented his place. He, like so many serial attackers, including Toronto's Paul Bernardo, was first reported to police for violence towards an ex-girlfriend whom police disbelieved. Donald Bakker was caught sexually torturing an aboriginal woman in the area park. He claimed as a defence in court that he had negotiated permission and a price for his violence with her and other women. He was caught with videos of as many as 30 other tortured women, as well as images of himself abusing children of both sexes as young as five in Asia (Lakeman, 2005).

It was stunning to witness the sense of male entitlement held by young, handsome university student Andrew Evans in 2007, explaining to a jury that he bought access to a young Aboriginal woman named Nicole Parisien in an apartment brothel listed on Craigslist, on his way home from an evening during which he had been sexually rejected. He had done this many times before, 'whenever he was lonely and horny'. With no prior plan for violence (beyond what the prosecutor called the 'ordinary business deal of prostitution'), Evans testified in court that he became enraged when *she* failed to maintain his erection and, fuelled by his sense of male entitlement, he dealt her an explosive blow with his shoe and strangled her. The only debate was which abuse killed her.

While patriarchy seeks to minimise the significance of such events, it is impossible to ignore the similarities between these cases, which all involve elements of men's sense of entitlement, racism, women's poverty, sex tourism and the rape of both children and women. Prostitution joins the list of violent acts against women, from wife assault to incest.

All require improved law enforcement to intervene in rape. Focused education and the politicising of community responses to the realities rather than the myths of rape would expose the role that violence against women plays in subjugating all women. But now, commercial media has digitalised and moved prostitution to the internet, evaded regulation (in part by globalising) and limited access to feminist perspectives by concentrating ownership of media technologies, the means of production, and outlets.

Canada is desperately in need of a communications strategy and measures to intervene in the propaganda war against women, from pornography and attacks on human rights mechanisms to the communalisation of social programmes. Neoliberalism has encouraged a perniciously ignorant cultural force that operates against women under the guise of individual agency. Faced with what is presented as unlimited freedom of choice, it becomes the woman's fault if she picks the wrong place to live, the wrong clothes or the wrong man. Women are frequently told they could have chosen something else and are thereby blamed for any sexist violence they suffer.

Those involved in the lobby for legislative change in the late 1970s and early 1980s hoped to fight some of those myths by reframing rape as a crime of violence rather than one of sex, and hoped that by shielding women from humiliating cross-examination at trial, sexual assault reporting rates would increase (McIntyre et al, 2000). But reporting rates did not significantly improve. Reporting rates have remained close to those seen in the early 1970s: according to data collected by CASAC centres, 70% of women choose not to report to police.

The numbers of unfounded reports persist. The 1999 audit of sexual assault investigation, conducted in Toronto in the aftermath of the Jane Doe case, found that a significant number of sexual assaults reported to the Toronto police service had been classified as unfounded, even though the file did not contain enough information to support such a finding. The audit also found that sexual assault reports were being classified as unfounded in cases where it was clear that a sexual assault had occurred (Auditor General of Toronto, 2004). In 2003, the Canadian Centre for Justice Statistics published an overview of its studies on sexual offences in Canada. One in six sexual offences (16%) reported to the police in 2002 was classified as unfounded. The rate at which reports were unfounded varied by type of offence. Sixteen percent of aggravated sexual assaults and 11% of other sexual assaults were unfounded. The rate at which reports of all sexual assaults were unfounded remained relatively stable between 1991 and 2002, but the rate at which reports of other sexual offences were classified as unfounded rose from 8% in 1991 to 15% in 2002. The rate at which reports of other violent crimes were unfounded remained at around 7% during the same period (Kong et al, 2003).

CASAC documented the same problem with a justice department researcher (Hattem, 2007). Women are confronted with an enormous amount of pressure in cross-examinations and are expected to meet very high standards when testifying about their rape (Gotell, 2007), as well as having to endure cross-examination by men that they have accused of rape.

Analysis of interventions

Twenty years ago, Dobash and Dobash compared the elements of feminist success against violence against women within the US and England (Dobash and Dobash, 1992). They examined criminal law and enforcement as well as the framework in which that law was embedded. Canadian feminists resisting systemic patriarchal violence thought they had the best of both systems: the provisioning welfare state with common law traditions and the mechanisms of constitutionally imbedded rights. Canadian women commonly use the political and legal as well as colloquial language of 'rights' to express their understanding of innate or natural entitlement, their aspirations and their disapproval of mistreatment by men or by the federal authorities. 'Rights', 'entitlement' and 'equality' considerations in public discourse link and frame 'violence against women' with all other women's issues and measures of women's advancement.

When Canadians entrenched equality rights in the Charter of Rights and Freedoms in the newly repatriated constitution of 1982, they began a comprehensive review of law and policy, believing those reviews might advance women. Women expected 'Charter-based' applications of law, including criminal law and social policy, to incorporate substantive notions of equality – special or specific government actions taken to establish equality of outcome for women, including reducing the social force of male violence against women. But globalised neoliberal ideology and multinational economic pressure meant that the federal government abandoned its interlocking, international, federal and local commitments and mechanisms to advance equality and redress inequality for women, even as it claimed to be addressing violence against women with law and order policies. Not only was change limited by formal rather than substantive understandings of equality, but patriarchy also reformed to incorporate neoliberalism and globalised capitalism. The imagined review and steady positive social change for women was warped by enormous structural reversals.

Against a background of economic pressure engendered by globalised capitalism, women face unprecedented setbacks in government cuts to social programmes and any immediate hope of reviving them. Provisions in welfare, healthcare, education and public services taken for granted for a generation have begun to disappear. Neoliberal restructuring has moved away from engagement with civil society and democratic consultative practices. Those ministries and programmes once designed for women and the advancement of women have been replaced by an open hostility to women's community-based advocacy and lobbying groups, in fact to women themselves.

The policy combination downloads, decentralises and disintegrates social programmes, rarely consults with non-profit civil society (much less feminists), explicitly refuses government funding for feminist advocacy and equality-seeking groups, and eliminates all internal mechanisms for overseeing the advancement of women. This cumulative and sweeping policy shift has restructured government, reducing the possibility for reversal. Rather than pinning their hopes on current policy, feminists have set their sights on a new framework for advocacy (Lakeman, 2005). In terms of dealing with violence against women, the 'welfare state' has been all but dismantled, and consequently the constitutional state imperative to equality has been circumvented.

Law and order policies have not resulted in laws that protect women from violence or even significantly criminalise violence. In cases where the criminal law on violence against women is applied, some sentences have been lengthened but the number of arrests and convictions has not increased. Moreover, while 'victim assistance' groups and associations of 'families of victims' or 'friends and neighbours' may receive funds, they tend to be disassociated from equality-seeking policies or from mandates to increase autonomy for women. While feminist or women-centred anti-violence groups are pressed to consider themselves as an important part of 'law and order' agendas, they are offered policies that offer vengeance – in the form of longer jail sentences, a victim's right to speak at sentencing, a seat in parole hearings to protest against prisoner release – rather than women's freedom. Meanwhile, probation services that could monitor released prisoners are cut, as are women's advocate programmes. It appears to be irrelevant that few men are ever arrested, much less convicted. Demonising the few men convicted of sex crimes does little more than reinforce the mythologies of rape. Nothing appears to be done to increase women's security, or provide exit from dangerous situations or protections for women's independence.

Thanks to 30 years of pressure from CASAC centres for improved police responses, most police now receive basic training in effective investigations. Originally many centres were directly involved in training police but withdrew when police hierarchies repeatedly refused to provide the necessary education, supervision, support, and promotion and dismissal procedures to change police practices. In recent years, victimised women ill served by the police have brought lawsuits against the government on the grounds that police have an obligation of care. The government has often shamelessly fought such women, sometimes blaming them for the sexist violence against them, as with Bonnie Mooney (*Mooney v Canada*) and Jane Doe. The cases are expensive for the government and the public and therefore still promising to have more effect than any training initiative on the part of centres. Jane Doe won a million-dollar settlement against police mistreatment of raped women in Toronto. However, even that settlement has not resulted in satisfactory police changes.

The federal Department of Justice has made several federal provincial cost-cutting arrangements that have damaged women's causes. The international agreement to criminalise violence against women is undermined by the process of diverting criminal violence against women out of the courts has been normalised through the use of 'victim–offender reconciliation' and 'restorative justice' initiatives such as 'circle sentencing', 'family group counselling', 'conditional sentences', prejudgement 'john's schools' (kerb crawler programmes) and 'mediation' in cases of family violence. Such measures have allowed the criminal justice system to avoid responsibility for necessary improvements in arrest, prosecution, conviction and sentencing for acts of rape and sexual assault as crimes of violence. The criminal justice system also colludes in covering up this violence through the use of plea bargains that rename such acts or leave them off the record, making future reform more difficult. The dismantling of the legal aid system, including the Court Challenges Program, completes the diversion by rendering it almost impossible for women to mount appeals to the court system on the basis of equality promised in the Charter of Rights and Freedoms.

Anti-rape centres have traditionally developed in every major population as spaces where women can gather apart from men to shield and comfort each other, and to document the nature and frequency of violent sexist abuses. Such documentation and growth of knowledge have been key to the successes achieved. From this base, women have advocated and campaigned for social change, building feminist praxis against oppression and towards equality. They have measured and revealed the severity and prevalence of violence against women buried in the practices of government, of the courts, and the police. They have documented, theorised and revealed the impact of that violence and they organised and mobilised the community to respond to that violence. The Statistics Canada 2002 publication *Assessing Violence Against Women: A Statistical Profile* (Federal-Provincial Territorial Ministers Responsible for the Status of Women, 2002) used six indicators to measure the prevalence and severity of violence against women, the impact of violence against women, risk factors associated with violence, institution and community-based responses to violence, the use of services by victims and, crucially, public attitudes and perceptions.

Conclusion

There are several threads of opportunity for resistance to and prevention of male violence in the Canadian context. These include:

- promoting human rights initiatives through state departments, ministries and government institutions, along the lines of those developed from the 1970s to the mid-1990s. This would require restructuring at the federal government level;
- encouraging Supreme Court judges to apply contextual analysis and substantive equality principles against sexist mythologies and national budget restrictions in cases where litigants are seeking equality;
- encouraging positive relationships (including funding) between government and non-governmental women's groups seeking equality. This would require a willingness on the part of government as a result either of its own ideology or public pressure;
- encouraging feminist 'conscientisation' through public education programmes and mass media campaigns;
- promoting direct action (including consciousness raising, participatory research and mutual aid particularly concentrated in feminist anti-rape services/centres).

The bench strength of the movement against violence was seen in the streets after the Montreal massacre in 1989, Jane Doe won the right to sue the police. That same year, significant changes were proposed by both the parliamentary report *The War on Women* and a national symposium on Women, the Law and the Administration of Justice. The Canadian Panel on Violence against Women was released but later shelved. Over the next five years, CASAC organised consultations with women's groups focuesd on (but not limited to) the proposed rape and rape shield law and made annual legislative and policy proposals that had some influence. However, none of the recommendations on violence against women included sentencing reform or proposals for cases of violence to be diverted from criminal courtrooms and processes. Anti-violence feminists warned against both 'law and order' and 'restorative justice' diversion mechanisms in crimes of violence against women.

Cost-cutting politics and right-wing rhetoric won out. As reforms to sexual assault laws were being implemented, so too were cuts to civil and criminal legal aid and sweeping sentencing reforms. Other departments saw cuts to social programmes such as welfare support for women and funding to equality-seeking women's groups). On the one hand, government argued a hard line on crime, although these reforms were implemented as a cost-cutting exercise to reduce incarceration. On the other hand, the government argued that it was taking a progressive stance in promoting restorative justice in order to restore offenders to the community by promoting restitution and centring the needs of the victims (in spite of funding cuts that prevented any successful efforts to do so).

In 2005, CASAC representatives gathered in Vancouver to consolidate a response to these issues. They reconfirmed demands for the effective application of the rule of law, for equal access to protections of law, for effective policing and fair trials. They confirmed the necessity to criminalise violence against women (including law reform to criminalise the buying of sex to protect women and children from the international sex trade). Participants voiced their disapproval of the tendency to divert cases of violence against women out of the criminal courts into private or community settings. They recognised that decriminalisation of violence against women comes in many forms: through restorative justice or other alternate dispute mechanisms, through diversion from court processes to religious, cultural or even commercial programmes, and through de-gendered, 'victim-centred processes'. They reconfirmed a recommendation that in legal cases of violence, those delivering judgments should do so in writing so that the extent of the equality provisions applied would be researchable and transparent. They reconfirmed and documented that the advocacy of an anti-rape centre greatly improved a woman's ability to access justice, including through the courts. Finally, they asserted women's claims on the state to intervene socially and politically on behalf of each woman attacked, and on behalf of women as a group.

Further reading
Lakeman, L. (2005) *Obsession, With Intent: Violence Against Women*, Montreal: Black Rose Books.

Doe, J. (2003) *The Story of Jane Doe: A Book about Rape*, Toronto: Random House.

Sheehy, E. (ed) (2010) Sexual Assault Law, Practice and Activism in a Post-Jane Doe Era, Ottawa: University of Ottawa Press.

References
Auditor General of Toronto (2004) *Review of the Investigation of Sexual Assaults: Toronto Police Service*, www.toronto.ca/audit/reports2004_sub4.htm

Benedet, J. and Hoogstraten, T. (2008) *A Critical Explanation of the New Legal Challenges to Canada's Prostitution Laws*, Vancouver: Vancouver Rape Relief and Women's Shelter, www.rapereliefshelter.bc.ca

Brickman, J., Briere, J., Lungen, A., Shepherd, M. and Lofchick, M. (1980) *Winnipeg Rape Incidence Survey Project*, Winnipeg: Canadian Association of Sexual Assault Centres.

Cohen, M.G. and Pulkingham, J. (eds) (2009) *Public Policy for Women: The State, Income Security and Labour Market Issues*, Toronto: University of Toronto Press.

Department of Health aand Welfare (1991) *The War Against Women: First Report of the Standing Committee on Health and Welfare, Social Affairs, Seniors, and the Status of Women to the House of Commons*, Ottawa: Department of Health and Welfare.

Dobash, R.E. and Dobash, R.P. (1992) *Women, Violence and Social Change*, London: Routledge.

Doe, J. (2003) *The Story of Jane Doe: A Book about Rape*, Toronto: Random House.

Federal-Provincial-Territorial Ministers Responsible for the Status of Women (2002) *Assessing Violence Against Women: A Statistical Profile*, Ottawa: Status of Women Canada.

Feminist Alliance For International Action (2010) *No Action, No Progress: Response to Canada's Report Back to the United Nations Committee on the Elimination of Discrimination Against Women*, www.fafia-afai.org

Gannon, M. and Mihorean, K. (2004) 'Criminal victimization in Canada', *Statistics Canada, Juristat*, vol 25, no 7, Ottawa: Statistics Canada.

Gotell, L. (2007) 'The discursive disappearance of sexualized violence', in D. Chunn, S. Boyd, and H. Lessard (eds) *Reaction and Resistance: Feminism, Law and Social Change*, Vancouver: University of British Columbia Press.

Hattem, T. (2007) *'Highlights from a Preliminary Study of Police Classification of Sexual Assault Cases as Unfounded'*, Canada: Department of Justice.

Johnson, H. (2006) *Measuring Violence Against Women in Canada: Statistical Trends*, Ottawa: Statistics Canada.

Johnson, H. (2011) 'Limits of a criminal justice response: trends in police and court processing of sexual assault', in E. Sheeny (ed) *Sexual Assault Law, Practice and Activism in a Post Jane Doe Era*, Ottawa: University of Ottawa Press.

Kong, R., Johnson, H., Beattie, S. and Cardillo, A. (2003) 'Sexual offences in Canada', *Statistics Canada, Juristat*, vol 23, no 6, p 6, Ottawa: Statistics Canada.

Lakeman, L. (1990) *99 Federal Steps Toward an End to Violence Against Women*, Ottawa: National Action Committee on the Status of Women.

Lakeman, L. (1992) 'Women, violence and the Montreal Massacre', in S. Crean (ed) *Twist and Shout, A Decade of Feminist Writing in This Magazine*, Toronto: Second Storey Press, pp 92-102.

Lakeman, L. (2004) *Canada's Promises to Keep: The Charter and Violence Against Women*, Vancouver: Canadian Association of Sexual Assault Centres.

Lakeman, L. (2005) *Obsession, With Intent: Violence Against Women*, Montreal: Black Rose Books.

L'Heureux-Dube, C. (2001) 'Beyond the myths: equality, impartiality and justice', *Social Distress and the Homeless*, vol 10, no 1, pp 89-90.

McIntyre, S. and Rodgers, S. (eds) (2006) *Diminishing Returns, Inequality and the Canadian Charter of Rights and Freedoms*, Markham: LexisNexis.

McIntyre, S., Boyle, C., Lakeman, L. and Sheehy, E. (2000) 'Tracking and resisting backlash against equality gains in sexual offence law', *Canadian Women Studies*, vol 20, no 3, p 74.

Rebick, J. (2005) *Ten Thousand Roses, The Making of a Feminist Revolution*, Toronto: Penguin Group.

Young, M., Boyd, S.B., Brodsky, G. and Day, S. (eds) (2007) *Poverty: Rights, Social Citizenship, and Legal Activism*, Vancouver: UBC Press.

FOUR

Introduction to the issue of rape in China as a developing country

Qihua Ye

Introduction

Rape, as a social issue, is an integral part of human history (Roberts, 1989; Wang, 2005; Jiang, 2007; Tang, 2007). In the development of humankind, rape has been used as a weapon both in mass conflicts, for example the rapes inflicted by Japanese soldiers on Chinese women during the Second World War, and in everyday battles. Within this context, pain is inflicted on women's bodies; their identity is attacked and they are deprived of their sexual rights. Rape is thus regarded by many as a gendered issue in society, as it is mostly perpetrated by men against women.

As proposed in the Declaration of Sexual Rights (1999), the right to sexual freedom encompasses freedom from all forms of sexual coercion, exploitation and abuse at any time and situation in life. Indeed, people should be free to enjoy equal sexual rights without being attacked or forced to engage in sexual activity. Likewise, the Universal Declaration of Human Rights (1948) states that 'all human beings are born free and equal with regard to dignity and rights'; being endowed with reason and conscience, people must treat each others as equals. However, in reality, women do not enjoy equal rights with men, which is most apparent in incidents of rape. Rape severely infringes on these fundamental sexual and human rights, as offenders violate the personal rights of their victims. Rape is a crime because it disturbs social order and affects people's – especially women's – mental and physical health (Jiang, 2007). Rape infringes on personal rights; considered by many to be the worst crime (Wang, 2005), acting as a social pollutant throughout the world (Chan, 2009; Yu, 2007). It has been reported that the rate of occurrences of rape is four times that of other criminal cases in China (Wang, 2005).

Within the context of the past 30 years of economic reforms, China's economic development has been extremely rapid. Since the 1980s, the number of rape incidents has increased in tandem with this development (Jiang, 2007). During the period 1981–86, the numbers of the rape cases put on file for investigation and prosecution were 30,808 in 1981, 35,361 in 1982, 37,712 in 1985 and 39,121 in 1986 (Wang, 2005), indicating that the number of reported incidents of rape has steadily increased. Furthermore, according to the *China Law Yearbook*, between 1991 and 2003, the numbers of the rape cases in China were respectively 50,331; 49,829; 47,033; 44,118; 41,823; 42,820; 40,699; 40,967; 39,435; 35,819; 40,600; 38,209; and 40,088. These figures show that the total number of rape cases during these 13 years was 551,771, with an average of more than 40,000 rapes reported in China every year. However, this figure may not be representative of the true number of incidents, because some cases may not be reported by the victims. As a rough estimate, if half the true number of rape cases were reported, the actual number of incidents would be 1,103,542 (Chen, 2006). Thus, it can be estimated that an average of more than 80,000 cases occur in China each year. In recent years, rape cases have represented about 15% of all criminal cases, which is testament to the serious impact that rape has on the stability of society and also on people's sense of security (Jiang, 2007).

Worldwide, rape is a social issue of increasing public concern. As a result, anti-rape campaigns, driven by the feminist movement, began in the late 1960s and early 1970s, particularly in the West (Roberts, 1989). A notable result of these campaigns was the establishment of Rape Crisis Centre, the first such centre being launched in the US in 1970, and the first in the UK six years later. However, no such organisations exist in China:

> Only some governmental organisations such as the All-China Women's Federation, [and] the Public Security Bureau, provide support to rape victims. Recently in China, a small number of non-governmental groups have been formed which aim to engage people with this social issue and to care for survivors of rape. (Alliance Regulations against Rape in China, 2006)

Cheng Yang, aged 28, received assistance from a non-governmental support group after she was raped while working in her office on 13 February 2005. She claimed damages on the grounds that she had suffered injury on the job (Xiang and Fu, 2006). Although her claim failed twice during the judicial procedure (Xi, 2006), the offender was eventually sentenced to six years in prison. Throughout the process, the group provided her with legal, psychological, social and emotional support.

As far as the legal situation is concerned, most countries have passed a series of laws against rape. In the UK, rape is judged in terms of sex crime law (Lu, 2007), while in China, rape crime is judged in terms of criminal law (Zhang, 1999; Li, 2007). These laws are intended to protect victims and punish offenders. A review of the literature on rape, however, shows that China has a number of weaknesses in its handling of the issue, for example in attitudes towards rape, and in terms of policy, legal and practical research approaches. Indeed, the deeper the assessment of the current situation, the more apparent the need for urgent work and study. This chapter will therefore introduce and discuss the following questions with respect to China: How does rape happen in China? How are laws in relation to rape crime stipulated? Are there weaknesses in the laws regarding rape? How is research on rape crime conducted? The analysis of these topics should highlight the key issues surrounding rape in China, which may aid further exploration of this crime.

Characteristics of rape in China

In China, rape is usually conceptualised as a male forcing a female to have sexual activity with him against her will, whether that be through the use of violence, threats or other means (Li, 2002; Sang, 2003; Yu, 2007). According to this definition, it is clear that rape infringes on women's sexual rights, while emphasising the paradigm of men as perpetrators of rape against women. Bearing these definitions in mind, it is vital to research and analyse the factors related to rape in China, as accumulating knowledge on these factors will affect a number of areas, from aiding the prevention of this crime in society to improving the law, with greater protection for rape victims and more appropriate punishments for perpetrators. There are many factors involved in the issue of rape, such as age, marital status, and professional and educational levels, which will therefore be considered below.

Age

People (mainly women) may be raped at any age (Yu, 2007). However, the number of female victims of rape does seem to vary somewhat between age groups. Guo's research (1997) showed that 48% of female victims of rape were between 18 and 25 years old. Twenty-six percent of those who had been raped were under 18, while 20% were aged between 26 and 35, and 6% were over 36 years old. Looking at these figures, it could be assumed that younger women are more likely to be raped (18-25 years old; 48%) than older women aged 26 and above (26%).

Male offenders may commit rape at any age. However, in line with the age of the victims, it is also more likely to be perpetrated by younger men. For example, Zhang (2005) analysed 36 rape cases by 38 offenders. At the time of committing the offence, 47.4% of offenders (18 of the 38) were between the ages of 18 to 25 years old, and 31.6% (12) were between the ages of 26 and 35 years old. In comparison, only 21% of perpetrators (eight) were aged between 36 and 60 years old. It can be inferred from these figures that rape can take place at any stage of a women's life, though young women are more likely than old women to be raped (Shang, 2003), and young men are more likely to be perpetrators (Zhang, 2001). This may be because young people prefer social activities and go out more frequently than old people. As a result, both young women and men may be in more situations where they could be a victim or perpetrator of rape. Yu (2007) suggests that this may because the former lack experience and awareness of self-protection when they enjoy social association with men, while the latter may neglect concepts of morality and duty for society when they come into contact with women in such situations. Thus, these increased levels of social activity may account for why rape incidents are more likely to occur between young men and women. However, this explanation is only partly valid, as rapes can take place in any situation, not only when young women and men are in the public arena. Moreover, rape is an issue of gendered power over women, and women should not be regarded as being responsible for the violation they experience.

Marital status

In China, marital status is usually divided into two categories: unmarried and married. The latter includes widows/widowers and divorced men and women. The likelihood of being a victim of rape may differ according to a woman's marital status. According to Guo's investigation (1997), nearly 80% of victims are unmarried women, while 22% of victims are married women (19% are married; 3% are widowed or divorced. These figures appear to show that young unmarried women may be more likely to experience rape than married women. Indeed, according to Guo's (1997) data, the majority of rape victims are unmarried (young) women. Furthermore, this data is paralleled by the aforementioned findings that young women (aged 18-25) are the most likely to be victims of rape. (Guo, 1997; Shang, 2003) It has been suggested that unmarried women are most likely to be raped because they lack self-protection and life experience, and may be vulnerable to being cheated or led by men into unwanted sexual experiences (Shang, 2003; Yu, 2007). However, it is important to note that this view comes close to holding young women responsible for rape, yet, as previously discussed, gendered abuse of power by men is the major cause of rape.

Professional and educational background

Today, a person's profession may be seen as a tool to distinguish his or her status in society. In rape studies, professional status may be a key issue because the number of reported rapes appears to differ depending on the profession of the victims. According to Guo's research (1997), the percentage of rape victims who worked as farmers was 34.4%, while the percentage of victims who were members of the urban working class was 21.9%; 19.8% of victims were students, while 8.3% were unemployed; 7.3% were office workers; 4.2% were retired; and 2% were self-employed. These figures suggest that most victims were farmers and working-class women. Moreover, students accounted for almost a fifth of all victims.

In terms of the professions of perpetrators, Zhang's study (2005) showed that offenders were also mainly farmers. The percentage of peasant/farmer perpetrators was 52.6% (20 out of 38). This rate was the highest among the groups assessed. Of the rape offenders assessed, those who were unemployed accounted for the second largest percentage (five; 13.2%). The rate of other occupations, first including workers[1] and taxi drivers was 18.4% (seven), and second including officers, teachers and students, was 15.8% (six).

Looking at all these figures, it appears that the peasants/farmers represent the occupational group most likely to be victims or offenders compared with other occupations. This may be because peasants/farmers make up the main body of society and form the highest proportion of the population in China. Moreover, within the context of the Chinese reforms, there is increased migration of both female and male peasants (mainly young peasants/farmers) to the cities. This may mean that male migrants are no longer regulated by family or local norms of sexual behaviour, and equally young female migrants may lack familial protection.

It may also be necessary to consider what impact educational levels have on the situation of rape victims and perpetrators. Guo's study (1997) reported that women with no or lower levels of education are most likely to be raped (48.9%). That study also found that 26.7% of victims had a primary level of education, while women with higher levels of education were less likely to suffer rape (14.4%). Zhang's study (2005) showed that the percentage of offenders with education at the junior level was 42.9% (nine out of 21) and those with primary level education was 23.8 % (five). The rate of offenders with graduate-level education was 14.3% (three), whereas the rate of offenders with postgraduate qualifications was 9.5% (two). In addition, the rate of offenders who were illiterate was 14.3% (three). The figures relating to the educational levels of victims and offenders therefore show that people with low levels of education are more likely to be raped or to rape women.

Relationship between victims and offenders

For a long time, it was thought that offenders and victims in rape cases generally did not know each other, and that offenders usually suffer from erotomania (Yu, 2007). However, this is rarely the case, as 73,6% of offenders know and are known to their victims, often in the capacity of neighbours (44.2%) or friends (21.5%). Yu (2007) studied a group of convicted rape offenders and found that in 38% of 140 rape cases, the relationship between rapist and victim was that of neighbour; and in 31% of cases, the relationship was that of teacher and student. A small proportion of rape offenders (10%) were friends with their victim, while 3% were related to their victim. Only 28% of the victims and offenders were unknown to one another. Similarly, Zhang's (2005) study of 36 rape cases found that that most cases (26; 73.2%) occurred between victims and offenders who were familiar with one another. Only 27.8% cases (10) occurred between victims and offenders who did not know each other (Song, 2005).

Given these figures, it is important to examine why most rapes occur between parties already known to each other. Yu (2007) suggests that offenders rape people who are known to them because they are aware of the personal details of their victims, such as their habits, family and address, thus creating more opportunities to contact and to rape their victims. Furthermore, victims often trust and depend on offenders. In this context, victims may be silent and not report the rape, because they forgive offenders who are known to them. While these are interesting theories, we need more research before we can conclude whether offenders choose victims for these reasons.

Time and space

Rape as a social phenomenon occurs in a certain time and space, and this may be related to the activities of victims. Studying these related factors may enable us to take and strengthen protection measures.

For the purpose of this analysis, we consider time in terms of season and time of day. With respect to season, Guo's study (1997) proposed that more rapes take place in summer (55.1%) than in spring (16.3%), in winter (15.3%) or in autumn (13.3%). These findings are in line with Jin's suggestion (2004) that rapes occurs most often in summer and spring. Shang (2003) and Yu (2007) suggest that rapes occur more in summer because of the short nights, meaning that women may go out for longer and associate more frequently with men in this season than in others. They also posit that women may be more likely to be raped by men in summer because they generally wear less at this time of year than in colder seasons. It is suggested that this tendency to blame the victim is almost universal in China, even without any more specific data. Finally, they address the possibility that in hot weather victims do not close their windows and doors, which provides a convenient chance for offenders who can easily enter victims' houses and sexually assault women. However, many of these theories would only apply to stranger rapes, and as we have seen, most rapes occur within relationships or where the perpetrator is known to the victim.

With respect to time of day, in Guo's investigation (1997), the most frequent time for a rape to occur was between 5 pm and midnight (44.2%), then between 8 am and 5 pm (38.9%) and finally between midnight and 8 am (16.8%). Accordingly, Yu (2007) suggests that most victims' activities take place in the daytime and early evening, while people are more likely to be at home in late evening. The rate of rapes in the evening (5 pm to midnight) may be the highest because offenders use the dark to avoid being seen or recognised by the victim, and because in the dark it is easier for offenders to leave the crime scene following the incident. In addition, the working day usually ends at 5 pm, and it is after this time that people are more likely to go out to socialise. Under these circumstances, women may be more likely to neglect self-protection and be targeted by rape offenders (Yu, 2007). However, these theories can also serve to blame women for their violation, and therefore need to be examined with care and caution.

When considering where rapes take place, there are variations across China in terms of geographical location. For a few years, incidents of rape have been more frequent in the Heilongjiang and Liaoning Provinces, located in the north of China (Zhang, 2001; Song, 2005; Yu, 2007). Comparing rural with urban areas, Guo's study (1997) showed that rape is more likely to occur on the outskirts of rural areas (35.4%) than in the space between urban and rural areas (27.3%), or in urban areas or rural areas (24.2% and 13.1%) respectively. According to a study by Liu and colleagues (2004), the level of rapes in the countryside was the highest (41.6%). The rate was 28.2% in towns, 18.6 % in cities and 8.1% in the area between urban and rural areas.

There were differences between Guo's (1997) and Liu et al's (2004) studies in terms of the number of rapes committed in the different areas, with subsequent shifts in the number of rape incidents over the seven years between the two studies. For example, Guo's (1997) data showed that, of all the areas, most rapes were committed in the outskirts (35.4%), while Liu et al's (2004) data suggested that the most rapes were committed in the countryside (41.6%). In 1997, a notable number of the rape crimes addressed occur in the area between the urban and the rural (27.3%), while in 2004, rape occurred less frequently in the area between the urban and the rural (8.1%). While rape crimes occurred in all areas in both studies, the likelihood of a rape being committed in a particular area differed depending on the study, and therefore it may be difficult to reach a conclusion about location and the incidence of rape.

The differences between these two studies demonstrate how difficult it is to ascertain whether the number of rapes in urban areas is higher than in rural areas or vice versa. Nevertheless, it would appear to be possible to identify the physical spaces where rape is likely to take place. Such a place is often the home of the victim and or the offender, a field or a deserted area. Rape occurs most often in the homes of victims (30.3%), then in the homes of offenders (25.3%) and then in fields (14.1%) (Guo, 1997). These figures suggest that most rape cases are likely to occur in an environment familiar to the victim, which does not conform to the idea that rape is more likely to occur in a hidden, unfamiliar place, or in a public place. Within this context of familiarity, victims may be more likely to be careless and to relax their vigilance with offenders (Zhou, 2005), especially when they know the offender. Some researchers such as Yu (2007) and Zhou (2005) suggest that women should be vigilant, even if they stay in familiar places, and that they need to have some way of protecting themselves that will reduce their chances of being raped. However, we need to be careful not to put the responsibility on women to protect themselves from rape, but rather to lay blame on the perpetrator.

Criminal law in China

Since ancient times, rape has been defined as criminal behaviour that seriously endangers social public order. Rape is one of the most serious crimes in Chinese criminal law (Zhang, 2007). In 1979 for the first time, the criminal law, rape, was specifically listed in Chapter Four, Sub-provisions, Part II: Infringement upon personal rights and democratic rights is defined as a crime (Wang, 2005; Jiang, 2007). Notably, this law was revised seven times between 1979 and 2009 (Chinese Criminal Law, 2009).

Rape is classed as a sex crime (Hu, 2004), which includes not only crimes of raping women, but also of forcing young girls to work as prostitutes, licentiousness, prostitution, incest, spreading pornographic videos and photos, and spreading sexually transmitted infections. Rape is considered a serious crime as it affects victims' health in both body and mind, as mentioned above. It can also lead to pregnancy of victims and to sexually transmitted infections.

Articles of Chinese criminal law that deal with sex crimes

In Chinese criminal law, rape constitutes a forced sexual act with a woman by violence, coercion and or any other means, as well as against her will. Notably, there is no explicit definition in Chinese criminal law in relation to specific standards of justice about what constitutes rape (Zhang, 1999; Wang, 2005). In other words, the law does not stipulate what types of forced sexual action (for example, vaginal penetration by penis, penetration of the anus, without consent and so on) constitute 'rape'. The articles described addressed below outline the provision for sex crimes within the Chinese criminal law.

First, the 236th article states that a person who rapes a woman by force, threat or any other means will be sentenced to a fixed-term imprisonment of no less than three years and no more than 10 years. This article particularly stipulates that the behaviour will be seen as a rape crime and offenders will be punished severely if they have sexual relations with the girls under 14 years of age. This article also states that offenders who rape women or young girls in any of the following circumstances will be sentenced to no less than 10 years' fixed-term or life imprisonment or death:

- raping a woman or having sexual relations with a young girl with flagrant circumstances;
- raping several women or sexual relations with several young girls;
- raping a woman in a public place;
- rape of the same woman in succession by two or more offenders;
- rape leading to serious bodily injury, death or any other serious consequence to the victim.

Second, the 237th article is related to obscenity and insult against women. It states that offenders who use obscenity against women will be sentenced to fixed-term imprisonment of not more than five years or to criminal detention. If offenders sexually insult or behave obscenely towards women in public, they will be sentenced to fixed-term imprisonment of not less than five years. If an offender acts indecently towards a child, they will be sentenced more heavily. Moreover, if offenders rape women who are abducted and trafficked, they will be sentenced more heavily (for example, fixed-term imprisonment of not less than 10 years or life imprisonment and concurrently to a fine or confiscation of property and so on) as the 240th article stipulates.

Finally, there are nine articles in the law that deal with other sex crimes. These articles stipulate how to punish offenders who spread a serious venereal disease by prostitution or forcing young girls (under 14 years of age) into prostitution. The articles also stipulate how to punish offenders who gather a crowd to engage in sex crimes and to make, copy, publish and sell pornography, including newspapers, magazines, books and videos.

From an examination of these articles, it is apparent that the law stipulates that certain kinds of sexual behaviour will be defined as crimes and awarded different degrees of punishment. In particular, the law indicates that rape directly and mainly affects women. The most serious punishments for perpetrators of rape are life imprisonment and the death penalty.

Chinese criminal law stipulates a series of specific items to punish offenders who violate sexually assault women. This aims to protect all women equally, with no additional conditions referring to victims who are 'pure' or who have a good reputation. Chinese criminal law shows that sexual behaviour by offenders will be defined as a crime as long as they force any women to engage in sexual activity against her will, perhaps via the use of violence or threats. This reflects respect towards women; the protection of women, and their sexual rights, are seen as human rights.

The 236th article and the protection of male victims

There is an issue in relation to lack of protection for male victims in the law on rape (Li, 2005; Feng, 2007; Li, 2007; Liu, 2007) because there is a difference between men and women in terms of the protection of their sexual rights (Ruan, 2003). In the matter of rape, Chinese criminal law focuses on male offenders and female victims (He and Gong, 2003), which could be seen as narrow and absolute.

This gendered distinction arises because historically, women have been seen as a vulnerable group, with men as the primary main breadwinners; women had to depend on men, while men both controlled and protected them. Women were thus regarded as subordinate to men. In terms of sexual rights, women were also seen as subordinate to men (Gu, 2001; Gao, 2005). Accordingly, legislators naturally focused on the legal protection of women's sexual rights (Gao, 2005; Li, 2005).

It has been suggested that as society has developed, particularly with reference to feminism, the relative status of men and women within society has gradually changed, and women can now contribute and partake in many of the activities that were previously thought of as male territory. Women's ideas and behaviours have changed, and their awareness of independence is increasing. People have begun to acknowledge the ways in which women play a role in initiating sexual behaviour, including coercive sexual behaviour (Kang, 2007; Zhou, 2007). It is therefore possible that a rape offender could be female (Gu, 2001; Li, 2006). However, Chinese criminal law only alludes to men, including young men from the age of 14, as perpetrators of rape bearing criminal responsibility in accordance with article 17 (Li, 2006).

Some Chinese academics have therefore started to address the fact that rape perpetrators can be male or female. They also suggest that rape by women is a genuine problem. For example, women may attract young men for the purpose of sexual activity, or to instigate or help someone commit rape (Gu, 2001; Li, 2006; Kang, 2007). Studies have concluded that anybody could be a victim or perpetrator of rape, regardless of their gender or sexuality (He and Gong, 2003; Ruan, 2003; Li, 2005; Li, 2007; Liu, 2007).

Yet, currently there is only anecdotal evidence to suggest that some women are perpetrators of rape (Bai, 2007; Li, 2007), meaning that precise figures are difficult to find. An (2002) describes the case of a male soldier being kept in captivity by five unmarried females working at an inn where the man had been staying. They reportedly wanted the man to have sex with them, and the soldier refused them. Both parties involved would not relent for the duration of the whole morning. By the afternoon, the five females had a discussion and decided to take matters further into their own hands. As a result, one of the females entered the man's room naked and threatened that she would claim that he had raped her unless he agreed to have sex with all the five women. The man felt helpless and, feeling compelled to submit to their demands, was raped by the women.

Another anecdotal example tells the story of a female mayor in her forties who attempted to use her position of power to maintain a long-term sexual relationship with a young man. For the first few years, the young man felt that he had to obey the woman. Finally, however, he reported her because he could not tolerate her behaviour and did not want to remain in an abusive relationship. The case went to court, but despite it attracting much attention, the woman received no sentence (Feng, 2007).

Thus, Chinese criminal law does not protect male victims or punish female perpetrators of rape. Other groups that need protection are gay and lesbian people, who may suffer rape from someone of their own sex (Li, 2007; Liu, 2007). More research needs to be done on the issue of male rape, and to measure the extent of the problem in Chinese society.

The 236th article and marital rape

Another feature of Chinese criminal law is that it does not deal adequately with marital rape, which is a real issue in China. For example, the Institute of Population, China Academy of Social Science (CASS) conducted an investigation among 9,033 couples aged between 20 and 54 in six cities and provinces (Xiong, 1994). Among these respondents, 19.84% of the urban husbands and 27.39% of the rural husbands believed that a wife cannot refuse to have sex with her husband when he wants it, and this viewpoint was also held by 18.66% of urban wives and 33.59% of rural wives. These figures suggest that there was virtually no difference in the prevalence of this attitude between urban husbands (19.84%) and wives (18.66%). The former figure is only 1.18 percentage points higher than the latter. But there was a difference in the prevalence of this attitude between rural husbands (27.39%) and wives (33.59%), the latter figure being 6.2 percentage points higher than the former. It should also be noted that there was a difference in the prevalence of this attitude between urban and rural husbands and wives. The rate of prevalence in rural husbands is 6.55 percentage points higher than that in urban husbands, with rural wives scoring 14.93 percentage points higher than urban wives. Comparatively, then, rural wives are more likely to have an attitude of subordination to their husbands in a sexual context.

In China, it is difficult to punish an offender for marital rape because the law does not define this behaviour as a crime; instead, it defines it as deliberate harm, insult and abuse, or even as guiltlessness (Bai, 2007). Some scholars suggest that marital rape should be defined as rape crime because husbands rape their wives, whereas some scholars think that it is not appropriate for the Chinese context to define marital rape as a crime because couples have a marital contract (Wang, 2005; Bai, 2007). In China, many people do not consider marital rape to be a crime. Due to this combination of traditional contexts and patriarchal views, there are no explicit articles in Chinese law that relate to marital rape (Bai, 2007).

Li (2006) argues that such weaknesses in Chinese criminal law should be addressed by adding a relevant article in relation to marital rape. Both husbands and wives should have the same sexual rights. In particular, wives should not be deprived of their sexual rights; they should be allowed to govern their bodies freely within marriage (Bai, 2007). If this right is violated, the victims should be protected by the law, yet such protection is difficult to obtain in China. The central government of China should consider revising the law not only to fit in with recent social development, but also to protect the rights of marital rape victims (Ruan, 2003; Li, 2005; Bai, 2007; Li, 2007; Liu, 2007).

Issues raised in recent Chinese studies

In China, rape has been a social issue since the communist years, unlike domestic violence, which has only recently begun to be discussed as a social problem (Han, 2004; Ye, 2008). The government has tried to combat rape crime through different means such as criminal law, education and media campaigns.

Researchers and practitioners are engaged in this topic and provide the government with research results. In particular, research into rape has begun to have some influence in combating the traditional research viewpoint that rape can only be committed by men on women, and has also begun to include homosexual as well as heterosexual rape. Researchers of rape are dealing with a variety of other topics, not only from a legal angle but also in an international context. In terms of the legal aspect, research tends to focus on the weaknesses of Chinese criminal law and ways in which it can be improved.

Chinese research thus covers three key areas: 'traditional' research about women victims; investigation of less stereotypical victim–

perpetrator dynamics, such as male victim–female perpetrator; and the study of the law in terms of its weaknesses and possible improvements. These studies focus mainly on exploring features of rape occurring in daily life, describing rape incidents and focusing on victims, and thus may not adequately address the causes and impact of rape. They also tend to use a quantitative rather than a qualitative approach, which leads to learning *what* but not *why*. Such studies therefore run the risk of failing to provide any novel findings or conclusions.

Moreover, Chinese researchers rarely use gender-based theories to analyse rape. While their findings have often reflected women's vulnerability within society, alongside their increased likelihood of being raped, researchers have frequently neglected to discuss the gender-based issues that lie behind such findings. Gendered approaches may be important in studies of rape because of the gender inequality inherent in rape cases involving men and women, and the different experiences of rape for women and men. However, this is rarely discussed in Chinese studies.

Victim blaming is another feature of some Chinese studies of rape. Some researchers believe that women tempt men to behave wrongly because they dress in revealing or sexy clothes (Shang, 2003; Liu and Zhang, 2009). This raises two important questions: first, why should women's wearing sexy clothes be related to rape?; and second, why should men's wearing sexy clothes be less likely to affect women's sexual behaviour? Women should have the same rights as men in their clothing choices. Rape cannot be blamed on the apparently 'sexy' clothes of the victim. Instead, we need to look at how men push or force women to have sex. Developing an understanding of why offenders hurt their victims via sexual assault is a key issue for exploration.

There are other attitudes towards rape crime that may have influenced recent studies. It is often difficult to investigate incidents of rape in China because some police officers, lawyers, members of the public and offenders hold victim-blaming attitudes towards rape crimes. They may also see the economy or money as an all-powerful force that plays an important role in rape. For the purposes of this research, the author informally interviewed a few professionals, including police officers, lawyers and teachers, between August and November 2009, to get their views on rape. Some were confused about why I wanted to explore the matter because they thought that rape was not an important issue. Some believed that paying for sexual services would lead to a decrease in the number of rape crimes. Some questioned how it was possible for rape to occur nowadays. Others thought that it was difficult to explore the issue because there are no publicly released official crime records in relation to rape (Chan, 2009). A common view of those interviewed was that there are normally two main ways to settle a rape incident: to report it publicly (to public security authorities or to court, for example) or to settle it privately (through negotiation or maintaining silence). Most victims choose the latter, so the handling of rape incidents is often kept quiet (Li, 2008). This is why, as discussed earlier in the chapter, it is difficult to ascertain accurate numbers of rape crimes in China.

One of the lawyers interviewed cited a case where a woman was raped by her colleague and subsequently reported the incident to the authorities. As part of the legal process, she was told that she could choose either monetary compensation or the sentencing of the offender. She chose to protect her human rights under the law and the offender was sentenced to seven years' imprisonment. However, she was unhappy, because, although the outcome was warranted, she was blamed for being unkind. People said that she should have taken the money as compensation from the offender so that he would not have had to go to prison. She came to regret her decision because she had lost her good reputation and the chance of monetary compensation.

Money often plays a key role in the response to rape incidents, most likely as a result of the economic reforms as China increasingly embraces consumerism and commoditisation. For example, on an evening in September 2000, 16-year-old Liu Yan went to an internet bar with two female friends, and while chatting, was dragged into a car, taken to a cornfield and raped by four men, Wang Bing, Wang Weimin, Jing Yongfeng and Wang Lei. According to the investigation report, the police caught the men in May 2001 after they admitted to the rape crime against Liu Yan. After a month, in accordance with approval from the People's Procuratorate of Jinshui, located in Zhengzhou, they were arrested. However, the evidence in the case suddenly changed when the four men were due to be sentenced. Two of the offenders (Wang Bing and Wang Weimin) denied that they had raped the girl, and claimed that she was a prostitute. Initially, the other two men (Jing Yongfeng and Wang Lei) admitted to raping the girl, but later also denied their crime. The victim, Liu Yan, also denied that Wang Bing and Wang Weimin had raped her, stating that she had voluntarily agreed to have sex with them. However, she stuck by her claim that she had been raped by Jing Yongfeng and Wang Lei.

At this stage, it was unclear why two offenders had withdrawn their confessions and, furthermore, why Lui Yan had withdrawn her accusation. Subsequent further careful investigation by the police established that the two offenders' fathers had asked Liu Zhi'an, the policeman handling the case, to help them, and had bribed both him and Liu Yan with money. As a result, on 2 December 2003, the judgement passed in the case resulted in Liu Zhi'an being sentenced to six years' imprisonment for manipulating the law to help the two offenders. The two offenders' fathers were sentenced to probation for bribery and for harm to a witness in a law court. Liu Yan was also punished and sentenced to probation for harbouring offenders. Wang Weimin escaped prosecution, but Wang Bing, Jing Yongfeng and Wang Lei were sentenced to a fixed-term imprisonment of 11, 12 and eight years respectively for raping Liu Yan (Wu and Li, 2004).

This case shows that financial inducements can lead to miscarriages of justice. Those involved rejected the law in favour of financial reward. Both the rape victim, Liu Yan, and the policeman in the case, Liu Zhi'an, accepted bribes. From their behaviour, it can be inferred that their attitude towards rape was determined by an external factor, in this case, financial benefit. A positive outcome, nevertheless, was that the offenders (with the exception Wang Weimin) were eventually punished by the law, indicating that the law can play its rightful role in exercising its power to seek justice and treat people equally.

Finally, although recent studies have revealed weaknesses in certain articles of Chinese criminal law, as discussed above, the author would suggest that academics' suggestions to improve the law may not reflect reality because they lack experience of practical investigation techniques and because they do not discuss or explain differing attitudes towards rape, including those of victims, offenders and the general public. For example, Wang (2005) argues that marital rape perpetrated by husbands cannot be seen as a crime at all because of the Chinese legal context and societal opinion. Wang's view on marital rape sticks to convention and, sadly, his view may be representative of certain sections of Chinese society. Those that hold this view may not understand the experiences of victims of marital rape. There are also very few reliable statistics about rapes where the perpetrator is female and the victim is male (Gu, 2001; Li, 2006; Kang, 2007; Zhou, 2007). This again reflects the lack of comprehensive research on rape in China and may influence the creation of sound law (Shang, 2003).

Conclusion

This chapter has introduced the issue of rape in contemporary China, and discussed the characteristics of rape crime as described in the literature, the legal situation and recent studies. From this analysis, it appears, first, that the prevalence of rape crime is relatively high in China, with an average of more than 80,000 cases occurring annually

(Jiang, 2007). A general assessment of factors associated with rape in China shows that age, marital status, profession and level of education are likely to be linked to the likelihood of becoming a victim or a perpetrator of rape. According to Guo's (1997) and Zhang's (2005) studies, 48% of rape victims are young women (between 18 and 25 years old), while 47.4% of rape perpetrators are young men (between 18 and 25 years old). It has also been observed that rape often occurs between victims and offenders who know each other (Yu, 2007). Early parts of the chapter described the time and place of rape incidents in terms of season, time of day and area. Rape is most likely to occur in summer (55.1%), between the hours of 5 pm and midnight (44.2%) (Guo, 1997).

Second, in relation to the law pertaining to sex crimes, it appears that the 263rd article, referring to rape crime in Chinese criminal law, contains a series of specific clauses designed to punish offenders who sexually assault women and young girls. It implies that women and young girls are protected equally by the law regardless of social status or wealth. Nevertheless, there are weaknesses in the law, including the fact that male victims are not protected and that marital rape is not defined as a crime. Accordingly, some scholars and researchers are appealing for improvements to the law to bring it in line with recent social developments.

Finally, it is evident that research into rape is being carried out both in the Chinese and the international context. For example, Chinese researchers have started to break through the traditional viewpoint that rape perpetrators are always male, and to explore the reality that perpetrators and victims can be of either sex, and that rape can happen in the context of same-sex and heterosexual relationships (Gu, 2001; Li, 2005; Zhou, 2007). Although research into rape is not a new phenomenon in China, it is possible that it may have stagnated during the ten-year Cultural Revolution (1966-76). Current studies may also lack depth, because they use more quantitative than qualitative data. In the other words, current studies may describe the prevalence of rape but not the experiences of victims and offenders. They describe and explain 'what' but not so much 'how' and 'why'.

In particular, current studies on rape in China do not fully address the following issues and questions:

- How many men have been victims of rape?
- What is the difference in experiences of rape for woman and men?
- What can offenders and victims tell us about rape?
- What attitudes do people have towards rape?
- What impact does rape have on victims?

In addition, these studies may only reflect the researchers' opinions about the reasons for rape rather than the actual reasons as reported by victims and offenders. Currently, there is a lack of more specific studies of rape, especially in relation to victims' experiences and the impact that rape has on them, to offenders' behaviour, and to people's attitudes towards rape. Research should focus not only on description but also on interpretation. This will allow researchers to provide useful suggestions to central government, which will in turn be able to make better laws and policies, and will help to raise people's awareness of rape.

The fact that recent studies are more likely to take a quantitative rather than a qualitative approach may have affected their findings as well as subsequent discussion. These studies show 'what' (the frequency of rape, when it occurs and so on), but do not tend to show 'how' or 'why' (for example, why offenders rape, and the impact of rape on victims). As Reinharz (1992) and Skinner and colleagues (2005) suggest, methods of social research should be plural. This methodological paradigm should be of general concern for Chinese researchers, as plural research methods allow researchers to explore rape further and in greater depth. Furthermore, a variety of methods will help researchers to obtain high-quality data, which will benefit investigations.

Of key importance is the attitude of central government and the Chinese people. They should increase their awareness of the issues surrounding rape and their concern for rape victims, but should not directly or indirectly blame victims. In particular, the government should be aware that rape should invoke the same concern as other social and economic development issues, because it destroys social stability and safety, specifically marriage, family and health. Economic reform cannot be successful without the backdrop of a peaceful environment. At the same time, the government should take positive measures to crack down on rape and other sexual crimes, specifically improving law and policy and providing financial aid for the establishment of organisations that support victims of rape. In this regard, China may lag behind other developed countries such as the US and the UK. Through the actions and efforts of both the government and the Chinese people, it is hoped that rape crime will be reduced and, ultimately, be eliminated in China.

Through this primary exploration of rape, it is the author's future aim to obtain more specific information in relation to professionals' and the general public's attitudes to rape, as well as victims' experiences and the effects of rape. It is hoped that the answers to the questions raised in this research will have useful and significant results for Chinese society.

Note

[1] In China the term 'workers' refers to people who stay in the towns and cities and gain their income directly through their work. The term is used to differentiate between 'workers' and 'farmers', the latter group who gain their income indirectly after selling their produce.

Further reading

Guo, J. (1997) *Victimology of Crime*, Beijing: Beijing University Press.

Wang, W. (2005) *Cases Study on Rape*, Beijing: The People's Court Press.

Zhang, G. (2005) *On Criminal Cases in Relation to Raping, Abducting and Selling Women*, Beijing: China Procurator Press.

References

Alliance Regulations against Rape in China (2006), http://blog.sina. com.cn/s/blog_4a1f4cec010006gx.html#comment

An, G. (2002) 'The study of rape crime: two cases', *Hebei Law Study*, vol 4, pp 24-6.

Bai, W. (2007) 'On the scope of the subject of rape crime in China', Unpublished Master's Thesis, Guizhou University.

Chan, K. (2009) 'Sexual violence against women and children in Chinese societies', *Trauma, Violence and Abuse*, vol 10, no 1, pp 69-89.

Chen, X. (2006) 'Looking at rape crime by the lawful view', http:// bbs.chinacourt.org/index.php?showtopic=182117

Chinese Criminal Law (2009) Chinese Criminal Law, www.szxingshi. com/95w9.html

Declaration of Sexual Rights (1999) Declaration of Sexual Rights, http://www.tc.umn.edu/~colem001/was/wdeclara.htm

Feng, H. (2007) 'The research on the legislative perfection of the crime of rape in our country', Unpublished Master's Thesis, Hunan University.

Gao, Q. (2005) 'Reflection on improving the criminal law in relation to the protection of sexual rights', *Journal of Tonghua Teacher's College*, vol 26, no 5, pp 37-9.

Gu, M. (2001) 'Definition of the subject and the object of rape', *Journal of Jiangsu Public Security College*, vol 15, no 3, pp 89-93.

Guo, J. (1997) *Victimology of Crime*, Beijing: Beijing University Press.

Han, H. (ed) (2004) 'Domestic violence does not include only physical violence', http://lady.anhuinews.com/system/2004/11/23/ 001053969/02.shtml

He, C. and Gong, T. (2003) 'Legislative proposal for crime of rape', *Modern Law Science*, vol 25, no 5, pp 64-9.

Hu, W. (2004) 'Reflection on improving sexual crime laws in China', *Journal of Hubei Police Officer College*, vol 80, no 5, pp 22-5.

Jiang, C. (2007) 'A comparative study on the makiing of rape laws between China and the West', Unpublished Master's Thesis, Sichuan University.

Jin, Q. (2004) *Criminology*, Beijing: China Fangzheng Press.

Kang, Y. (2007) 'Weakness and improvement of rape crime legislation in China', Unpublished Master's Thesis, Xinan University of Politics and Law.

Li, H. (2007) 'On a lack of enacting sex crime law based on protection for men's sexual rights', Unpublished Master's Thesis, China University of Political Science and Law.

Li, J. (2005) 'On protection by criminal law for male sexual right', Unpublished Master's Thesis, Sichuan University.

Li, W. (2006) 'Research on the scope of the subject of rape', Unpublished Master's Thesis, Jilin University.

Li, Z. (2002) *The Origin and Development of Law in Relation to Sex*, Beijing: The Mass Press.

Lie, H. (2008) 'Why didn't the women report when they were raped?', http://wenwen.soso.com/z/q37741490.htm

Liu, B. (2007) 'On penal protection for male sexual right', Unpublished Master's Thesis, Jilin University.

Liu, S. et al (2004) 'Offenders and victims in rape: the analysis on 71 rape cases', *Criminal Study*, vol 4, pp 50-2.

Liu, Y. and Zhang, X. (2009) 'Methods of Interrogating Suspects of Rape', *Journal of Liaoning Police Academy*, vol 54, no 2, pp 41-3.

Lu, J. (2007) 'A comparative research on rape between the UK and China', http://qzq333.fyfz.cn/blog/qzq333/index.aspx?blogid=289271

Reinharz, S. (1992) *Feminist Methods in Social Research*, Oxford: Oxford University Press.

Roberts, C. (1989) *Women and Rape*, London: Harvester Wheatsheaf.

Ruan, J. (2003) 'On the analysis of protection of criminal law for male sexual right', *Journal of Guangxi Public Security Management Cadres Institute*, vol 2, pp 59-61.

Sang, B. (2003) 'Why is rape a crime?', *North West College of Politics and Law*, vol 3, pp 49-55.

Shang, X. (2003) 'An analysis on causes in relation to the female raped', *Jiangsu Police Officer College* vol 18, no 5, pp 20-2.

Skinner, T., Hester, M. and Malos, E. (eds) (2005) *Researching Gender Violence: Feminist Methodology in Action*, Cullompton: Willan Publishing.

Song, H. (2005) *Criminology*, Beijing: Chinese People's Public Security University Press.

Tang, Y. (2007) 'Research on several questions of rape crime', Unpublished Master's Thesis, Shandong University.

Universal Declaration of Human Rights (1948), www.un.org/Chinese/hr/issue/udhr.htm

Wang, W. (2005) *Study of Rape Cases*, Beijing: The People's Court Press.

Wu, H. and Li, Q. (2004) 'Rape or whore?', *Out Eight Hours*, vol 4, pp 13-5.

Xi, L. (2006) 'A woman who was raped in the office has demanded a claim damage and will receive psychological therapy (continuing report)', *Chengdu Evening News*, http://edu.beelink.com.cn/20060316/2045092.shtml

Xiang, Q. and Fu, Y. (2006) 'A young lady who was raped in the office claimed damages but her application was rebutted twice', *Chengdu Evening News*, 15 March, p 10.

Xiong, Y. (1994) 'Power to make Chinese women's own decisions in marriage, birth and sex', *Collection of Women's Studies*, vol 3, pp 32-5.

Ye, Q. (2008) 'The issue of gender in relation to domestic violence cannot be neglected within the context of Chinese development', in T. Zhang, X. Qiu and Y. Shen (eds) *Women and Social Development*, Shanghai: Shanghai Academy of Social Sciences Press.

Yu, H. (2007) 'Research on the victims of rape', Unpublished Master's Thesis, Jilin University.

Zhang, G. (2005) *On Criminal Cases in Relation to Raping, Abducting and Selling Women*, Beijing: China Procurator Press.

Zhang, Q. (1999) 'Argument against definition of rape crime', *Jiangsu Police Officer College*, vol 5, pp 54-6.

Zhang, R. (2007) 'Research on the legal interest of rape', Unpublished Master's Thesis, Suzhou University.

Zhang, Y. (2001) *Principles of Criminology*, Beijing: China Law Press.

Zhou, C. (2007) 'On women becoming the subject of rape', Unpublished Master's Thesis, Xinan University.

Zhou, M. (2005) *On Criminology*, Beijing: Beijing University Press.

FIVE

Still little justice for rape victim survivors: the void between policy and practice in England and Wales

Nicole Westmarland

Introduction

The past decade has seen huge advances in rape law and policy in England and Wales. However, there are still significant problems with the ways in which rape victim survivors are treated, and most men who rape go unpunished. This chapter explains the national context and gives an overview of law and policy, focusing particularly on developments during the reign of the New Labour government from 1997-2010. It describes three key issues that remain problematic. First, it analyses problems with policing and prosecuting rape using two recent serial rape cases (Reid and Worboys) that resulted in official complaints. Second, it describes the continuing problem of negative attitudes towards rape victims and analyses the implication of this problem. The third and final key issue outlined is the Rape Crisis funding crisis, which has resulted in a number of Rape Crisis Centre closures and continues to be a significant problem. The chapter concludes that there is now a range of well-developed laws and policies, but that in practice these are not being carried out. There exists a large 'implementation gap' (Brown et al, 2010a) as well as a 'funding gap', both of which must be closed before substantial improvements can be seen.

Rape in England and Wales

In England and Wales there is no national non-government rape prevalence study. The most reliable figures available come from the government's British Crime Survey (BCS), which measures self-reported victimisation across a range of different crime types on an annual basis. Rape is part of a special self-completion module on intimate violence. Data published in 2009 from the 2007/08 BCS (Roe, 2009) showed that nearly one in four women (23.3%) and one in 33 men (3%) men had experienced some form of sexual assault (including attempted sexual assault) since the age of 16. Corresponding figures for rape (including attempted rape) were nearly one in 21 women (4.6 %) and one in 200 men (0.5 %) since the age of 16.

These figures are slightly lower than international self-report studies have found, although this can partly be explained by known methodological limitations of the BCS, which has always had problems with the way it measures rape and other forms of intimate violence. In its early days, very few women reported rape to the BCS; for example, in the 1983 sweep, only one woman disclosed an attempted rape (Hough and Mayhew, 1983). This led to a period of time where the results for rape were simply not included in BCS publications because so few disclosures were being made (Percy and Mayhew, 1997). This continued until the late 1990s when the new computer-assisted self-interviewing method was introduced (Mirrlees-Black, 1999; Walby and Allen, 2004). There are a number of reasons why rape may be still under reported in the BCS. For example, framing questions within the context of crime may reduce the likelihood of people reporting acts such as forced sex that they do not label as 'criminal' (Walby and Myhill, 2001), and those who are excluded from the survey (people who are homeless or living in temporary accommodation such as refuges and hostels) may be populations that experience particularly high rates of intimate violence (Hagemann-White, 2001; Walby and Allen, 2004). In addition, the fact that the BCS only asks about intimate violence that has happened since the age of 16 and does not survey participants over the age of 59 significantly restricts its ability to measure the true prevalence of sexual violence.

In 2008/09, the police recorded 12,165 incidents of 'rape of a female' (an increase of 5% compared with 2007/08) and 968 incidents of 'rape of a male' (a decrease of 4%) in England and Wales (Roe et al, 2009). Previous years (2006/07 to 2007/08) had seen a substantial decrease in reported rapes for both females and males (of 8% for females and 13% for males) (Hoare and Povey, 2008). However, as with the BCS, police-recorded rape figures also have significant limitations. Only a minority of people who are raped will report the crime to the police. Just 10% of women using Rape Crisis Centres have made a police report (Women's Resource Centre and Rape Crisis, 2008) and only 11% of serious sexual assault victims in the BCS made a police report (Roe, 2009). Recorded crime rates may also be distorted by changes in police recording practices (Hoare and Povey, 2008). Therefore, it is not known whether the aforementioned changes in recorded rapes represent true variation in the number of rape crimes, or whether they are due to other factors such as changes in victims' likelihood to report (possibly linked to confidence in the police) or differences in police recording rates. (Although there have been no official changes to the way rape is recorded over this period, different police forces are known to apply the same recording rules slightly differently.)

Rape conviction rates have been a matter of national concern since the late 1990s, following campaigns by feminist organisations such as the Truth About Rape, Campaign to End Rape, and Rape Crisis England and Wales, as well as academic research (Lees and Gregory, 1993; Lees, 1996a, 1996b). Since then, rape conviction rates have stayed at between 5% and 8% (Harris and Grace, 1999; Kelly and Regan, 2001; Lea et al, 2003; Kelly et al, 2005), with large variations between police force areas (Fawcett Society, 2008). Lovett and Kelly (2009) tracked attrition in reported rape cases across Europe. They found that out of 22 countries, four were categorised as having a low conviction rate (defined as 10% or under) with England and Wales the second lowest at 6%, Scotland the lowest at 3%, and Ireland and Sweden also categorised as low at 7% and 10% respectively.

Feist and colleagues (2007) conducted a logistical regression analysis to investigate which factors best predict whether or not a rape case will result in conviction. After controlling for other variables, they found that in each of the following circumstances the odds of an offence resulting in a conviction at court increased:

- where assault was linked to a sexual offence against a separate victim (accounting for only 7% of crimes but a third of convictions);
- where the offender threatened the victim (accounting for less than 10% of crimes but 38 % of convictions);
- where forensic evidence was recovered;
- where the victim's medical history was obtained;
- where witnesses were present.

Interestingly, they also found that for adult victims, the police force area that investigated the rape was a highly significant factor. This is important because it suggests that police knowledge, resources, skills and experience (or lack of these) play a role in the rape conviction rate (see also Fawcett Society, 2008). Encouragingly, this means that there are actions that can be taken to increase the effectiveness of investigations and prosecutions that may lead to increased conviction rates.

Relevant laws and policies

One of New Labour's pledges when it gained power in 1997 was to help victims of sexual offences obtain justice. Sexual offences legislation had previously been altered through piecemeal changes, meaning that a number of different Acts had to be accessed in order to clarify the law. A range of case law advances confused the situation even more and the Home Office itself described the situation as a 'patchwork quilt of provisions' (Home Office, 2000, p iii). A Sexual Offences Review was initiated in 1999 to review legislation, which resulted in the drafting of a Sexual Offences Bill, and then the 2003 Sexual Offences Act which came into force in May 2004 (See Westmarland, 2004, for overview of the reform process).

Rape is now defined, under the 2003 Sexual Offences Act, as:

> (1) A person (A) commits an offence if –
>   (a) he intentionally penetrates the vagina, anus or mouth of another person (B) with his penis,
>   (b) B does not consent to the penetration, and
>   (c) A does not reasonably believe that B consents.

The Sexual Offences Review concluded that penile penetration of the mouth should be included within the definition of rape on the basis that '… forced oral sex is as horrible, as demeaning and as traumatising as other forms of penile penetration' (Home Office, 2000, p 15). This was a key change, because previously penile penetration of the mouth had been classified as indecent assault and carried a lesser maximum sentence than rape. This means that rape remains a gender-specific offence with regard to the perpetrator (that is, the act requires a penis so only a man can rape) but a gender-neutral offence with regard to the victim (a woman or a man can be raped).

A new assault offence, 'assault by penetration', was established under the 2003 Sexual Offences Act. This is not gender-specific for either the victim or the perpetrator and refers to penetration of the vagina or anus with any part of the body (for example, digital penetration) or anything else (such as a weapon or bottle). As with the crime of rape, assault by penetration has a maximum punishment of life imprisonment.

As with many crimes, there are two elements that must be proven in a rape case – the *actus reus* (the guilty act – that the defendant committed an act that meets the legal definition of rape) and the *mens rea* (the guilty mind – that the defendant knew that the victim was not consenting). The 2003 Sexual Offences Act altered both elements. Along with the widening of the definition of rape (to include penile penetration) and the creation of the new offence (of assault by penetration), there were two other significant changes – clarification of what is meant by 'consent' and the inclusion of the word 'reasonably'.

The 1976 Sexual Offences (Amendment) Act was the first to use the term 'consent' in statute; previously it had been force that was named as the relevant factor. The 2003 Sexual Offences Act was the first to provide a statutory definition of 'consent', stating that 'a person consents if he agrees by choice, and has the freedom and capacity to make that choice' (s 74). In addition, it lists six situations where consent is 'presumed to be absent' and two where it is 'conclusively presumed' to be absent. In these situations there is now an evidential burden on defendants to demonstrate the steps they took to ascertain consent. However, definitional problems continue. Judicial interpretation of the consent definition in cases involving intoxication has also continued to be particularly problematic (discussed further later). It is worth noting that that rape of a child under 13 is a separate offence and does not include the consent element of the definition.

The other significant change was the inclusion of the word 'reasonably' (that 'A' does not *reasonably* believe that 'B' consents). Previously if the defendant committed the *actus reus* (the guilty act) but he honestly believed that the other person was consenting, regardless of how unreasonable that belief was, he could not be convicted of rape because the *mens rea* (guilty mind) was not present. This was known formally as the 'mistaken belief' clause and informally as the 'rapist's charter' (Temkin, 1987), because it meant that a person could be actively non-consenting, even shouting 'no' and struggling to free herself, and the defendant could still be acquitted of rape[1]. It was a defence that was difficult, if not impossible, to disprove because of its reliance on what was going on the defendant's mind.

Feminist groups had campaigned for many years to have the 'mistaken belief' clause removed or, alternatively, for a test of 'reasonableness' to be introduced. In the aforementioned Sexual Offences Review, there was much debate, but no clear agreement was reached. Around a third of the respondents to the rape and sexual assault section of the review argued that mistaken belief in consent clause should be changed so that a belief must be both honest and reasonable (Home Office, 2000). Alongside these responses, a postcard campaign to the then Home Secretary Jack Straw was organised by the feminist activist group Campaign to End Rape, which called for a total removal of the mistaken belief clause. The debate within the review was not whether the clause *should* be changed (since nearly all agreed it should be), but rather *how* it should be changed, and what, if anything, should replace it. After much debate, the word 'reasonably' was inserted, whereby the belief is considered to be reasonable after 'regarding all the circumstances, including any steps A may have taken to ascertain whether B consents'.

Despite the massive overhaul of rape laws, the perception in the eyes of the public is that rape law is unfair to victims and that rape is a difficult crime to prove persists. Brown et al (2010b) compared opinions on rape in 1977 with those in 2010 and found that 78% in 1977 and 70% in 2010 agreed or strongly agreed that the law on rape is unfair to the victim. In addition, 78% in 1977 and 74% in 2010 agreed or strongly agreed that rape is difficult to prove in a court of law.

Government policy was slower to develop for rape than it was for domestic violence, and it was not until April 2007 that the first national policy document was published – the *Cross Government Action Plan on Sexual Violence and Abuse* (HM Government, 2007). There was nothing that was specifically 'new' in the action plan. Rather, its intention was to bring together into one document all the current and planned measures that would help deliver on three key objectives:

- to maximise prevention of sexual violence and abuse;
- to increase access to support and health services for victims of sexual violence and abuse;
- to improve the criminal justice response to sexual violence and abuse.

An online implementation guide was published alongside the action plan to set out the roles and responsibilities of 'delivery' agencies (police, courts, local authorities and so on) and partnerships (local criminal justice boards and so on).

The key measures in the action plan to maximise prevention included the management of sex offenders through multi-agency public protection arrangements; the introduction of a new vetting and barring scheme for people who work with children; and the implementation of new strategies for treating sex offenders. To increase victims' access to support and health services the key measures included providing funding to Rape Crisis and other voluntary sector support organisations; expanding the network of Sexual Assault Referral Centres (SARCs, statutory services providing enhanced health and criminal justice responses); and evaluating government-funded Independent Sexual Violence Advisor services (ISVAs, which provide advocacy and support to victims). The action plan's key measures to improve the criminal justice response were focused on increasing reporting and the investigation and prosecution of sexual offence cases, and included rolling out national training programmes for specialist police officers, strengthening the capacity of specialist rape prosecutors and expanding the use of special measures (such as video links) to make it easier for vulnerable victims to give evidence in court. It is important to emphasise again that these were ongoing, planned measures rather than new actions that were introduced as part of the action plan. Accordingly, some had already been introduced by the time the action plan was published, while others have yet to be implemented. At the time of writing (July 2010), it was unknown whether the new Conservative–Liberal Democrat coalition government would continue with the action plan.

Following the 2007 sexual violence action plan, in February 2008 a new action plan on tackling violence was published (Home Office, 2008). This document mainstreamed sexual and domestic violence (including street prostitution, human trafficking and other forms of sexual exploitation) alongside other priority violent offences such as gun, knife and gang-related crime. Its aim in relation to rape was 'to drive forward work on sexual violence, with a particular focus on improving the investigation and prosecution of rape and protecting children from sex offenders' (Home Office, 2008, p 5). The key actions were mainly in line with those contained within the sexual violence action plan published just 12 months earlier, for example expanding the number of SARCs; continuing to improve the investigation and prosecution of serious sexual offences; implementing measures to protect children from sex offenders (including online protection in relation to internet-facilitated abuse).

Arguably the most significant step forward in terms of rape policy came in November 2009, when the first integrated plan to tackle violence against women – *Together We Can End Violence Against Women and Girls: A Strategy* (hereafter referred to as the VAWG strategy) – was published (HM Government, 2009). This represented the first cross-government attempt to join up a range of action plans and measures to provide a more coherent strategy to *end* violence against women. It was also the first time in many years that an official government document had explicitly recognised in linguistic terms the gendered nature of violence and abuse, using the term 'violence against women and girls' rather than 'intimate partner violence' or 'violence and abuse'. Although this may seem relatively insignificant, in reality it reflected a major shift in opinion, as previously violence against women tended to be regarded solely as a crime issue and the wider gender equality framework was largely ignored (Sen and Kelly, 2007).

It is fair to say that the Labour government had come under a substantial amount of pressure to develop an integrated approach. The End Violence Against Women coalition represents seven million individuals and organisations across the UK and one of its four aims is 'for the UK government and devolved administrations to develop integrated and strategic approaches to ending violence against women' (www.endviolenceagainstwomen.org.uk). The lack of an integrated strategy was highlighted in a number of submissions to the United Nations Committee on the Elimination of Discrimination Against Women (the body responsible for overseeing the Convention on the Elimination of All Forms of Discrimination Against Women, or CEDAW; see, for example, Sen and Kelly, 2007; Women's National Commission, 2008; Women's Resource Centre, 2008). Subsequently, the UK was specifically questioned on its lack of such a strategy during its examination by the committee in 2008, despite its protestations that such a strategy existed in 'all but name' (United Nations, 2008, p 9).

The VAWG strategy attempts to provide an integrated approach to tackling violence against women and girls and supporting victims in terms of prevention, provision and protection (often referred to as 'the three Ps'). As would be expected within such a strategy, some actions are focused specifically on rape and other forms of sexual violence, while others have a wider scope. Wider actions include the development of a national communications strategy on public attitudes towards violence against women and girls; steps to improve safety for women and girls on public transport; and lessons on violence against women and gender equality in the school curriculum. The three key actions specific to rape and other forms of sexual violence are the development of a new 24-hour sexual violence helpline; the further development of SARCs (with a commitment to at least one per police force area by 2011); and protected funding in 2010/11 for ISVAs with a view to expanding the service. Rather confusingly, a second government rape review was conducted by the Victims' Champion (Sara Payne), which overlapped with the VAWG consultation period. The findings from this review are available in a separate report (Payne, 2009) and are also referenced within the VAWG strategy. Many of the recommendations overlapped, for example the inclusion of lessons about healthy relationships in the school curriculum and the commitment to challenge public attitudes, while others were additional, for example improved multi-agency working and more training for police and members of the Crown Prosecution Service.

In September 2009, a major independent review of rape was announced by the government and launched by Harriet Harman in her role as Minister for Women and Equality. It was led by Baroness Vivien Stern (Stern, 2010), who was given the task of investigating the response of public authorities to rape complainants (known as the Stern Review). She concluded that the policies currently in place are the right ones, but that their implementation is patchy and must be improved. A total of 26 recommendations were made, and the Labour government published an official response outlining how it intended to meet the review's recommendations (Government Equalities Office/ Home Office, 2010). However, it is unclear how the new Conservative– Liberal Democrat coalition government, which came into power soon after the recommendations were published, will respond.

Policing and prosecuting rape

In 1982, Roger Graef's fly on the wall documentary, Police, caused a public outcry when police officers were shown aggressively interviewing a rape victim about her behaviour and the truthfulness of the allegation. This documentary led the Home Office to establish a Sexual Offences Commission and to issue guidance through two Home Office circulars (25/83 and 69/86). However, problems continued both in relation to 'no criming' (in which the police file an incident as no crime having taken place) and in relation to victim care in cases other than stranger rape (see, for example, Smith, 1989; Temkin, 1999).

As mentioned earlier, the issue of low conviction rates in rape cases became a matter of national concern in the late 1990s, and this meant that both police and prosecutors were subjected to further scrutiny. This time it was not solely through concern for the victim; rather, it aimed to attain more successful prosecutions via thorough investigation and appropriate decision making. In 2001, a joint thematic inspection was carried out by Her Majesty's Crown Prosecution Service Inspectorate (HMCPSI) and Her Majesty's Inspectorate of Constabulary (HMIC) (HMCPSI/HMIC, 2002). Its purpose was to discover the reasons behind the declining conviction rate by analysing and assessing police and crown prosecution policy, procedures and practice. One of the most frequent words used within the report was 'inconsistent', since a large variation in practice was found between different forces. This included variation in the efficiency and quality of victim care, the investigation of cases, the training of police and forensic medical examiners, and in levels of forensic knowledge. Virtually all of the 18 recommendations from this inspection were accepted, resulting in the development of the government's *Rape Action Plan* (HM Government, 2002).

However, problems continued. The rape conviction rate showed no sign of increasing and serious policing problems were still evident. In 2006, a Dispatches television documentary featuring an undercover police officer revealed that there were still significant failings. The programme showed police failing to take the rape of a woman involved in prostitution seriously and failing to collect forensic evidence from a rape scene, and a woman officer saying that if she were raped she would rather 'do herself in' than report it to the police. Pornographic posters were on display in staff-only areas at the police station, and one scene showed police laughing at extreme pornography images on a mobile phone.

In 2006, a further HMCPSI/HMIC inspection took place (HMCPSI/HMIC, 2007), to evaluate to what extent the situation had improved since the previous inspection and to look at the implementation of previous recommendations. It found that only one of the 18 recommendations had been achieved, while three were described as having made 'substantial progress'. There had been no significant progression towards the attainment of the remaining recommendations, although there was 'some' or 'limited' progress towards a few. The report found a 'considerable amount of good practice' (p 5) but continued to find significant challenges and, again, inconsistencies. It concluded that:

> ... in many cases it is not necessarily about changing what is done, but ensuring instead that what is done is effective and is carried out to a consistently high standard, and that the efforts of those involved are properly supported and co-ordinated. In many respects, the policies are sound and in place. It is not a question of changing the approach, but of ensuring that what should be done is actually done in practice and that full effect is given to the existing sound policies and good practice. (HMCPSI/ HMIC, 2007 p 5)

A further 12 recommendations were made, and progress will be evaluated through a third joint inspection in 2010.

The Worboys and Reid cases

Since the 2006 inspection, further problems have come to the fore. Two high-profile cases in particular have challenged any notion that police and prosecutor practice has substantially improved. Both cases involved serial sex offenders (Worboys and Reid) and both investigations were referred to the Independent Police Complaints Commission (IPCC).

John Worboys was the driver of a black cab in London (known as the 'black cab rapist'), who committed a range of serious sexual offences against more than 80 women, although over 60 of these women had not initially reported the incident to the police and only came forward following a media appeal. The IPCC (2010) reported a total of 81 offences were identified as a result of this appeal and Worboys was charged with 23 offences that occurred between 2006 and 2008. He was sentenced in 2009 for an indeterminate period for 19 of these charges, including rape and a range of sexual assaults. Worboys' *modus operandi* (MO) was that he told the women he picked up in his cab that he had just won a significant sum of money, and wanted them to celebrate with him. He would then give them a glass of champagne, which was spiked with drugs, and proceed to commit a range of sexual offences once the victim was unconscious.

When the case hit the media, there was a public outcry questioning how Worboys had been able to get away with committing so many sexual offences with the same MO. Ironically, the emphasis in London at the time had been on warning women about using unlicensed minicabs and recommending that they use black cabs (Westmarland, 2009). Official complaints were made by two of the victims on how the police had handled their reports. Many elements of the complaints were upheld, and some of the police officers involved received either official written warnings or 'words of advice' (similar to a verbal warning). The IPCC found that the police had failed to conduct a thorough investigation, and appeared to doubt the victims from the very start. For example, no search of Worboys' home or cab had been conducted:

> There appears to have been minimal thought in relation to what evidence may be found at Worboys' home or in his cab. The victim had mentioned a bag of money and tablets being offered, yet no attempts appear to have been made to corroborate her account. This was a serious error of judgement. (IPCC, 2010, p 10)

A further example can be seen in the wording used by the officer in charge on the first crime report, described by the IPCC as 'indicative of a mindset that had already been formed' (p 10), who wrote: 'The victim cannot remember anything past getting in the cab, it would seem unlikely that a cab driver would have alcohol in his vehicle let alone drug substances' (IPCC, 2010, p 10).

In the Kirk Reid case, the issue was again one of missed investigatory opportunities. A range of attacks and indecent assaults on women took place in south-west London between 2001 and 2006 and a number of proactive police operations took place in an attempt to identify and arrest the offender. Reid was first identified as a potential suspect in 2004 after being found acting suspiciously in the area, but it was not until 2008 that a DNA sample was requested and matched to Reid. As with the Worboys case, once these details hit the media, questions were asked about why it took so long for the police to stop the attacks and whether any of them could have been prevented.

The IPCC (2010) concluded, with regard to both the Reid and the Worboys cases, that: 'The overwhelming themes in these cases are of an actual or perceived sceptical or insensitive police response to victims of sexual violence, investigations that lack rigour and during which the victims feel they are not being kept informed' (p 15).

It seems clear, therefore, that serious problems remain in relation to the policing of rape. Responding to press coverage about the Reid and Worboys cases, John Yates, the Association of Chief Police Officers' lead for rape at the time, made the insightful and bold statement that 'we are policy-rich and implementation-poor' (*The Guardian*, 26 March 2009), echoing the conclusion of the 2007 joint HMCPSI/ HMIC inspection. This difference between policy and practice, termed by Brown et al (2010a) as the 'implementation gap', therefore appears to be the factor that requires the most attention and effort in the future.

Attitudes to rape

There is widespread agreement that the problems faced in rape prosecutions cannot be dealt with solely through legal reforms (HM Government, 2007, 2009; Temkin and Krahé, 2008). Alongside such reforms, a shift in attitudes is needed throughout society, and recognition of this has resulted in a renewed commitment to the importance of tackling rape myths and other rape-supportive attitudes in society. The *Cross Government Action Plan on Sexual Violence and Abuse* (HM Government, 2007), for example, states:

> We are aware that we need to do more to address the myths and stereotypes associated with sexual violence and childhood sexual abuse that are prevalent in society. We will look at what more can be done with our statutory and voluntary sector partners to raise awareness in this area. (p 40)

The most influential rape myth research in recent years in England and Wales has been the 2005 Amnesty International poll, where telephone interviews were conducted with a national random sample of 1,095 adults (Amnesty International/ICM, 2005). As well as showing that a general ignorance exists about the prevalence of rape and about the low rape conviction rate, the poll used a scale to measure levels of agreement on a range of attitudes towards rape victims. The main results were:

- 34% of interviewees believed the victim was 'partially' or 'totally' responsible if she behaved in a flirtatious manner;
- 22% of interviewees believed that the victim was 'partially' or 'totally' responsible for rape if she had had many sexual partners;
- 22% of interviewees believed that the victim was 'partially' or 'totally' responsible for rape if she was alone in a dangerous/deserted area;
- 30% of interviewees believed that the victim was 'partially' or 'totally' responsible if she was drunk;
- 26% of interviewees believed that the victim was 'partially' or 'totally' responsible for rape if she was wearing sexy/revealing clothing.

The poll received a high level of media coverage, demonstrating that between a fifth and a third of the population held some level of rape-condoning attitudes.

Similar questions were asked again in 2009, this time in a government-commissioned poll of 915 adults (Home Office, 2009). Results that compared badly with the 2005 poll were as follows:

- 43% of interviewees believed that the victim should be held at least partly responsible if she was flirting heavily with the man beforehand (up 9% compared with the 2005 poll);
- 36% of interviewees believed that the victim should be held at least partly responsible if she was drunk (up 6% compared with the 2005 poll).

Therefore, the picture does not look optimistic in terms of attitudinal changes over recent years. The poll also found evidence of other rape-condoning attitudes that were not directly examined in the 2005 poll. For example, 26% agreed that the victim should be held at least partly responsible if she was out in public wearing sexy or revealing clothes; 14% were in agreement if she was out walking alone at night; 42% if she was using drugs; 47% if she worked as a prostitute; and 49% if she did not clearly say no to the man.

In 2010, Brown and colleagues compared opinions on rape to a previous study conducted in 1977 (Brown et al, 2010b). They found that there was positive change over time for some opinions. For example, fewer respondents in 2010 agreed or strongly agreed that if a woman gets raped it is usually her own fault (34% in 1977 compared with 15% in 2010). Likewise, fewer respondents in 2010 agreed or strongly agreed that prior sexual experience of the woman should be taken into consideration when considering punishment for rape (42% in 1977 compared with 19% in 2010). Westmarland and Graham (2010) also reported cautious optimism in a qualitative study into the way rape myths are both promoted and resisted.

Rape-supportive and condoning attitudes are problematic for at least three key reasons (in addition to the psychological effect they may have on victim survivors and the people close to them). First, there is evidence of a correlation between rape myth acceptance (generally measured using a variation of Burt's (1980) rape myth acceptance scale) and the perpetration of rape. For example, Greendlinger and Byrne (1987) found a correlation between male students' self-reported likelihood to rape and rape myth acceptance, and Muehlenhard and Falcon's (1990) research was able to predict rape proclivity in male students based on the rape myth acceptance scale. Bohner et al (1998) argue that their research actually shows a causal link between rape myth acceptance and self-reported likelihood to rape.

Second, there are a range of studies that have shown that people who hold negative attitudes towards rape victims and believe in rape myths attribute blame to victims rather than defendants, which has obvious ramifications in terms of jury decision making. Gray (2006) distributed questionnaires to 180 students and found that those who had a high rape myth acceptance score were significantly more likely than those with low scores to state they were confident that a man was innocent of rape after reading a 'date rape' scenario. Temkin and Krahé (2008) conducted three studies using student and non-student samples in England and Germany to investigate the impact of rape myths on judgements in rape cases. They consistently found that the participants who believed that women precipitate rape (for example, through behaviour or appearance) were the most likely to blame the complainant and least likely to hold the defendant liable. In a series of mock rape trials conducted by Ellison and Munro (2009), jury deliberations were analysed to explore the impact of the complainant's conduct on assessments of her credibility. They found that a complainant's lack of injury, delayed reporting and a calm demeanour in court all independently led to a finding that her evidence was not credible.

The third key reason why rape-supportive and condoning attitudes are problematic is that they affect the way that rape victim survivors are treated by professionals. This may have an impact on the way investigations and prosecutions are handled and also on victims' help-seeking behaviour. Both US and UK studies have shown that police officers believe a high proportion of rape allegations are false (Kelly et al, 2005; Page, 2008). Male police officers are (statistically) significantly more likely to accept rape myths than female officers (Brown and King, 1998), and significant gender difference has also been demonstrated with medical students, with female students more positive in their responses to victims (Williams et al, 1999).

The Rape Crisis funding crisis

Rape Crisis Centres are the longest-running services for rape victim survivors in England and Wales, with over 30 years' experience. Most are members of Rape Crisis (England and Wales) and are women-led, women-centred, feminist organisations that provide support to women and girls by women. As well as direct service provision (for example, telephone helplines, advocacy, group work and counselling), they actively challenge the oppression of women in society, for example supporting campaigns against the sexual objectification of women and girls (see Jones and Cook, 2008, for an excellent history of the Rape Crisis movement in England and Wales). There are currently around 40 Rape Crisis Centres in England and Wales.

While central government funding for rape and abuse did increase substantially over the last six years of Labour's period in office (before the new Conservative–Liberal Democratic government came into power in May 2010), this funding was mainly used to support initiatives explicitly linked to the criminal justice system (for example, SARCs and ISVAs). Importantly, initiatives were funded that attempted to increase public confidence in the criminal justice system by improving the experience of victims going through the criminal justice system to ultimately raise conviction rates. However, this emphasis on 'victims' and 'criminal justice' (and therefore rapes that are reported to the police) had a detrimental effect on the Rape Crisis movement and led to what has been termed the 'Rape Crisis crisis' (Westmarland, 2008). Nine out of ten women who contact Rape Crisis do not report rape to the police (Women's Resource Centre and Rape Crisis, 2008) and a significant proportion are adult survivors of child rape and other sexual abuse, and as a result do not fit neatly into the criminal justice agenda.

A joint report by the Women's Resource Centre and Rape Crisis in 2008 provided details of this crisis and the hoops that Rape Crisis Centres had to jump through in order to gain funding. For example, it describes one Rape Crisis Centre that receives its annual funding of £77,000 from a total of 14 separate funders, which results in the centre being forced to spend valuable time it could be spending working with women completing funding applications and monitoring forms instead. It also describes centres with no or few funders, for example one centre that had to close for part of the year because it had no income at all and another with an annual fund of just £306. Nearly seven in 10 centres (69%) described themselves as financially 'unsustainable', and nearly eight in 10 grants (79%) were for one year or less. Six centres reported situations where they had not been able to pay their staff, but where these staff had continued to work without pay during periods of financial crisis. However, despite this remarkably high level of staff dedication, nine Rape Crisis Centres had been forced to close in the five years between 2003 and 2008. The report concluded:

> While Rape Crisis centres have always been marginalised and suffered from underinvestment, the sector, en masse, is now at crisis point. Any further losses of centres, and their specialist expertise and experience, will, undoubtedly, impact heavily on survivors of sexual violence, their families and society as a whole. (Women's Resource Centre and Rape Crisis, 2008, p 8)

There were slight improvements following the report's publication in that no Rape Crisis Centres closed through lack of funding between 2008 and the time of writing (July 2010) and some new centres are now being (re-)established in major cities including Leeds, Bristol and Bath. However, it remains the case that the future of the Rape Crisis movement is far from secure and short-term grants continue to be the norm. Furthermore, many Rape Crisis Centres fear substantial cuts to funding under the new coalition government.

Conclusion

Compared with a decade ago, there has been a seismic shift in the importance accorded to rape. Alongside a complete overhaul of the criminal law, a number of important policy developments have been advanced. New initiatives, such as the expansion of SARCs and ISVAs, have undoubtedly improved the way in which some rape victim survivors are treated. However, these and other improvements are inconsistently implemented and resourced. As such, they are far from fulfilling their true potential. As I have argued elsewhere (Westmarland, 2008), the optimistic reading of this situation is that the hard work has been done and the policies, strategies and workplans are in place. We have developed a large body of knowledge about what works and what victim survivors want. Now is the time for the new coalition government to establish an appropriate funding regime to support Rape Crisis Centres and to put in place proper penalties for those professionals who fail to adhere to policies and guidelines. A 'culture of silence' still exists, whereby most victim survivors still do not feel able to report rape to the police. A 'culture of scepticism and blame' still exists, whereby large numbers of the general population and key professionals (including some police, prosecutors and judges) believe rape myths such as 'most women lie about rape' and that women should be held partly responsible for rape if they engage in activities such as drinking alcohol or dressing 'provocatively' (as discussed earlier). If improvements are to be seen in the future, these detrimental cultures need to be replaced by a 'culture of action'. This 'culture of action' should include sustainable funding for Rape Crisis and other rape support initiatives, adherence to policies and guidelines (and penalties for those who do not adhere) and a shift in public and professional attitudes towards rape so that excuses for rape are eliminated.

Note

[1] The 'mistaken belief' clause was applied to rape in the case of Morgan in 1976 when a husband colluded in the rape of his wife by three of his friends. He allegedly told his friends that his wife would struggle and say 'no', as though she did not want to have intercourse with them, but that this 'turned her on' because she was 'kinky'. The accused men claimed that they honestly believed she had consented and was enjoying it and that they did not intend to rape her – in other words, they never had a guilty mind. Although in the Morgan case the men were convicted, and the husband convicted of aiding and abetting, this case established a precedent that if a man honestly believed that a woman consented, regardless of how unreasonable this belief was, he could not be found guilty of rape.

Further reading

Brown, J., Horvath, M., Kelly, L. and Westmarland, N. (2010a) *Connections and Disconnections: Assessing Evidence, Knowledge and Practice in Responses to Rape*, London: Government Equalities Office.

McGlynn, C. (2010) 'Feminist activism and rape law reform in England and Wales: a Sisyphean struggle', in C. McGlynn and V. Munro (eds) *Rethinking Rape Law: International and Comparative Perspectives*, London: Routledge-Cavendish.

Rape Crisis (England and Wales) website, www.rapecrisis.co.uk (see also Facebook page)

Truth About Rape website, www.truthaboutrape.co.uk (see also Facebook page)

Links to other work by Nicole Westmarland: http://nicolewestmarland.pbworks.com

References

Amnesty International/ICM (2005) *Sexual Assault Research Summary Report*, London: Amnesty International/ICM.

Bohner, G., Reinhard, M.A., Rutz, S., Sturm, S., Kerschbaum, B. and Effler, D. (1998) 'Rape myths as neutralising cognitions: evidence for a causal impact of anti-victim attitudes on men's self-reported likelihood of raping', *European Journal of Social Psychology*, vol 28, no 2, pp 257-68.

Brown, J., Horvath, M., Kelly, L. and Westmarland, N. (2010a) *Connections and Disconnections: Assessing Evidence, Knowledge and Practice in Responses to Rape*, London: Government Equalities Office.

Brown, J., Horvath, M., Kelly, L. and Westmarland, N. (2010b) *Has Anything Changed? Results of a Comparative Study (1977-2010) on Opinions on Rape*, London: Government Equalities Office.

Brown, J. and King, J. (1998) 'Gender differences in police officers attitudes towards rape; results of an exploratory study', *Psychology, Crime & Law*, vol 4, no 4, pp 265-79.

Burt, M.R. (1980) 'Cultural myths and support for rape', *Journal of Personality and Social Psychology*, vol 8, pp 217-230.

Ellison, L. and Munro, V. (2009) 'Reacting to rape: exploring mock jurors' assessments of complainant credibility', *British Journal of Criminology*, vol 49, pp 202-19.

Fawcett Society (2008) 'Regional rape conviction rates 2006', www.fawcettsociety.org.uk/documents/Regional%20Rape%20Conviction%20Rates%20-%20Final%20Map.pdf

Feist, A., Ashe, J., Lawrence, J., McPhee, D. and Wilson, R. (2007) *Detecting Recorded Offences of Rape*, Home Office Online Report 18/07, London: Home Office.

Gray, J.M. (2006) 'Rape myth beliefs and prejudiced instructions: effects on decisions of guilt in a case of date rape', *Legal and Criminological Psychology*, vol 11, pp 75-80.

Government Equalities Office/Home Office (2010) *Interim Government Response to the Stern Review*, London: Government Equalities Office/ Home Office.

Greendlinger, V. and Byrne, D. (1987) 'Coercive sexual fantasies of college men as predictors of self-reported likelihood to rape and overt sexual aggression', *Journal of Sex Research*, vol 23, pp 1-11.

Hagemann-White, C. (2001) 'European research on the prevalence of violence against women', *Violence Against Women*, vol 7, no 7, pp 732-59.

Harris, J. and Grace, S. (1999) *A Question of Evidence? Investigating and Prosecuting Rape in the 1990s*, London: Home Office.

HM Government (2002) *Rape Action Plan*, London: HM Government.

HM Government (2007) *Cross Government Action Plan on Sexual Violence and Abuse*, London: HM Government.

HM Government (2009) *Together We Can End Violence Against Women and Girls: A Strategy*, London: HM Government.

HMCPSI/HMIC (2002) *A Report on the Joint Inspection into the Investigation and Prosecution of Cases involving Allegations of Rape*, London: HMCPSI/HMIC.

HMCPSI/HMIC (2007) *Without Consent. A Report on the Joint Review of the Iinvestigation and Prosecution of Rape Offences*, London: HMCPSI/ HMIC.

Hoare, J. and Povey, D. (2008) 'Violent and sexual crime', in C. Kershaw, S. Nicholas and A. Walker (eds) *Crime in England and Wales 2007/08*, Home Office Statistical Bulletin 07/08, London: Home Office.

Home Office (2000) *Setting the Boundaries: Reforming the Law on Sex Offences*, London: Home Office.

Home Office (2008) *Saving Lives, Reducing Harm, Protecting the Public. An Action Plan for Tackling Violence 2008-11*, London: Home Office.

Home Office (2009) *Results from the Ipsos Mori Poll of Telephone Interviews with People in England and Wales Regarding their Opinions on Violence against Women*, London: Home Office.

Hough, J.M. and Mayhew, P. (1983) *The British Crime Survey*, Home Office
Research Study 76, London: HMSO.

IPCC (Independent Police Complaints Commission) (2010) *IPCC Independent Investigation into the Metropolitan Police Service's Inquiry into Allegations against John Worboys*, London: IPCC.

Jones, H. and Cook, K. (2008) *Rape Crisis: Responding to Sexual Violence*, Lyme Regis: Russell House Publishing Ltd.

Kelly, L., Lovett, J. and Regan, L. (2005) *A Gap or a Chasm? Attrition in Reported Rape Cases*, Home Office Research Study 293, London: Home Office.

Kelly, L. and Regan, L. (2001) *Rape: The Forgotten Issue? A European Research and Networking Project*, London: Child and Woman Abuse Studies Unit, University of North London.

Lea, S.J., Lanvers, U. and Shaw, S. (2003) 'Attrition in rape cases; developing a profile and identifying relevant factors', *British Journal of Criminology*, vol 43, pp 583-99.

Lees, S. (1996a) *Carnal Knowledge: Rape on Trial* (1st edn), London: Hamish Hamilton.

Lees, S. (1996b) 'Unreasonable doubt: the outcomes of rape trials', in M. Hester, L. Kelly and J. Radford (eds) *Women, Violence and Male Power*, Milton Keynes: Open University Press.

Lees, S. and Gregory, J (1993) *Rape and Sexual Assault: A Study of Attrition*, London: Islington Council.

Lovett, J. and Kelly, L. (2009) *Different Systems, Similar Outcomes? Tracking Attrition in Reported Rape Cases in 11 European Countries*, London: Child and Woman Abuse Studies Unit, London Metropolitan University.

Mirrlees-Black C. (1999) *Domestic Violence: Findings from a New British Crime Survey Self-Completion Questionnaire*, London: Home Office.

Muehlenhard, C.L. and Falcon, P.L. (1990) 'Men's heterosexual skills and attitudes towards women as predictors of verbal sexual coercion and forcible rape', *Sex Roles*, vol 23, pp 241-59.

Page, D.A. (2008) 'Gateway to reform? Policy implications of police officers' attitudes toward rape' *American Journal of Criminal Justice*, vol 33, no 1, pp 44-58.

Payne, S. (2009) *Redefining Justice. Addressing the Individual Needs of Victims and Witnesses*, London: Ministry of Justice.

Percy, A. and Mayhew, P. (1997) 'Estimating sexual victimisation in a national crime survey: a new approach', *Studies on Crime and Crime Prevention*, vol 6, no 2, pp 125-50.

Roe, S. (2009) 'Intimate violence: 2007/08 British Crime Survey', in D. Povey (ed) *Homicides, Firearm Offences and Intimate Violence 2007/08* (3rd edn), Home Office Statistical Bulletin 02/09, London: Home Office.

Roe, S. Coleman, K. and Kaiza, P. (2009) 'Violent and sexual crime', in A. Walker, J. Flatley, C. Kershaw and D. Moon (eds) *Crime in England and Wales 2008/09*, Home Office Statistical Bulletin 11/09, London: Home Office.

Sen, P. and Kelly, L. (2007) 'Violence against women in the UK: shadow thematic report for the Committee on the Elimination of All Forms of Discrimination Against Women', www2.ohchr.org/english/bodies/cedaw/docs/ngos/UKThematicReportVAW41.pdf

Smith, L.J.F. (1989) *Concerns About Rape*, Home Office Research Study No 106, London: HMSO.

Stern, V. (2010) *The Stern Review*, London: Government Equalities Office/Home Office.

Temkin, J. (1987) *Rape and the Legal Process*, London: Routledge and Kegan Paul.

Temkin, J. (1999) 'Reporting rape in London: a qualitative study', *The Howard Journal*, vol 38, no 1, pp 17-41.

Temkin, J. and Krahé, B. (2008) *Sexual Assault and the Justice Gap: A Question of Attitude*, Oxford: Hart Publishing.

United Nations (2008) 'Committee on the Elimination of Discrimination against Women, forty-first session, summary record of the 843rd meeting', http://daccess-dds-ny.un.org/doc/UNDOC/GEN/N08/417/32/PDF/N0841732.pdf?OpenElement

Walby, S. and Allen, J. (2004) *Domestic Violence, Sexual Assault and Stalking: Findings from the British Crime Survey*, Home Office Research Study No 279, London: Home Office.

Walby, S. and Myhill, A. (2001) 'New survey methodologies in researching violence against women', *British Journal of Criminology*, vol 41, no 3, pp 502-22.

Westmarland, N. (2004) *Rape Law Reform in England and Wales*, School for Policy Studies Working Paper Series, Paper No 7, Bristol: School for Policy Studies, University of Bristol.

Westmarland, N. (2008) The Rape Crisis crisis, *The New Statesman*, 18 March, www.newstatesman.com/politics/2008/03/rape-crisis-centres-women

Westmarland, N. (2009) 'Rape: answers needed. How did the London 'black cab rapist' evade the police for so long?', *The Journal*, 23 March, www.journal-online.co.uk/article5626-rape-without-warning

Westmarland, N. and Graham L. (2010) 'The promotion and resistance of rape myths in an internet discussion forum', *Journal of Social Criminology*, vol 1, no 2, pp 80-104.

Williams, L., Forster, G. and Petrak, J. (1999) 'Rape attitudes amongst British medical students', *Medical Education*, vol 33, pp 24-27.

Women's National Commission (2008) 'Submission to the United Nations' Committee on the Convention on the Elimination of all forms of Discrimination against Women', www2.ohchr.org/english/bodies/cedaw/docs/ngos/WNC_UK41.pdf

Women's Resource Centre (2008) 'The state of the women's NGO sector: shadow report submitted to the United Nations Committee on the Elimination of Discrimination against Women (CEDAW) in response to the United Kingdom's 6th periodic report', www2.ohchr. org/english/bodies/cedaw/docs/ngos/WRCUK41.pdf

Women's Resource Centre and Rape Crisis (2008) *The Crisis in Rape Crisis*, London: Women's Resource Centre.

SIX

Controlling women's sexuality: rape law in India

Geetanjali Gangoli

... when a woman is ravished, what is inflicted is not merely physical injury, but the deepest sense of some deathless shame.... (Justice Iyer, *State of Maharasthra v Chandraprakash Kewalchand Jain*, 1990)

Rape is linked with power, that is, the power that men enjoyed in society.... Rape brings out, and enlarges opposition between the sexes nakedly, unlike other forms of gender based oppression, such as lower wages for women. Rape, and the fear of rape therefore is an instrument for terrorising and paralysing women, contributing to a low sense of self worth. (Gothoskar, 1980)

Indian feminist movements have recognised rape as a form of male oppression and control over women since the 1970s. However, the Indian legal system prefers to see it as an issue of loss of honour of the raped woman. This chapter will address the long-standing conflicting relationship between Indian feminists and the legal system.

The national context in relation to rape

Rape continues to be a serious issue for Indian women. The latest crime statistics released by the Home Ministry's National Crime Records Bureau (NCRB, 2007) show that every hour 18 women become victims of rape. The number of reported rapes a day has increased nearly by 700% since 1971, when such cases were first recorded by the NCRB. It has grown from seven cases a day to 53. In general, violent crimes showed a decline of 16% between 1971 and 2006, but rape cases increased by 678%. The rape conviction rate in 2007 was 26.4%, which is in the same range as some other violent crimes, including kidnapping, armed robbery and arson, but lower than conviction rates for others including dowry-related homicides, robbery and murder.

In India as in other parts of the world, the question of rape is linked to women's 'status' within society. As the author has argued elsewhere, it is difficult to measure the 'status of women', especially in the context of a large and diverse country such as India (Gangoli, 2007), but it can be noted that Indian women do possess a number of legal rights. These include certain fundamental rights incorporated in the Indian constitution such as equality under the law for men and women (article 14), equal accessibility to public spaces (article 15), equal opportunity in matters of public employment (article 16) and equal pay for equal work (article 39). In addition, there are statutory provisions that guarantee these rights, such as the 1976 Equal Remuneration Act and the 1976 Maternity Benefit Act. There are also a number of legal provisions criminalising dowry[1], such as the 1961 Dowry Prohibition Act, and domestic violence. Women also have rights to property under personal laws (Kishwar, 1994).

In spite of these rights, women's position in Indian society is highly variable, and depends to a large extent on class and caste. While some Indian women have attained prestigious posts in the judiciary, education, politics, IT, medicine and a myriad of other fields, they are mainly upper-caste, upper-class women, and many of the benefits they enjoy are denied to the majority of women in the country. The mean age at marriage for females is 18 years while for males it is 22.6 years. However, more than half (51%) of illiterate females currently married were below the legal age at marriage, that is, 18. Nearly 20% of the 1.5 million girls married under the age of 15 years were already mothers (Census of India, 2001). Most women have limited control over various aspects of their lives including visiting their natal family, making healthcare provisions and making expensive purchases. National data also reveals that domestic violence is endemic (Kishor and Gupta 2004), as are dowry demands at marriage and son preference (Sunder Rajan 2003), leading to female infanticide, sex pre-selection and the abortion of female foetuses.

Further, there is some evidence that globalisation since the early 1990s has exacerbated class divisions and contributed to increasing poverty. Structural factors such as caste, community and class status can contribute to sexual violence, and affect women's ability to access the criminal justice system. Women from working-class, minority or lower-caste Dalit groups are particularly vulnerable to sexual violence, and this can sometimes be in the context of riot or conflict situations. For example, Dalit women from lower castes in some parts of the country are very vulnerable to sexual violence from upper-caste men (NCRB, 2007). A study conducted by People's Union for Democratic Rights (PUDR), a Delhi-based civil liberties group, looked at 10 cases of rape by police personnel and revealed that in most cases, the victim was a working-class woman. In almost all cases, the accused was acquitted; some have been reinstated in their old posts (PUDR, 1994). Communalisation and the social and economic marginalisation of Muslims in post-independence India has resulted in sexual assaults perpetrated on Muslim women, as was apparent in the anti-Muslim riots in Gujarat in 2002 (Hameed et al, 2002).

As Susan Brownmiller (1975) has persuasively argued, women's fear of rape can prevent them from participating in public life, even though rape and sexual assault is not confined to the public domain. This is further complicated in the Indian context by constructions of the ideal woman as sexless, or one whose sexuality is confined within marriage. Within this context, non-marital sex, whether coercive or voluntary, is considered problematic for women and is seen as potentially shameful for the community or family. Thus rape is experienced as something more than violence against individual women; members of the communities of both the perpetrators (Hindus) and the victims (Muslims) experience the rape of minority women as symbolic dishonour of the community. In the case of the Gujarat riots, it has also been persuasively argued that the nature of violence against minority women – stripping, beating, throwing acid, raping, burning, killing pregnant women, and killing children before their parents' eyes – went beyond collective dishonouring. It was meant to destroy or punish the fertile Muslim female body and to destroy future generations (Sarkar, 2002).

Defining rape: existing laws and policies

In India, rape is legally defined as penile penetration into the vagina, which makes it a gender-specific crime, where only men can be perpetrators and only women can be victims of rape. The rape law was first enacted in 1860 as a part of the Indian Penal Code (IPC), which was partly amended in 1983. However, the definition of rape continues to remain the same as when it was first introduced in 1860, and under s 375, the IPC states that a man is said to commit the offence of rape if he has sexual intercourse with a woman in the following circumstances[2]:

- against the victim's will;
- without the victim's consent;

- with her consent, when her consent has been obtained by putting her or any person known to her in fear of death or harm;
- with her consent, when the man knows that he is not her husband;
- with her consent, when at the time of giving such consent she was intoxicated, or suffering from unsoundness of mind and unable to understand the nature and consequences of that to which she has given consent;
- with or without her consent when she is under 16 years of age.

However, the law makes an exception in the case of rape within marriage, except where the wife is under 15 years of age. The rape law also allows the victim's sexual history to be adduced during trial, under s 155 of the 1872 Indian Evidence Act, which states that: 'When a man is prosecuted for rape or an attempt to ravish, it may be shown that the prosecutrix was of generally immoral character'. The same section does not apply to the accused. Section 54 of the 1872 Indian Evidence Act states that: 'In criminal proceedings (including rape) the fact that the accused has a bad character is irrelevant, unless evidence has been given that he has a good character, in which case it becomes relevant'. It has been suggested that the legal concern with defining rape as an offence was to regulate the sexuality of the woman, not to protect her bodily integrity (Das, 1996). This is certainly borne out by the exemption to marital rape within rape law, and more specifically in the cases of rape that led to a national feminist movement in the late 1970s on the issue of 'power' rape or custodial rapes, which in turn led to amendments to the rape law. As non-consensual penile penetration into the vagina is defined as rape, only women or girls can be raped, and only men can be charged under this law. However, s 377 IPC criminalised all sex between men, consensual and non-consensual, and male rapes by men can only be prosecuted under this Act[3].

Three cases in the late 1970s and early 1980s created a public debate around the issue of rape, and fed into the newly emerging feminist movement in India. This movement created a nationwide campaign on the issue of rape, which led to amendments to the rape law in 1983.

The first case was that of Rameezabee, a Muslim working-class woman from Hyderabad. In April 1978, she and her husband were arrested by the police for 'loitering' when they were returning from a late-night visit to the cinema. The police demanded a fine. The husband went home to bring the money. During his absence, Rameezabee was raped by three policemen. When the husband returned, he was beaten to death by the police. Rameezabee was prosecuted for enticing minor girls into prostitution. She was convicted on this charge, and was subsequently released on probation for a year (Farooqi, 1984).

The second case was that of Mathura, a tribal agricultural labourer from Maharashtra, aged around 14-16 years. She developed a relationship with Ashok, the cousin of Nushi, her employer. Ashok and Mathura decided to get married. On 26 March 1972, her brother, Gama, complained to the local police that Mathura had been kidnapped by Nushi and Ashok. Nushi, Ashok, Mathura and Gama were brought to the police station for questioning, and to record their statements. At 10.30 pm, when they were leaving the police station, the head constable, Tukaram, and constable Ganpat held Mathura back. She was subjected to rape by Ganpat and attempted rape by Tukaram. Mathura came out of the police station and announced to the crowd outside that she had been raped. The crowd surrounded the station and exerted enough pressure to ensure that a case of rape was registered.

While the Sessions Court acquitted the accused, the Bombay High Court reversed the judgment, and convicted sentenced Tukaram and Ganpat for rape. The court held that since the police were strangers to Mathura, it was unlikely that 'she would make any overtures or invite the accused to satisfy her sexual desires'. Justice Koshal, Supreme Court, reversed the High Court judgment. According to the judge, as there were no injuries shown in the medical report, the story of 'stiff resistance having been put up by the girl is all false' and the alleged intercourse was a 'peaceful affair'. Justice Koshal dismissed Mathura's testimony that she had raised an alarm, and further held that under s 375 IPC, only the 'fear of death or hurt' could vitiate consent for sexual intercourse. There was no such finding (quoted in Dhagamwar, 1992, p 253)

The third case was that of Maya Tyagi, a young middle-class woman, who, on 18 July 1980, was driving to her parents' house in Haryana. The car broke down on the way, and while it was being repaired a policeman in civilian dress tried to molest Maya and was beaten up by her husband. The officer returned with a contingent of policemen. The police opened fire and shot her husband dead. Maya Tyagi was dragged out from her car, beaten, stripped and paraded through the town. She was finally taken to the police station, where she was raped by the police. She was charged with being a dacoit (armed robber), and subsequently released on bail.

The three cases described above have several points in common. In all three cases, the victims were innocent of having committed any crime. Hence, the action of the police in holding them in custody was in itself illegal. Rameezabee and Mathura were socially and economically disadvantaged. Rameezabee was a Muslim and Mathura a tribal woman.

In both these cases, the victim's testimony was suspected. Mathura was held to be a 'shocking liar', as she was not a virgin prior to the rape and had a lover. As she was 'habituated to sex', the judge concluded that she had consented to sexual intercourse with the accused. In two of the three cases, the women was re-victimised by having false cases filed against them – Rameezabee was convicted of procuring minor girls into prostitution, and it was further alleged that her marriage was illegal, and that she was sexually promiscuous. Maya Tyagi was accused of being a dacoit. Mathura was castigated by the Supreme Court of indulging in pre-marital sex and of lying.

The three cases, both individually and collectively, led to a major campaign on the issue of rape in custody. Following the Rameezabee incident, there was public protest in the city of Hyderabad. The police opened fire on the protesting crowd, and several people were killed. As a result, a commission of inquiry was set up headed by Justice Muktadar, a sitting judge of the Andhra Pradesh High Court. Justice Mukhtadar found the accused guilty of the offences of rape, murder and assault. He recommended that they be prosecuted for these offences. The judge further held that the inquiry revealed the 'pitiable conditions of suspect women particularly of the poor classes at the hands of the police in the police station' (Kannabiran, 1996, p 120). However, the accused were acquitted by the Sessions Court of the charge of rape and were admonished for wrongful confinement.

The Mathura case led to a major nationwide campaign on the issue of custodial rape, following the open letter written in September 1979 by four law teachers – Upendra Baxi, Lotika Sarkar, Vasudha Dhagamwar and Raghunath Kelkar – to the Chief Justice of India. The Maya Tyagi case was discussed in the Lok Sabha (House of Parliament) on over four days, after which a judicial inquiry was initiated by the Uttar Pradesh government (Gangoli, 2007).

The open letter referred to earlier deserves special mention. It questioned the validity of a judgment passed by the Supreme Court. The authors of the letter identified themselves as Indian citizens and as teachers of law. The letter described the Mathura judgment as 'an extra ordinary decision sacrificing human rights of women under the law and the constitution'. The authors enumerated their reservations on the judgment, stating that a young girl could not be expected to successfully raise the alarm for help when trapped by two policemen inside a police station. They pointed out that the absence of marks of injury on Mathura's body need not imply absence of resistance. They further stated that there is a clear difference in law and common sense between submission and consent. The letter went on to state:

Could not their Lordships have extended their analysis of 'consent' in a manner truly protective of the dignity and rights of Mathura? One suspects that the Court gathered an impression from Mathura's liaison with her lover that she was a person of easy virtue. Is the taboo against pre marital sex so strong as to provide a licence to the Indian police to rape young girls? Or to make them submit to their desires in police stations? (Baxi et al, 1979, p 1)

The letter was circulated among civil liberty groups and women's organisations, initiating a campaign. Meetings were held in various parts of the country. In Bombay, the Forum Against Rape, which was made up of feminists from various organisations, was formed on 12 January 1980. In Delhi, demonstrations were held outside the Supreme Court. At a national level, the feminist campaign focused on demanding amendments to the rape law, asking for legal recognition of rape by men in authority, formal recognition of rape within marriage, and an expansion of rape beyond penile penetration to reflect the experiences of women.

Rape law amendment

On 12 August 1980, a Bill was introduced in the Lok Sabha to amend certain provisions of the rape law. The Bill suggested four major changes. The first was a prohibition on press coverage of any incident of rape or any publicity that revealed the name of the offender or the victim. The second was a new section, which attempted to define consent more clearly. In this definition, rape is held to have taken place when a man has sexual intercourse with a woman 'without her free and voluntary consent'. A further amendment was that the marital rape exemption would not be applicable in cases of judicial separation. A final, major amendment was the introduction of s 376 to the IPC, which introduced a new category of rape – rape by members of the police within their official jurisdiction, by public servants, by superintendents or managers of jails, remand homes, or hospitals, against women in their custody. Gang rape was included within this category, punishable more severely than other forms of rape. Under s 376, the onus of proof was shifted from the victim to the accused, that is, 'if the woman stated that she did not consent, the court would presume that she did not consent'. This was a reversal of the generally applicable legal principle. Finally, the Bill provided that under s 228A, rape cases be conducted 'in camera', that is, unlike other trials, they would not be subjected to and open to public scrutiny and attendance (Bill No 162 of 1980). The Bill was referred to a joint committee comprising representatives from both houses of parliament, which consulted with women's groups, lawyers and the press (The Gazette of India, 1982).

The Joint Committee Report, voicing the concerns of some feminist groups, opposed s 228A, holding that under certain circumstances, publicity may be 'necessary for proper investigation' and may be desired by the victim. Further, the committee suggested that provisions regarding rapes by policemen be strengthened; that s 376 be extended to all the staff of a jail, not merely the supervisory staff; that rapes in hospitals be extended to include visitors, as well as patients; and that rape of minors be included under the section. The committee also believed that not all cases of sexual assault need be held in camera (The Gazette of India, 1982).

Other general recommendations made by the committee included that women should not be arrested after sunset and before sunrise; that medical examination of the accused and of the complainant be performed immediately on complaint; that social welfare officials be associated in the procedures; and that compensation for social ostracism be given to rape victims. However, the report did not accept the recommendations of the Law Commission and various women's organisations that the past sexual history of the woman not be adduced in the evidence or during cross-examination.

The final law did acknowledge the importance of custodial rape, but did not take up many suggestions made by the women's groups. For example, the new law continued to treat the past sexual history of the woman as relevant, and press restrictions on the trial were imposed. Further, marital rape continued to be outside the remit of the rape law, although the amendments allowed rape charges to be brought in the case of judicially separated couples. While this was a significant shift, the amendment did not go far enough in challenging patriarchal assumptions about women's rights within marriage (Mishra and Singh, 2003). Finally, rape continues to be defined exclusively as penile penetration into the vagina. The rape law therefore is based on, and legitimises, several patriarchal presumptions and attitudes regarding male and female sexuality, including the idea that within marriage women are the sexual property of their husbands. At the time of writing, recommendations have made to the Lok Sabha by the Law Commission addressing some of these anomalies, and these are likely to be implemented in the near future (see section below on analysis of policies and interventions).

Key criminal justice issues

Some of the key issues faced by women in accessing justice in rape trials relate to social perceptions that influence the criminal justice system. Women's bodies are seen as repositories of community or familial shame and honour, leading to a dichotomy between virtuous and suspect women. Further, working-class women are seen as sexually available, as they are less secluded and consequently less 'respectable' than middle-class women. This section exams some key themes emerging from case law on rape.

The police and custodial rape

As discussed above, the police, far from providing women with protection in rape cases, have often been identified as potential perpetrators of sexual assault. Cases of custodial rape by the police are treated as 'routine' cases, negating the amendments made to the IPC in 1983, and rates of conviction in cases of custodial rape are very low (PUDR, 1994). This seems to indicate a benevolence on the part of custodians of law and order towards perpetrators, analogous to that displayed by the patriarch of a family towards a straying prodigal son.

Perceptions of working-class sexuality

Judicial interpretations in cases of custodial rape following the 1983 amendment demonstrate that in spite of the change in the law that shifted the onus of proof in these cases on to the accused, judicial interpretations remained centred on questions of the 'character' of the complainant. As most cases of custodial rape are perpetrated against working-class women, class assumptions regarding sexuality are also apparent. In an incident in a village in the state of Bihar in 1988, a large group of policemen gang-raped 19 women following a quarrel between a policeman and local villagers. The case attracted much press coverage, and the state government awarded the women Rs 1,000 as an ex-gratia payment. However, as the investigation by the local police was not carried out properly, and included just a perfunctory medical examination, there was insufficient evidence to convict the accused, and the judge remarked: 'It can not be ruled out that these ladies might speak falsehood to get a sum of Rs. 1000 which was a huge sum for them' (quoted in Baxi, 1995, p 128). Further, the judge noted the defence counsel's argument that 'the women could not be equated with such ladies who hailed from decent and respectable societies, as they were engaged in menial work, and were of questionable character' (quoted in Baxi, 1995, p 129).

Pre-marital sex

In the Suman Rani case, representations of women's sexuality were based on diverse understandings of pre-marital sex. Suman Rani, a minor, had eloped with Ravi Shankar in March 1984. Her family had filed a case for abduction. The police arrested the absconding couple on 31 May 1984 at Bhiwani bus stop on the way to Jammu, where they were headed. Suman Rani and Ravi Shankar were put in separate rooms in the Patram Gate police post, where Suman Rani was raped by two policemen, one of whom was Premchand. Ravi Shankar was charged for abduction and rape under s 366 of the IPC. In the Sessions Court, Bhiwani Khera, Ravi Shankar and the two policemen were tried together, and convicted on the charge of rape, the policeman getting the minimum sentence of 10 years under s 223 (*Premchand and Another v State of Haryana*, 1989). Significantly, the Sessions Court judge dismissed the plea that Suman Rani was 'habituated to sexual intercourse', and therefore was not raped. He stated:

> And all things said and done, even a girl of easy virtue is also entitled to all the protection of law and can not be compelled to sexual intercourse against her will and without her consent. Offences of rape and other allied offences are created for the protection of fallible, earthly mortals and not for goddesses. (*Premchand and Another v State of Haryana*, 1989)

The Sessions Court judgment was overturned by the Punjab and Haryana High Court at Chandigarh. Ravi Shankar was acquitted, as it could not be proved that Suman Rani was below 18 years, and it was held that she had had sex with Ravi Shankar of her free will. The conviction and sentence of the two policemen was confirmed. The accused appealed to the Supreme Court. The Supreme Court did not dispute that Suman Rani had been raped in custody. However, Justice S Ratnavel Pandian and Justice B C Ray were reluctant to award the minimum punishment under s 223, accepting the argument that 'the victim was a woman of questionable character and easy virtue with lewd and lascivious behaviour' (*Premchand and Another v State of Haryana*, 1989).

Rewarding the 'good Indian woman'

While judgments like these bring out the more obvious misogynist and conservative aspects of judicial functioning, one finds that even seemingly 'positive' judgments can be based on similarly anti-women sentiments. The central point of rape cases is the role of corroborative evidence under the 1872 Indian Evidence Act, which is often reduced to physical injuries suffered by the victim (1972 Cri L J 824 Raj) or other witness statements (*Naravan v State of Rajasthan*, 2007). However, some judges have argued that insistence on corroborative evidence is tantamount to a denial of justice. In a case of custodial rape, in which a co-petitioner was a Nagpur-based women's group, the judges held that to disbelieve a woman, especially a 'young girl', was to insult womanhood, and they suggested that Indian women are unlikely to lie about rape:

> Ours is a conservative society where it concerns sexual behaviour. Ours is not a permissive society, as in some of the western or European countries. Our standards of decency and morality are not the same as in those countries.... Courts must also realise that ordinarily a woman, more so a young girl, will not stake her reputation by levying a false charge concerning her chastity. (*State of Maharasthra v Chandraprakash Kewalchand Jain with Stree Atyachar Virodhi Parishad v Chandraprakash Kewalchand Jain*, 1990).

In an earlier case, the judge had similarly commented on the perceived differences between eastern and western cultures, suggesting that, in the Indian setting, women and girls would be bound by tradition and the stigma of rape and non-marital sex. They would therefore fear being ostracised by society, and their natal and marital family, thus risking the family honour. Further, women and girls would be reluctant to face interrogation by the court. It was stated that it was conceivable that western women might lie about rape for several reasons, such as financial considerations, psychological neurosis, revenge, notoriety or publicity, hatred of one or all men or a desire for sympathy. However, in the Indian context, these did not apply and 'refusal to act on the testimony of a victim of sexual assault in the absence of corroboration as a rule, is adding insult to injury' (*Bharwada Bhoginbhai Hirjibhai v State of Gujarat*, 1983). In an earlier case, it was argued that insisting on corroborative evidence was to 'cling to a fossil formula', and the ruling stated that: 'No woman of honour will accuse another of rape, since she sacrifices thereby what is dearest to her' (*Rafiq v State of Uttar Pradesh*, 1980).

Within this context, a woman is therefore only believed if she is a 'woman of honour'. What to the judicial mind constitutes an honourable woman? It is a respectable married woman or a virginal daughter? In another case of custodial rape, a married woman was raped by a policeman, after being threatened that her husband, a labourer, would be arrested if she did not consent. While the Bombay High Court acquitted the accused on the grounds that the woman did not raise an alarm, and that there were no injuries on her body, the Apex Court reversed the judgment on the grounds that she was threatened by the police, and because she was not a prostitute (*State of Maharashtra v Prakash and Another*, 1984).

Shame and honour: lost chances

The judicial mind also exercises sympathy where the victim is a young and virginal child. While deciding on an appeal made to the Supreme Court 10 years after a child of nine was raped, the judges noted that the loss of virginity had blighted her chances of a happy married life:

> ... the victim who is now 19 years old, after having lost her virginity still remains unmarried undergoing the untold agony of the traumatic experience and the deathless shame suffered by her. Evidently, the victim is under the impression that there is no monsoon season in her life and that her future chances for getting married and settling down in a respectable family are completely marred. (*Madan Gopal Kakkad v Naval Dubey and Another*, 1992)

These judgments reveal a number of assumptions about male and female sexuality. Most obvious is that the courts constantly emphasise the 'chastity' of the raped woman, or its absence. Even in 'positive' judgments, when the woman conforms to the standards of womanhood held as ideal by the judge, the focus is on the loss of honour and shame suffered by the woman. Rape is not seen as a violation of bodily integrity, but as a loss of family honour.

Rape as crime of passion

Some case law also projects rape not as an act of violence, but as a crime of passion, and rapists as 'lusty brutes' (*Madan Gopal Kakkad v Naval Dubey and Another*, 1992). In the case of the abduction and gang rape of Shashibala, a minor, the judge called the rape a 'bestial act of lust' (*Krishnalal v State of Haryana*, 1980). In another case, where a 22-year-old man raped his cousin, the judgement uses language that verges on pornography:

> A philander of 22, appellant Phul Chand, overpowered by sex stress in excess, hoisted himself into his cousin's house next door, and in broad daylight, overcame the temptingly lonely prosecutrix [female prosecutor] of 24, Pushpa, raped her in hurried heat, and made an urgent exit having fulfilled his erotic sortie. (AIR 1980, SCC 249, 1980 Cri L J 8)

The language used converts an act of violence into a sexual odyssey, while the description of the woman as 'temptingly lonely' objectifies her. In a further attempt to reduce the seriousness of the crime, Justice Krishna Iyer lists several 'mitigating' factors. He reluctantly admits that 'rape is a violation with violence, of the private person of a woman', but goes on to state that 'excessive punishment of the offender can be counterproductive' and the accused is described as a 'hyper sexed Homo Sapien' (AIR 1980, SCC 249, 1980 Cri L J 8).

Another 'extenuating' factor mentioned in the judgement is the perceived shift in Indian society towards sexual licentiousness, as evident in the following quote:

> It may be marginally extenuating to mention that modern Indian conditions are drifting into societal permissiveness on the carnal front, prompting proneness to pornos [sic] in real life, what with libidinous 'brahmacharis', womanising public men, lascivious dating and mating by unwed students. Isolated prosecutions and annual suppression rhetoric will stultify the law, where the vice is widespread and the larger felons are left loose. (AIR 1980, SCC 249, 1980 Cri L J 8)

The judgement therefore fails to distinguish between consensual sexual activity and violent, coercive sex. The inherent moralistic tenor projects 'pre-marital' sex – sex being defined only in terms of marriage – as ushering in a social situation in which men have the unconditional 'right' to rape, and women, no right to refuse any sexual initiative from men.

Analysis of policies and interventions

Feminists soon realised that the 1983 IPC amendment did not yield positive results at the level of women's lives, nor did it lead to any substantial improvement in judicial and police procedures. A feminist lawyer pointed out that the amendment and the campaign behind it could not succeed in 'evolving a new definition of rape beyond the parameters of ... notions of chastity, virginity, premium on marriage and fear of female sexuality' (Agnes, 1993). The rate of convictions in cases of custodial rape is low, perhaps because stricter laws and increased punitive measures make judges cautious in awarding the full punishment available to them. In addition, as mentioned above, feminist understanding of custodial rape as being limited to rape by policemen might have been governed by political exigencies in the early 1980s. However, an inability to extend custodial rape to include other categories, including rape of minors or adult women within the family, or of married women by their husbands, meant that a substantial area of women's experience was never centrally addressed.

In 1992, a Bill on sexual violence was proposed by feminists and approved by the National Commission for Women that aimed to expand the law on rape to reflect the experiences of women and children:

> The present law (on rape) has become so outdated in terms of language and intent that it fails to acknowledge the true nature of sexual assault. In particular, the existing law does not address the increasingly visible offence of child sexual abuse ... a substantial number of child sexual abuse cases are occurring within the family. (1992 Sexual Violence Bill[4])

The Bill attempted to extend the definition of rape beyond that of penile penetration of the vagina. Hence, it included a range of non-consensual sexual activities, that is: introduction by a man of his penis into the vagina, external genitalia, anus or mouth of another person; the introduction by one person of an object or a part of the body of another person; the uttering of any word, making of any sound or gesture, or exhibiting any object or part of the body for sexual purpose. The charge of 'aggravated sexual assault' included assault by a police officer, a member of the Armed Forces, a public servant or anyone in a position of trust, authority, guardianship or with economic and social domination over someone 'under such trust, authority or dominance'. After much deliberation, the age of consent was fixed at 18 years. While there were some concerns that this would lead to consensual sex between adolescents being treated as an offence, it also provided for the criminalisation of rape within marriage, as it included any sexual intercourse between a married couple if the wife was under 18.

This Bill, however, was not adopted by the Indian state, and Saakshi, one of the organisations involved in drafting the Bill, filed a writ petition to the Supreme Court in 1997:

> ... praying for (a) issuance of a writ in the nature of a declaration or any other appropriate writ or direction declaring inter alia that 'sexual intercourse' as contained in section 375 of the Indian Penal Code shall include all forms of penetration such as penile/vaginal penetration, penile/oral penetration, penile/anal penetration, finger/vaginal and finger/anal penetration and object/vaginal penetration and (b) to issue a consequential writ, order or direction to the respondents in the Writ Petition and to their servants and agents to register all such cases found to be true on investigation. (Law Commission of India, 2000)

As a result, the Law Commission was directed by the court to file a report on this matter. The Law Commission made the following recommendations:

- changing the focus from rape to 'sexual assault', expanding the definition beyond penile penetration to include penetration by any part of the body and objects;
- deleting s 155(4) of the 1872 Indian Evidence Act, which had previously allowed for a victim to be cross-examined about her sexual history;
- introducing different gradations of punishment for rape, with higher punishment for rape committed by the relatives and persons in 'trust or authority', public servants, and superintendents, management and staff of hospitals;
- introducing a new section of s 376(E), to include sexual harassment in the workplace;
- shifting the burden of proof of consent in all rape cases to the accused;

- introducing specific provisions to deal with the medical examination of the victim and the accused by a registered medical practitioner, and guidelines to the police to question minor victims of rape;
- providing compensation in some cases of sexual assault;
- treating sexual assault as a gender-neutral crime, allowing both women and men to be prosecuted under the law; and men and women to be treated as potential victims under the law;
- deleting s 377, as sexual assault was treated as gender-neutral.

The Law Commission's recommendations have been submitted to parliament and are likely to be applied in the main.

Suggested amendments in the law

While meeting many of the concerns of feminist groups, the recommendations of the Law Commission do not go far enough in some areas. The shift from penile penetration to other forms of sexual assault (including sexual assault in the workplace) is a welcome step, as it is based more widely on the experiences of women and children. The deletion of the clause allowing the woman's sexual history to be adduced in trial is similarly a step in the right direction, as it could make rape trials less traumatic for women and encourage more women to come forward to report rape. Further, the focus on child rape, the guidelines for medical examinations and police procedure in cases involving children are useful.

However, the Law Commission does not take into account marital rape, other than by raising the age of consent within marriage from 15 to 16 years. While commenting on recommendations by feminist groups that the exemption to marital rape be removed, the report states that 'that may amount to excessive interference with the marital relationship' (Law Commission of India, 2000, p 14). The report therefore continues to support the view that women are the sexual property of their husbands.

Further, while the suggested deletion of s 377 – that is, the law criminalising male homosexual activity – can be seen as highly desirable, some feminists have argued that the proposed gender neutrality could be problematic, as it could lead to false claims made by men against women, and increase scrutiny of women's sexual behaviour in a patriarchal context (PRISM, 2006). In addition, Mumbai-based LABIA (Lesbians and Bisexuals in Action) has suggested that the gender neutrality introduced within the Sexual Assault Bill may work against the interests of gay groups. Representatives of LABIA suggest that while the suggested decriminalisation of voluntary male homosexuality is a positive development, the proposed Bill introduces for the first time legal recognition of the sexuality of lesbian women in the context of perpetrating violence. It is suggested that this could be problematic in a predominantly homophobic social and legal context (Shah, 2006).

Finally, the question of compensation in rape cases remains a vexing issue for Indian feminists. As mentioned above, case law can sometimes treat women who accept compensation with scepticism. However, women from working-class backgrounds may need compensation in order to rebuild their life after a sexual assault, especially if they are likely to face stigmatisation from wider society.

Conclusion

This chapter has highlighted some of the complex debates within social, legal and feminist perceptions of rape in India. Rape and the fear of rape continues to be an issue for many Indian women, even though the conviction rate for rape stands at over a quarter of all cases charged and brought to trial. While this may seem impressive, it should be noted that case law reveals that judges are more likely to pass positive judgements when they consider the victim to fit into the societally acceptable norms of the 'good' woman, that is, a virginal, unmarried girl or virtuous, married woman. Rape is associated with loss of honour for the family or community, and therefore raped women often do not file a report with the police. Also, while Indian feminists have campaigned on the issue of rape, it has been primarily in the area of demanding legal reforms and solutions, and there has been no concerted Rape Crisis movement in India. Furthermore, feminist shelters for rape victims are few and far between. This has led to rape victims becoming dependent on their families and often lacking support when they need it most. This could be another reason why many Indian women do not report rape. However, there are no reliable statistics on the proportion of rape cases reported (compare Gangoli, 2007).

The proposed changes to rape law in India will potentially contribute to reducing the stigma of rape, as discussions on the character and sexual history of the victim will no longer be considered legally relevant. However, as noted above, marital rape continues to be unrecognised by the law, and the issue of gender neutrality may cause problems in a society that remains, in part, deeply patriarchal and conservative, as it can increase sexual scrutiny of women, who could be seen as perpetrators of sexual violence. Nevertheless, the suggested changes, based as they are mainly on feminist understandings of violence against women, are a step in the right direction.

Notes

[1] Dowry in the Indian context can be defined as money or property given by the woman's family to the husband's family at the time of marriage.

[2] There are currently changes being proposed to the rape law; see conclusion.

[3] In July 2009, following years of concerted efforts by gay rights groups, the Delhi High Court revoked the provision of s 377 of the Indian Penal Code that criminalised consensual sexual acts of adults in private, holding that it violated the fundamental right of life and liberty and the right to equality as guaranteed in the Indian Constitution. This is currently not applicable to the rest of the country.

[4] Under existing law, s 376 of the IPC does criminalise child rape as a category warranting greater punishment than some other forms of rape, but does not address intra-family rape in particular.

Further reading

Gandhi, N. and Gandhi, S. (1992) *The Issues at Stake: Theory and Practice in the Contemporary Women's Movement in India*, New Delhi: Kali for Women.

Sunder Rajan, R. (2003) *The Scandal of the State. Women, Law and Citizenship in Postcolonial India*, New Delhi: Permanent Black.

Articles and research papers on Indian society and various aspects of gender-based violence are available at www.indiatogether.org

References

Agnes, F. (1993) 'The anti rape campaign. The struggle and the setback', in C. Datar (ed) *Violence Against Women*, Stree: Calcutta, pp 125-40.

AIR (1980) SCC 249, 1980 Cri L J 8.

Baxi, P. (1995) 'The normal and the pathological in the construction of rape. A sociological analysis', Unpublished MPhil Thesis, Department of Sociology, Delhi School of Economics, University of Delhi.

Baxi, U., Sarkar, L. and Dhagamwar, V. (1979) Open Letter to the Chief Justice of India, 16 September, on file with Akshara (women's resource centre, Mumbai).

Bharwada Bhoginbhai Hirjibhai v State of Gujarat (1983) AIR 753 1983 SCR (3) 280.

Brownmiller, S. (1975) *Against Our Will: Men, Women, and Rape*, New York, NY: Simon and Schuster.

Das, V. (1996) 'Sexual violence, discursive formations and the state', *Economic and Political Weekly*, vol 31, no 35-7, pp 2411-23.

Dhagamwar, V. (1992), *Law, Power and Justice. The Protection of Personal Rights in the Indian Penal Code*, New Delhi: Sage Publications.

Farooqi, V. (1984) 'A woman destroyed. An interview with Rameezabee', in M. Kishwar and R. Vanita (eds) *In Search of Answers. Indian Women's Voices from Manushi*, London: Zed Books.

Gangoli, G. (2007) *Indian Feminisms. Campaigns against Violence and Multiple Patriarchies*, Aldershot: Ashgate.

Gothoskar, S. (1980) 'Politics of rape', Paper presented at National Conference on Perspectives for Women's Liberation, Bombay, 1 November.

Hameed, S., Manorama, R., Ghose, M., George, S., Naqvi, F. and Thekaekara, M. (2002) 'How has the Gujarat massacre affected minority women? The survivors speak', http://cac.ektaonline.org/resources/reports/womensreport.htm

The Gazette of India (1982) *Joint Committee Report on the Bill to amend the Indian Penal Code, 1860, the Criminal Procedure Code, 1973, and the Indian Evidence Act, 1872*. The Gazette of India, Extraordinary, Part II, Section II, 2 November.

Kannabiran, K. (1996) 'Challenge of communalism', in M. Datta, F. Agnes and N. Adarkar (eds) *The Nation State and Indian Identity*, Calcutta: Samya.

Kishor, S. and Gupta, K. (2004) 'Women's empowerment in India and its states. Evidence from the NFHS', *Economic and Political Weekly*, vol 39, no 7, pp 649-712.

Kishwar, M. (1994) 'Codified Hindu law. Myth and reality', *Economic and Political Weekly*, vol 29, no 33, pp 2145-61.

Krishnalal v State of Haryana AIR (1980) SCC 1252.

Law Commission of India (2000) 'One hundred and seventy second report on review of rape laws', http://Lawcommissionofindia.Nic.In/Rapelaws.Htm

Madan Gopal Kakkad v Naval Dubey and Another (1992) Insc 140 (29 April 1992) 1992 SCR (2) 921 1992 SCC (3) 204 JT 1992 (3) 270 1992 SCALE (1)957.

Mishra, S. and Singh, S. (2003) 'Marital rape – myth, reality and need for criminalisation', PL WebJour12.

Naravan v State of Rajasthan 2007 Insc 383 (10 April 2007) Criminal Appeal No 526 of 2007 (Arising out of Slp(Crl.) No 4179 of 2006).

National Crime Records Bureau (2007) 'Statistics on crimes', http://ncrb.nic.in/cii2007/home.htm

PUDR (People's Union for Democratic Rights) (1994) *Custodial Rape*, New Delhi: PUDR.

Premchand and Another v State of Haryana (1989) Cri L J 1246.

PRISM (2006) *PRISM on the Sexual Assault Bill*, New Delhi: PRISM.

Rafiq v State of Uttar Pradesh (1980) Cri L J 1344.

Sarkar, T. (2002) 'Ethnic cleansing in Gujarat. An analysis of a few aspects', *Akhbar*, vol 3, p 2.

Shah, C. (2006) 'Gendered and sexual: a queer feminist look at the recent sexual assault law debates', Paper presented at Workshop on Towards a Theory of Law and Social Movements, organised by the Hauser Centre for Nonprofit Organisations at Harvard University, Bangalore, 26-27 June.

State of Maharashtra v Prakash and Another (1922) Cri L J 1984.

State of Maharasthra v Chandraprakash Kewalchand Jain with Stree Atyachar Virodhi Parishad v Chandraprakash Kewalchand Jain (1990) Cri L J 889.

Sunder Rajan, R. (2003) *The Scandal of the State. Women, Law and Citizenship in Postcolonial India*, New Delhi: Permanent Black.

SEVEN

Breaking the silence: rape law in Iran and controlling women's sexuality

Nadia Aghtaie

Introduction

Iran has a population of over 70 million and, as a non-Arab, predominantly Shia country, differs considerably from most other countries in the region. After the 1979 Islamic Revolution, religious authority found its way into both public and private policy. Prior to the Islamic Revolution, religion was a private matter; it was the choice of the individual whether to pray, fast or wear the *hejab* (the Islamic covering for women). After the revolution, however, the state began to enforce the religious mandates. As a result, the Shari'a law was declared the law of the land, meaning that the state is founded on the doctrine of *velayat-e faqih* (rule of the Islamic jurist). In order for the government not to transgress the framework of Islamic law, a powerful body called the Guardian Council[1] must approve all of the Bills passed by parliament, and can veto them if it considers them inconsistent with the constitution and Islamic law.

After the revolution, therefore, many laws and policies were abolished because they contradicted the Shari'a. New policies were introduced and gender became quite significant. The government believed that women were susceptible to anti-Islamic influences and could easily slip from being 'honourable' and 'respectable', while men could easily become victims of sexual temptation. As a result, women's participation in some social activities was banned and a significant emphasis was put on women's domesticity. The Islamic republic's idea of women's domesticity was based on Motahari's[2] ideology on the notion of gender difference. This meant that due to physiological and psychological differences, husbands and wives in the family and women and men in society were to have different roles and expectations (Moghadam, 2003). This presumption was prevalent among other religious scholars:

> The female brain has a larger capacity for dealing with emotions, creativity, and spirituality, whereas the male brain has more capacity to deal with deliberate and abstract thought. In light of these differences, men and women are believed to have equal but different rights. (Bahonar, 1984, p 155)

The 1967 Family Protection Law was immediately annulled and a new Family Law was created. This had an enormous impact on women's position in society. The new law reduced the age of marriage to puberty for girls, denied women the right to initiate divorce and reinstated men's unilateral right to divorce and practise polygamy. Laws such as compulsory veiling and gender segregation were introduced to protect men's inherent vulnerability to women's bodies. Moral police were created to patrol the streets to implement these laws and make sure that women appeared modest in public. Thirty-two years after the revolution, moral police are still active in the public domain. Although men are sometimes cautioned or are taken away, it is mainly women who are at the receiving end of the moral police's disciplinary actions. Women, especially young women who are *bad hejab* (not veiled properly) and do not adhere to strict moral codes are perceived as a source of potential moral decay that needs to be cautioned and disciplined. *Bad hejab* is a loose concept and can vary from showing your hair and wearing make-up or tight or see-through clothing to looking different from the norm. A *bad hejab* woman could be fined or imprisoned for a period of 10 days to two months (Centre for Women's Participation, 1999), the sentence depending on the discretion of the moral police due to a lack of clarity in the application of the law. However, there is no written law against men who do not adhere to strict rules of modesty such as having long hair or wearing westernised shirts bearing foreign words that are perceived as satanic. Marriage is encouraged sooner rather than later to avoid illegitimate outlets for sexual gratification and therefore moral ill. *Sigheh* (temporary marriage) is allowed as a way preserving public modesty and sexual corruption through legitimising a sexual union between women and men[3].

Since the revolution, there has been a dramatic increase in female literacy rates from 52% in 1987 to 72% in 1997 (Mehran, 2003) and in 2006 the rate rose to 96.1% for those aged between 15 and 24 (UNESCO, 2007). In 2000, women's university enrolments exceeded men's (Mehran, 2003). Female university students are currently able to gain admission to almost all disciplines. Women's literacy rates have also had an impact on fertility rates. Research has suggests that women's level of education is a sound predictor of fertility rates (Mehran, 2003). However, women's employment rates are not reflective of their educational level. There is a high unemployment rate in Iran for both genders, but women's is considerably higher than men's. The Ministry of Planning and Policy Affairs announced in 2003 that 43% of women aged 15 to 22 who had previously joined the labour market are now jobless (*Iran Official*, 2003; Roudi-Fahimi and Moghadam, 2006). Iran is also grappling with other social issues such as a high divorce rate. According to *Faslnameh-ye Refah-e Ejtema'i*, a Tehran-based social welfare quarterly, the national average divorce rate is 120 per 1,000, rising to 200 per 1,000 in the capital Tehran (Afary, 2009). There is also a high incidence of suicide among rural married women in violent and abusive marriages. In 2000, the average rate of such suicides reached 25-30 per 100,000 women (Afary, 2009). In 2001 alone, 350 women set themselves on fire in Ilam (Amiri, 2001).

The national context of rape in Iran

In Iran, there are no official statistics on the number of reported rape crimes. The Iranian government has not published any official data on conviction rates where women have been able to prove their cases. Likewise, there are no academic articles or published books solely on rape in Iran. There is limited information in legal books, and these are targeted mainly at professionals and legal experts such as lawyers and judges. In these books, the words 'rapists' or 'perpetrators' are not used; rather, the term for someone who commits rape is *zani* (adulterer) or 'the accused'.

The only available statistics on rape are sporadic pieces of information in various newspapers based on interviews carried out with police forces and lawyers. For example, the Iranian Student News Agency (ISNA, 2007), through an interview with a police official, reported that sexual attacks on women are one of the top priorities of the police force because of their harmful consequences. The police officer declared that 40% of rapes in Iran are the outcomes of hidden friendships between boys and girls and false marriage promises made by boys. He believed that parents should raise their daughters' awareness of these issues and give them sufficient attention and love to avoid such harmful incidents. This seems to be a pattern in the state-controlled media, where the focus is on girls and women as the party able to avoid rape and sexual attacks by altering their behaviour and observing modesty at all times.

In another interview (ISNA, 2008), a police official stated that the numbers of reported rape cases had increased. He believed the increase in the number of reported cases was due to a project established by Iranian President Ahmadi-nejad that aimed to raise safety levels in public spaces: "Now people trust us and have realized that police forces are going to deal harshly with offenders. Therefore, the victims are more likely to come forward". However, he stressed the fact that even if police forces do their jobs efficiently, it is up to the judges to decide the appropriate sentence for offenders and admitted that sentences could vary between inflicting lashes to the death penalty. He also repeated the assertion that girls and women could avoid sexual attacks and were partly to blame for rape crimes: "The main aims of perpetrators are young girls and women. They are the ones who take the first steps and fall into men's trap". This statement demonstrates how women in Iran are expected to self-regulate their sexuality due to their presumed inherent seductive nature as well as men's uncontrollable desire for sexual gratification.

In addition, the police sometimes attempt to downplay the number of reported rape crimes. For example, ISNA (2009b) reported that the head of police in Naja rejected the claim that there was an increase in the number of reported rape crimes. He stated that the media should not create public anxiety because of one or two incidences. He blamed 'cultural invasion' through western TV programmes transmitted via satellite, the increase in the average marriage age and unemployment for different forms of rape, including incest.

Resalat, an Iranian-based newspaper, conducted an interview with the head of Society for Social Pathology (Anjoman-e Asibhay-e Raftari), Dr Yeganeh, regarding incestuous rape. Yeganeh declared that in Tehran there are 4,000 files on brothers raping their sisters and 1,200 cases of fathers raping their daughters. He believed that these cases were all drug-related (Anjomanhaye Iran Pardis, 2007). It has also been claimed that the high rate of maternal mortality in Iran is due partly to illegal abortions and that some of these abortions are the result of rape (Asgari-Nejad, 2005).

Cultural perceptions of rape

Rape is probably the only crime in which, in most cases, the victim not only feels ashamed, but may even be blamed for the incident. Unfortunately, in Iran, rape victims are often blamed for provoking the incident. Even if the perpetrator is charged with the crime, the victim will still feel ashamed. Therefore, it could be argued that many victims of rape and sexual harassment stay silent in order to avoid public humiliation.

The orthodox Islamic culture of Iran is turning a blind eye to this issue and does its best not to publicly address or discuss rape. It is not surprising, therefore, that there is no actual word in the Iranian dictionary that means 'rape'. The terms *tajovoz jensi* or *taroz jensi*, meaning sexual attack or sexual harassment, are used as synonyms for 'rape'. People often just use the words *taroz* and *azaar*, which translate as 'bothering' and 'harassment' with no reference to 'sexual'.

In Iran there is still a *bavare omumi* (deep belief) that there can be no rape within marriage or an intimate relationship. Therefore, if a boyfriend rapes his girlfriend, it is seen as a part of the sexual relationship rather than rape. In countries like Iran where traditional norms are still very strong, there is the perception that if something is not spoken of publicly, it has not happened. The state-run media tries to glorify the dominant traditional norm by stating that the statistics on rape in western countries are the result of their lack of morality (Shahidian, 2002).

The reason why there are no official records or statistics is that according to Islamic teaching, sexual acts, whether voluntary or forced, should not be part of public discourse because this would affect public morality. Furthermore, the victims of rape and their families are too ashamed to talk about it. State and self-censorship therefore preclude any public discourse and debate on the issue. Even when the state media highlights the issue of rape, it is presented as something that does not happen very often, and when it does, it is the fault of the victim. Shortly after the launch of Ahmadi-nejad's 'raising social safety project', a programme on Iranian state-run TV showed a young rape victim whose face was obscured to hide her identity. She had been raped in the middle of the day in a deserted road by two men. The interviewer asked her whether she was wearing an appropriate *manto* (an overcoat, normally worn at knee length) and whether it was too tight. The girl repeatedly said that her *manto* was of standard size and that she had not used much make-up, but the interviewer insisted that the perpetrators had claimed that "your manto was too tight and your make-up was too provocative and that is why they did it". Finally the victim said: "I admit I had some make-up on and my *manto* was above my knees but that does not give them the right to rape me unless they are animals" (Rezaie, 2008). There appears therefore to be an expectation that any attire that accentuates a women's body and beauty should be repressed, with women being perceived as the main bearers of public morality. Shahidian (2002, p 212) states how the Islamic state of Iran believes that: 'Modesty in dress, especially women's hejab, secures society against chaos and individuals against self-incurred harmful thoughts and deeds'.

Legal framework

The Iranian Penal Code was passed by the judiciary committee of the Islamic Consultative Assembly on 30 July 1991 (8 Mordad 1370) and was approved with amendments by the Majma-e Tshkhis-e Maslahat-e Nezam (Council on the Determination of the Regieme's Welfare) on 28 November 1991 (7 Azar 1370). The code has four main sections containing 729 articles. Article 12 introduces five kinds of punishment that deal with various crimes: *hodud, qasas, diyat, ta'zirat* and prohibitive punishments[4].

Hadd [singular of *hodud*] is a punishment whose characteristics have been described by Shari'a law. *Qasas* is a retaliatory punishment where the perpetrator receives a punishment equal to the crime committed. *Diyeh* [singular of *diyat*] is an amount of compensation, money or property payable for the crime and determined by the legislator. *Tazir* [singular of *ta'zirat*] is a punishment whose characteristics have not been defined in Shari'a law and are therefore at the judge's discretion. The punishment determined by the judge could include imprisonment, fines or flogging. The punishment received must be less than *hadd*. Finally, prohibitive punishments are determined by the government to maintain public order.

Crimes punishable by *hadd* are *zena* (sex outside marriage), sodomy, lesbianism, pimping, sexual malicious accusation, intoxication, civil unrest and theft. Rape, which is referred to as *zena-e ba onf va ekrah* (adultery with force and duress) falls under the category of *zena*. This section focuses on the law that specifically concerns rape, that is, the fourth subsection of article 82 of the Iranian Penal Code. It is important to note that there are other articles that judges sometimes refer to in rape cases, but they are not central to the discussion of rape and its legal framework and therefore will not be discussed here. According to article 82, regardless of the age or marital status of the offender, the punishment for *zena*, sex outside marriage, in the following circumstances is the death penalty:

- *zena* with incest (blood relatives who are non-marriageable according to religious law);
- *zena* with one's stepmother, in which case the man would receive the death penalty and the step mother would be stoned[5];
- *zena* with a non-Muslim man, in which the man would receive the death penalty (the woman would be sentenced to 100 lashes if unmarried and death penalty if married);

- *zena-e ba onf va ekrah* (adultery with force and duress, that is, rape) outside marriage, in which case the rapist would receive the death penalty.

As explained above, voluntary sex outside marriage is also punishable under the Iranian law. The aim of the government is to regulate sexuality by confining sex to the marital bed and any deviation from this is punished harshly. Same-sex relationships are also seen as deviation from 'healthy' sexuality and denounced.

Zena-e be onf va ekrah

As mentioned earlier, there is no synonym in Farsi language for the word 'rape'. *Zena-e ba onf va ekrah* in Iranian law means forced sexual intercourse with a woman to whom the culprit is not married. Penile penetration can be either into the vagina or anus. There is no law prosecuting forced oral sex. The word *onf* means force or violence, and suggests that resistance is shown by the victim. *Ekrah*, however, could include a situation in which the victim did not show any signs of resistance because she was scared or threatened but the intention to protest was there. Threats to kill or hurt a woman are therefore included in the definition of coercion. However, neither of these definitions includes rape while the victim is unconscious. On 4 April 1995, the Supreme Court issued the death penalty for a man who had used a general anaesthetic to put a woman to sleep in order to have sexual intercourse with her. However, this is not a uniform practice across the country; different jurists have issued different rulings in similar cases. For example, Ayatollah Musavi Ardabili, a *marja taghlid* (religious leader[6]), believes that unless the victim shows signs of resistance before being put to sleep, sexual intercourse is not classified as rape, whereas Ayatollah Makarem Shirazi declares that if a woman is unwilling to have sex whether awake or sleep, intercourse constitutes rape and the verdict would be the death penalty (Hadadzadeh-Nayeri, 2008).

General *zena* can be proved in court in the following circumstances:

- confession before the judge. This has to be done four times before the designated punishment can be set. If it is done less than four times, the punishment is at the judge's discretion (article 68). However, article 71 indicates that a denial made after a confession can result in the verdict being changed from stoning or the death penalty at the judge's discretion;

- on the testimony of four just men or three just men and two just women in cases where the designated punishment is either stoning or flogging (article 74). It is important to note that there is no specific definition in the legal texts about who can be identified as a just man or a just woman; this depends on the personal views of the judge;
- on the testimony of two just men and four just women in cases where the designated punishment is flogging (article 75). The testimony of women alone or in conjunction with the testimony of only one man cannot be used to prove *zena*, instead it can it be regarded as *Qazf* (false accusation), which is liable to punishment (article 76). *Qazf* constitutes wrongly accusing a person of *zena* or sodomy, and is punishable by 80 lashes (article 139). In addition, article 79 indicates that the witnesses should give their accounts one after the other without any lapse of time. If some of the witnesses testify and others are not present to testify immediately or decide not to testify, *zena* cannot be proven. In this situation, the witness will be subject to punishment for false accusation (*qazf*);
- where the judge uses his own knowledge to prove *zena*, although this is not a uniform practice. In this situation, the judge has to make the source of his knowledge transparent (article 105). Some judges use tools such as medical evidence to help them make a decision. Others believe that only prescribed religious evidence, that is, confession and witness testimony, is valid.

As will be demonstrated in the following section, because of a lack of uniformity in court procedures, the verdicts in such cases vary greatly depending on individual judges and the way they deal with each case.

It is important to highlight that the law does not punish a non-married woman for becoming pregnant unless her adultery is proven by one of the methods highlighted above (article 73).

The following example illustrates how rape may be dealt with in the Iranian courts. It is important to bear in mind that this case by no means represents all rape cases in Iran. It was chosen specifically from seven other cases because it was documented in detail.

On 20 April 1999, a case was presented in the Supreme Court[7]: A 24-year-old girl, Kolsum, filed a complaint of rape against three men, stating[8]:

> I went to another city with my dad to visit a relative in hospital. I got separated from my dad by accident and got lost in the city. I was upset and crying. Muhammad came over and asked me what had happened. He took me to his

cousin's house. The next day I was taken to his friend's house.
I was told to tell the wife, Khavar, that I was Muhammad's
sister (Khavar cut her hair and gave her some make-up
to wear). I was then taken to another house where three
men, Teymour, Nasir and Nabi raped me while I was under
duress, while being threatened with a knife. I first tried to
resist Teymour by kicking him but he smashed my head
against the wall and I stopped. Muhammad came after the
incident, he took me home. Prior to my departure Nabi
gave me 50,000 Rial.

Nasir escaped, Nabi and Teymour were arrested and charged with
zena-e ba onf va ekrah (rape), dishonouring and deflowering Kolsum
and were given the death penalty by sword. Muhammad was charged
with kidnapping and pimping, and was given five years in prison, 75
lashes and 10 months' exile to another city.

The defendants' lawyers appealed against the case twice, with a
number of issues being raised by the defence team in the subsequent
several sittings. First, they questioned why Kolsum did not go to the
police station or the hospital to seek help, rather than going with an
unknown man (Muhammad). For the defence team, it was hard to
believe that a 24-year-old girl could be lost in a city, which led them
to conclude that she was looking for customers for sex. Likewise, it
was questioned why Kolsum accepted the money from Nabi if she
was not a consenting party.

Kolsum was asked by one of the judges whether she enjoyed having
sex with the defendants. In this context, it was argued that Kolsum's
reported acceptance of Khavar's suggestion to wear make-up was an
indicator of her willingness to have sex with the defendants. It was also
stated that Kolsum had several opportunities to get away, yet she failed
to do so. According to the defence team, this illustrated her willingness
to spend a period of time with the unknown men. It was also claimed
that Kolsum's accounts were contradictory.

As a result of these concerns, as raised by the defence team, it was
suggested that there was lack of sufficient evidence to prove *zena-e ba onf
va ekrah*. However, there was evidence for general *zena*. The confessions
of the defendants were not valid because they were not repeated four
times (article 68) and they were not made before the judge. Even if the
confessions were valid, the defendant, Nabi, denied the act of rape after
the initial confessions. According to the article 71 of the penal code, if
the defendant denies the charge after confession, she/he can no longer
be considered for the death penalty (especially by sword). Therefore,

article 120, which indicates that the judge can make a verdict based on his knowledge (one element being the accused's confession), is not applicable here as the defendants denied the claim after confessing.

However, this law is unsuitable because defendants have become adept at manipulating the current system to their advantage, which is evident in the counterarguments to the initial arguments of the defence team. Indeed, Nabi confessed to raping Kolsum at different times during the interrogation, which was argued to be enough for a conviction. Denial following confession should not overturn the verdict. This law was introduced to deal with general *zena* in order to prevent it becoming a public affair, yet this is *zena-e ba onf va ekrah* and is therefore already in the public domain.

Furthermore, Kolsum was a young woman from a small village who could not easily articulate her experiences. Her lack of the economic means required to employ a lawyer to present her case effectively should not have hindered her ability to seek and receive justice. It is also unlikely that Kolsum would have come forward willingly and filed a complaint if she had been making a false accusation. Another factor to consider that Kolsum was proven to be a virgin prior to the incident, so Nabi should also have been liable to pay compensation for this. It was argued that Nabi's previous convictions for robbery discredited him as an honourable person.

The case went to the Supreme Court and it was finally decided that there was not sufficient evidence to charge the defendants of *zena-ba onf va ekrah*. The fact that Kolsum did not call for help, accepted money, wore make-up and pretended to be Muhammad's sister played a significant role in the verdict. Muhammad was subsequently acquitted. The case was referred back to the local court to decide the appropriate charges for Teymour, Nabi and possibly Kolsum. It was stated that if the case turned on general *zena* rather than *zena-e ba onf va ekrah*, Kolsum would also be liable for punishment. The court then had to clarify whether any of the involved parties were married because sentences would vary for each party depending on their marital status. If any of the parties are married, *zena* is deemed to be *mohsana*, meaning that adultery has occurred between adults of sound mind who are in a marital relationship.

There are no further details about the case and the final charges. If the local court decided on a verdict of general *zena*, Kolsum would have received 100 lashes if single (she would have received death by stoning if she were married). Teymour, if married would be sentenced to stoning or to 100 lashes. In this case, we know that Nabi was married. However, during the court's procedure, his lawyer stated that Nabi's wife was in another city when the incident occurred. The lawyer, envisaging the outcome of the trial, made this clear during the appeal, arguing for Nabi's sentence to be reduced from stoning to 100 lashes on the grounds that his wife's absence had deprived him of the opportunity for sexual intercourse.

This case highlights several issues with regard to rape law. It is very difficult to prove rape crime within the framework stipulated. For example, it is difficult to provide any witnesses in rape cases, especially the numbers required under the current law – four men or three men and two women. In addition, as discussed earlier in the chapter, the term 'judge's knowledge' can mean different things for different judges depending on their personal views. One could include the perpetrator's confession as the 'judge's knowledge', for example, while in this case the Supreme Court judge believed that denial after confession could not be counted as such. Furthermore, perpetrators can annul the punishment by denying their crime after confession or by repenting prior to testimony (article 81), thus providing an easy escape for the offender, while the fact that victims can receive punishments for not being able to prove their claims may prevent them from filing complaints in the first place.

The case described above also illustrates how a woman's claim can be dismissed if she is not identified as a 'good woman'. According to the state's gender ideology, the way a woman presents herself could be seen as a threat to the public morality and she could be blamed for encouraging and arousing male strangers. Some of the judges in this case assumed that if Kolsum had agreed to wear make-up, this meant that she was willing to have sex with the defendants. These matters will be analysed in greater depth in the following section.

Key issues faced by women in Iran

Iranian society, particularly the legal system, perceives the virginity of an unmarried woman as a signifier of her chastity, and losing her virginity outside marriage is perceived as a colossal disaster for both her and her family. Not only might it ruin her marriage prospects, it will have an impact on her honour and her father's honour. Laws such as *arsholbekareh* (compensation for losing one's virginity outside wedlock) and customs like the provision of certified documents verifying a girl's virginity prior to marriage[9] or the illegal practice of hymenoplasty[10] for girls who have lost their virginity prior to marriage demonstrate how patriarchal society controls women's sexuality. The stigma attached to rape and the honour-related issued involved make it very difficult for women to report a rape crime.

Sex outside marriage is prohibited in Iran, and boys and girls who are not related are not supposed to mingle with each other. This makes it difficult for girls who have been raped by their boyfriends to come forward and file a complaint because they risk being blamed for having a boyfriend in the first place. They would probably be told that they 'asked for it'. This issue was raised several times by participants in an empirical research conducted in Iran in 2008 looking into the attitudes of Iranian students towards violence against women. Some participants stated that Iranian society perceives girls who have boyfriends as social deviants who get what they deserve if they are raped (Aghtaie, 2010). However, male sexuality and men's desire to have unlimited sex are treated as something natural and beyond their control. As demonstrated in the case above, one of the lawyers asserted that because Nabi's wife was out of town, and therefore he did not have opportunities for sex with her, his sentence for the crime of *zena* should be reduced from stoning to 100 lashes. While the author is not condoning stoning as a punishment, it is surely right to question the portrayal of women as sexless and men as creatures incapable of controlling their desire for sex, and to query a verdict where an unmarried man or a married man deprived of his usual opportunities for sexual intercourse receives a lesser punishment for adultery. Considering marital rape as within the remit of legality exemplifies the assumption that men have inherent vulnerability to women's naked bodies. In rape cases where perpetrators are sentenced to death, they are punished not because they have violated a woman's sexual rights, but because they have threatened another man's property.

Iranian state-run television sometimes broadcasts programmes in which young, 'deviant' rape victims are interviewed with their backs to the camera or their faces obscured. They are asked questions about the underground parties they attend and whether they drink alcohol or take drugs, where they were raped (at night or in the middle of the day in a deserted street?), and whether their clothes or make-up were provocative. The state portrays a dichotomous vision of women, *najib* (virtuous) or *nanjiab* (non-virtuous), in which the behaviour or appearance of the latter invites men to take sexual advantage. Consequently, this type of woman is regarded as not deserving of societal respect. If she becomes the victim of sexual harassment or rape, she is therefore considered to be the main guilty party. This was demonstrated in Kolsum's court case. The final letter written by the Supreme Court clearly stated that one of the issues that had an impact on the reversal of the charge from rape to adultery was the fact that Kolsum had consented to wearing make-up.

The presence of moral police patrolling public places to ensure that women have covered themselves appropriately to protect men's inherent vulnerability to sexual temptation demonstrates the state's perception of women as people who could affect moral chastity in public. The fact that victims of rape could themselves be blamed for the crime probably means that many incidents are not reported. In the case described above, not only was Kolsum unable to prove her claim, but she may well also have been accused of adultery, which is punishable by 100 lashes. Consequently, in the Iranian courts, victims of rape become co-defendants, as they have to prove their own innocence in order to avoid punishment. Likewise, if women try to defend 'their honour' themselves, they may well be harshly penalised for it.

Golku, a student in her twenties, writes in her public web log, a popular means for women in Iran to talk about taboo subjects such as sex and boyfriends, that women in Iran are cornered by the lack of legal protection they face in rape cases: 'Which of us does not put a knife in our purse, when we leave our house? All of us contemplate about how to defend ourselves, if we feel unsafe in a situation' (Sadr, 2003).

Fereshteh Ghazi, a journalist for the Tehran-based daily newspaper *Etemad*, told the presidents of the executive, legislative and judiciary branches of the Islamic government that women who are victims of rape do not have the support of the state under Iranian law. She was referring to Afsaneh Nowrouzi, a 34-year-old mother of two, spent seven years on death row for sexually mutilating and killing the head of security police in Kish Island for trying to rape her in his house while her husband was out of town. She was released in 2001 after widespread protests by various human rights and media organisations, and some female members of parliaments. Finally, the Supreme Court reversed the death sentence on the grounds of 'technical difficulties'. What these cases and messages indicate to women is that it is best to remain silent if they want to avoid state-sanctioned punishments (Sadr, 2003). In her testimony, Afsaneh Nowrouzi stressed that when the rape occurred she had been wearing a pair of trousers under her skirt, her hair was covered with a scarf and she had wrapped a veil round her waist (a common practice by traditional women), indicating that she wanted to ensure that the judge perceived her as 'an honourable woman' who was protective of her modesty. Mohammadinia (1992) states in his book *What a Woman Must Know* that:

> ... an honourable woman is so solemn that she discourages male strangers. Her monotonous speech does not arouse men ... she wears long pants ... the cut and colour of her dress must not stimulate the eye. Her walk ought not to draw attention. Hence high heels are ruled out because of their exciting sounds. (pp 174 and 178)

It seems that the state often fails to perceive rape as violence against women or sees it as a power issue stemming from unequal gender relations and male domination, but with women as agents rather than victims. This perception is portrayed in some newspaper articles, for example in '*Tajavoz-e beh onf farjam-e dustiy-e khiabani*' ('Rape[11] as the result of street friendship'), an article that describes how a 20-year-old girl was raped by her 24-year-old boyfriend when he tricked her into going to his office to collect some money for the cinema (ISNA, 2008).

The judges in Kolsum's case had contradictory views regarding the impact of women's appearance and its relation to rape crimes. The Supreme Court judge believed that Kolsum's acceptance of wearing make-up indicated her consent to sex, whereas the local judge disagreed with this. This shows the effect of judges' personal views and their perception of gender ideology on the outcomes of verdicts. There are many examples of cases in which different judges have defined *zena-ba onf va ekrah* differently. As discussed above, for example, some religious authorities believe that a charge of rape is invalid in cases where the victim has been drugged unless she can proved that she resisted being put to sleep, whereas others declare that in cases where a woman is unwilling to have sex whether awake or asleep, a claim of rape is justified and the verdict is the death penalty (Hadadzadeh-Nayeri, 2008). On 18 January 2005 (29 Dey 1383 [Persian Calandar]), a dentist in Iran was convicted and charged with using general anaesthetic to sexually assault and rape his female patients, and filming the assaults. Ten of his victims filed a complaint against him for rape. Despite confessing to 79 assaults, and despite various videotapes of his victims' ordeals being found in his apartment, he was given eight years and six months' imprisonment[12], 192 lashes and banned from practising dentistry. During the trial, the defendant explained how he stopped his patients from reporting him to the police by threatening to show the film to their families or posting them on the internet, thereby ruining their reputation and honour. The judge declared that if he wanted to charge him with *zena-e ba onf va ekrah*, the process would have been different, although it is not exactly clear what he meant by this statement (*Etemad*, 2005). Because of the controversial outcome, Ayatollah Shahroudi, the head of the judiciary, ruled that the case be examined again. After months of examination, it was decided that because the women were not 'harassed under force' and the defendant only threatened to disclose the films, the charge could be not *zena-e ba onf*. The defendant may well have been given the death penalty, however, if he had been prosecuted by a different judge. This case illustrates how varied the sentences are for committing the same crime. Punishment can vary from 100 lashes to imprisonment or the death penalty depending on the judges' personal views on the matter. This leaves the decisions in rape cases totally at the judges' discretion. The ambiguity in the law and the resulting variation in verdicts for the same crimes are also evident in domestic violence cases in Iranian courts (Mir-Hosseini, 2000; Aghatie, 2006).

It was also demonstrated in Kolsum's case that the contradictory nature of some of the laws makes it very difficult to prosecute any rape offender. For example, as described above, one of the ways in which a rape crime can be proven is if the offender confesses (article 68). However, the offender can then be acquitted of the crime by rescinding his confession (article 71). In Kolsum's case, although Nabi confessed that he was standing behind the door when Teymour raped Kolsum and could hear them scuffling before going in and raping her himself, they both were acquitted on the grounds of Nabi's later denial. The judge's personal view, and what was perceived as 'the judge's knowledge', played a significant role in deciding the outcome of the case. However, concerns are now being expressed over what should be admissible as the 'judge's knowledge' and whether a defendant's subsequent denial can overrule the initial confession.

Analysis of policies and interventions

As we have seen, both women and men can be subject to the inhumane punishment of stoning under Iranian law. In 1980, Ayatollah Khomeini announced that stoning should be banned. However, after his death, some judges continued to mete out this punishment (Zahedi, 2009). In 2002, Ayatollah Shahroudi, the head of the judiciary, declared a freeze on the practice. His declaration has not been implemented thoroughly throughout the country, as the practice has not been formally outlawed. Such punishments are still given out in some small villages; in one such case in January 2009, two men were stoned. The judiciary's response to the event was that the freeze on stoning was not legally binding and was only a recommendation (Erdbrink, 2009). Due to political pressure from various groups such as lawyers, academics and activists, a Bill on banning stoning has been under consideration by the government since

July 2009. It is important to note, however, that there have been more cases of women being punished by stoning than men (Tohidi, 2009).

The requirement to provide eyewitnesses to the act of rape is unreasonable, as rape normally happens in the private sphere. In addition, basing the credibility of the testimony on gender sends the message to perpetrators that they live in a society where gender discrimination and inequality is legally sanctioned and women are second-class citizens (Kar, 2000). Imagine, for example, that at a women's gathering, one of the attendees is raped by several male intruders, but none of the other women present are eligible to be called before the judge as eyewitnesses because they are female. Even if they could testify, they open themselves up to the charge of *qazf* (slander), punishable by 80 lashes (article 76). This is clearly detrimental to justice.

Kar (2000), a prominent Iranian lawyer, points out the shortcomings of the legal system with regard to violence against women and rape. She comments on the grave vulnerability of women in rape cases because of judges being over-reliant on witness testimony. She declares that medical examination on its own does not have legal validity and an expert's opinion is of little weight unless the victim was a virgin prior to the rape. In any case, the expert can only verify whether it has been 10 days or less since the victim lost her virginity or indicate when sexual intercourse last took place. Lawyers therefore tend to advise their clients not to pursue the matter unless there is a high chance of conviction. In addition, if a woman loses the court case, she could be subject to punishment for *zena* along with her rapist. This means 100 lashes if the woman is single or stoning if she is married, or she could receive 80 lashes for *qazaf* (false accusation). Women therefore have to be extra cautious in filing a complaint, as they could be the one to be punished for being raped.

In summary, the combination of Iranian society's perception of women and various shortcomings in Iranian legislation makes it difficult for the victims of rape to report the crime to the police. Even when they do, such a crime is very difficult to prove. Moreover, there is a great deal of discrepancy between the minimum and maximum sentences for the same crime. According to Tohidi (2009), various discussions are taking place among Iranian media and non-governmental organisations regarding violence against women, but various political and cultural factors have prevented systematic studies covering different forms of violence including sexual violence.

Legalised rape

Although the average age of marriage in Iran is 23.9 for females and 26.7 for males, and the number of child marriages has decreased dramatically, legally girls and boys can marry at the ages of 13 and 15 respectively. They can even marry at a younger age with parental permission (Daniel and Mahdi, 2006). It has been reported that in rural areas of the south-eastern province of Sistan and Baluchestan, the practice of child marriage still exists and some parents marry their children off before they have reached puberty (Afary, 2009). This in itself is legal rape. There have been attempts by various human rights activists to change the law and increase the age of marriage. The One Million Signature Campaign is a good example of human rights groups demanding changes to discriminatory laws such as marriage age. Campaigners declare that their demands are not contradictory to Islamic principles, and they have had the support of some prominent Islamic scholars such as Ayatollah Sanei and Ayatollah Bojnourdi, who have called for the reforms of laws that discriminate against women. However, the Iranian state has been repeatedly clamped down on the campaigners. In June 2006 during a peaceful demonstration, 70 demonstrators were arrested. Some were given jail sentences and others received lashes.

Men's legal right to rape their wives is known, in religious terms, as *tamkin khaas*, which means full submission. According to Shahidian (2002, p 179), 'heteromarital intercourse – "marital relationship" – is thus defined as the only appropriate sexuality in which the man has virtually unlimited claims on a woman's sexuality'. Women are supposed to submit to their husbands' sexual desires any time that he wishes and in return husbands have to financially support their wives. This means if a woman refuses to have sex with her husband, he does not have to pay his wife *nafaqeh* (maintenance), money for food, clothing and lodging. This is a law that clearly illustrates women's blatant subjugation to men's pleasure, and, in other words, legalises rape within marriage.

Orthodox jurists have supported this claim by citing verses of the Quran that talk about women's and men's duties within marriage, for example, 'Women are your fields: go, then, into your fields as you please' (Quran 2:223). Khomeini sustains this by stating in his thesis: 'A woman must surrender to her husband for any pleasure' (Khomeini, n.d., p 386).

However, there are others who interpret the Quran differently and believe that its verses should not be translated literally but rather put into context. The concept of *tamkin khaas* (wife should sexually submit herself to her husband whenever he desires) has been challenged:

> In a human relationship that depends on the feelings and state of minds of individuals for its formation, one cannot reduce the woman to just an instrumental creature that has to be at all times under control and available for exploitation.... It is the height of injustice, if a woman – who carries social, economic ... and family responsibilities and has a delicate and gentle temperament – would be required, regardless of her own emotional and affectionate state of mind, to always submit to the sexual demand of her husband, just because she receives provisions.... The health of a relationship, which according to psychologists is not a one-sided satisfaction but fulfils the inner happiness of and builds mutual trust between the two, is dependent on the physical and mental readiness of the both. Such considerations should be taken into account for the woman as much as for the man. (Shukri and Labriz, 1992, pp 58–63)

Authors such as Shukri and Labriz bring to our attention the discriminatory laws in Iran, opening the field for discussion on issues of equality of men and women in marriage, women's sexuality and health. Although to a western feminist view these arguments may not seem too liberating, they have had the impact of raising awareness among the general public, including women, creating the room for discussion on the legitimacy of some of the laws. Women's status and the laws affecting them are discussed repeatedly in various women's magazine. *Zanan* magazine was one of 29 publications devoted solely to women issues, but was shut down in 2008 after two decades. It had a feminist agenda and ran sophisticated articles on women's legal issues such as child custody, divorce and sexual violence. It also translated the articles of authors such as Mary Wollstonecraft and Virginia Woolf (Afary, 2009). One of *Zanan*'s most important contributions was articulating an alternative interpretation of Islamic doctrines. It declared that some of the current laws and policies pertaining to women are anti-Islamic and suggested a more egalitarian interpretation (Kar, 2001).

Suggested amendments in the law

First, there should be a separate section in the Iranian Criminal Code that deals directly with rape. Having rape as a subsection to *zena* leaves women in a vulnerable situation, where they have to be co-defendants as well as complainants in rape cases. In addition, the gender of the witness should not affect the credibility of the testimony. Indeed, many religious scholars suggest that the current laws are a misinterpretation of Islam and are demeaning to women (Ahmed, 1992). It should be noted that there are others who believe that any legal reforms with gender equality in mind entail the separation of religion from politics and, in the case of Iran, such reform would only be possible if the Islamic state were dismantled. According to Mojab (2001), this is because it has been constructed on the basis of unification of the two. Scholars such as Mojab do not accuse Islam of being exclusively responsible for repressive gender practices, but they believe in taking into account the immense implication of Islamisation in Islamic countries for women (Moghissi, 1999; Mojab, 2001; Shahidian, 2002)[13].

There should also be clarity in what is meant by 'the judge's knowledge'. This would avoid a significant discrepancy between minimum and maximum punishment for committing the same crime. In addition, the inhumane practice of stoning should be outlawed. Some of the highest-ranking clerics in Iran, such as Ayatollah Makarem Shirazi, Ayatollah Sanei and Ayatollah Mousavi Bojnourdi, have spoken against the practice (Ebadi, 2007). Alasti (2007) argues that it is possible to ban stoning by reinterpreting Islam and believes that the practice is clearly a human rights abuse.

The age of marriage should be raised and rape within marriage should be criminalised. Muslim feminists and women's rights advocates have objected to the notion of *tamkin khaas*. They have stated that it is not reflective of true Islam, and have insisted that reading and interpreting the Quran from a woman's perspective is more appropriate to the modern world. Otherwise, the Iranian state could be seen as having legalised rape under the flag of Islam. By amending the laws relating to women's rights, some scholars believe the Iranian state would be conveying the message that Islamic laws do not favour men (Afshar, 1998; Mir-Hosseini, 2002) and do not support rapists at the cost of gender equality and justice. Finally, the state should fund organisations that could provide counselling for the victims of rape.

Conclusion

This chapter has sought to analyse the way in which the Iranian Penal Code responds to rape. Within this framework, it has broadly discussed how rape and sexual intercourse are perceived outside marriage. It is important to note that in recent years, there has been what Afary (2009) calls a 'sexual awakening' in the Iranian society:

> Medical doctors had reported marital rape on the wedding nights for over a century. In an effort to reduce sexual and psychological trauma for young women who might be virgins until their wedding, doctors now advised a couple to wait until both were mentally and physically prepared and reminded them of the importance and impact of the first sexual encounter, especially on women. (Afary, 2009, p 347)

The state has acknowledged the increase in the number of reported cases and has announced that court cases relating to rape and kidnapping should be dealt with as quickly as possible. It has also called for prompt, transparent media reporting of the outcomes of such cases (ISNA, 2009a). It is hoped that this chapter has shed some light on the ambiguities of Iran's Penal Code on rape and that it will highlight the issue of rape crime, within both the private and public sphere, in the public discourse. Amendment of the relevant laws could potentially increase the number of reported rapes, as victims would have more hope of proving their case without fear of brutal chastisement if they fail. Bringing the issue of rape into the public discourse will also help fight the stigma long associated with this crime and alter perceptions of cultural stereotypes surrounding rape victims.

Notes

[1] The Council of Guardians (www.spiritus-temporis.com/council-of-guardians) comprises 12 jurists, six of whom are appointed by the Supreme Leader. The head of the judiciary recommends the remaining six, who are officially appointed by parliament. The Council of Guardians is vested with the authority to interpret the constitution and determines whether the laws passed by parliament are in line with Islamic law. Hence, the council can exercise veto power over parliament. If a law passed by parliament is deemed incompatible with the constitution or the Shari'a, it is referred back to parliament for revision. The council also examines presidential and parliamentary candidates to determine their fitness to run for a seat. For example, the council rejected most of the 33 Bills introduced by women in the Sixth Majles, all on the grounds that they were incompatible with the Shari'a law. For more information, see www.amnestyusa.org/news/document.do?id=ENGMDE130242006

[2] Motahari, who was Khomeini's foremost ally, is considered one of the important influences on the ideologies of the Islamic Republic. On 1 May 1979, Morteza Motahari was assassinated by gunshot by a member of opposition group, Furqan.

[3] Temporary marriage, *sigheh*, is only acceptable in Shia Islam. It is a legal contract that can be formed between a man and an unmarried woman. A man can take an unlimited number of temporary wives for a period lasting from one hour up to 99 years (in order for the marriage to be valid, the duration of the contract needs to be specified). This is in addition to four permanent wives. A woman, by contrast, can only enter one permanent or temporary marriage at a time (see Haeri, 1989, for a more detailed explanation). However, temporary marriage is socially frowned on. Some refer to it as prostitution in religious garb and those women who enter such marriages keep it a secret for fear of stigmatisation.

[4] For further reading on Iranian law relating to women, see Kusha (2002).

[5] A non-married girl who has sexual intercourse with her stepfather will receive 100 lashes.

[6] *Marja taghlid* is the second-highest authority on religion and law in Shia Islam after the prophet and Shia imams.

[7] This case is documented in 'Mozakerat va ara-e heyat-e omumi' ('Negotiations and votes of the Supreme Court')(1378/1991) divan-e ali-e keshvar (the Supreme Court). Edareh vahdat-e raviyeh va nashr-e mozakerat (The publisher).

[8] This is a summary of what had happened and it is not a direct quote. In the original document, the case is explained in 23 pages and contains letters exchanged between different judges. The points made here derive from an analysis of the case by the author.

[9] 'The very practice of verification of female virginity upon their marriage is called virginity examination ... in spite of unreliability of virginity examination as a dependable tool for gaining knowledge of a female sexual history, these examination [sic] are practices in many middle Eastern and North African societies as well as in some immigrant minorities in Western multicultural context. The (lack of) presence of the practice depends on class, religiosity, level of education, urban and rural backgrounds, among other factors. The test usually [sic] performed before the wedding night but sometimes it is done after

the wedding night in case the woman has failed to leave a blood sign on the white bed sheet. Since the failure of bleeding holds up the assumption that the woman violated the prohibition of sex outside marriage, written official documentation assists those who may have failed to leave blood sign due to the inborn "lack" of hymen or the extra elasticity of the hymen' (Farahani, 2007, p 80). Afary (2009) believes that in contemporary Iran, young women more than ever engage in premarital non-vaginal sexual intercourse or same-sex relationships.

[10] 'The modern operation includes the use of gelatine capsules containing red dye that will rupture during nuptial intercourse, stimulating the physical markers of virginal sexual experience' (Afary, 2009, p 338).

[11] The article use the words 'aggression by force' instead of 'sexual attack' or 'rape'.

[12] Different Iranian newspapers quoted different prison sentences, from eight to 10 years.

[13] For further reading on Islam, feminism and gender equality, see Mojab (2001), Moghissi (1999), Rajaee (2007).

Further reading

Afary, J. (2009) *Sexual Politics in Modern Iran*, Cambridge: Cambridge University Press.

Afshar, H. (1998) *Islam and Feminisms: An Iranian Case Study*, Basingstoke: Palgrave.

Mojab, S. (2001) 'Theorizing the politics of Islamic feminism', *Feminist Review*, no 69, pp 124–46.

Moghissi, H. (1999) *Feminism and Islamic Fundamentalism*, London: Z Books.

Rajaee, F. (2007) *Islam and Femininisms: An Iranian Case Study*, Basingstoke: Palgrave.

Shahidian, H. (2002) *Women in Iran: Gender Politics in the Islamic Republic*, Westport, CT: Greenwood Press.

References

Afary, J. (2009) *Sexual Politics in Modern Iran*, Cambridge: Cambridge University Press.

Afshar, H. (1998) *Islam and Feminisms: An Iranian Case Study*, Basingstoke: Palgrave.

Aghtaie, N. (2006) 'Clash between policy and religion in relation to women's rights in Iran', Unpublished Master's Thesis, University of Bristol.

Aghtaie, N. (2010) 'Comparative study of Iranian students attitudes to violence against women in Iran and UK', Bristol: University of Bristol, PhD submitted to University of Bristol.

Ahmed, L. (1992) *Women and Gender in Islam*, New Haven, CT: Yale University Press.

Alasti, S. (2007) 'Comparative study of stoning punishment in the religions of Islam and Judaism', *Justice Policy Journal*, vol 4, no 1, pp 1-38.

Amiri, F. (2001) '*Ilam sarzamin-e zanan Sholevar. Zanan 77 (tir)*', in J. Afary (2009) *Sexual Politics in Modern Iran*, Cambridge: Cambridge University Press, pp 10-16.

Anjomanhaye Iran Pardis (2007) 'Negahi be padideh Zena ba Maharem' ('An overview of incest'), www.iranpardis.com/archive/index. php/t-13376.html_

Asgari-Nejad, H. (2005) 'Kanun-e zanan-e Irani: death of hundred thousands Iranian mothers due to illegality of abortion', http://zanan. iran-emrooz.net/index.php?/zanan/more/4222

Bahonar, M.J. (1984) 'Islam and women's rights', *Al-Tawhid*, vol 1, no 2, pp 155-65.

Centre for Women's Participation (1999) *Ghavanin va Moghararate vizheh-ye Zanan dar Jomhury-e Islamy-e Iran (Special Laws and Regulations for Women in the Islamic Republic of Iran)*, Tehran: Centre for Women's Participation.

Daniel, E.L. and Mahdi, A.A. (2006) *Culture and Customs of Iran*, Westport, CT: Greenwood Press.

Ebadi, S. (2007) 'Practice of stoning is in our law', *Medan-e Zanan (Women's Roundabout)*, http://meydaan.net/English/showarticle. aspx?arid=133&cid=46_

Erdbink, T. (2009) 'Iran stones 2 men to death; 3rd flees', Washington Post, 14 January, www.washingtonpost.com/wp-dyn/content/ article/2009/01/13/AR2009011302174.html

Etemad (2005) 'Dandanpezeshke Sheitan Sefat dar Astaneh Mojazate Marg Tabraeh Shod', http://forum.iran-egold.com/showthread. php?t=1559

Farahani, F. (2007) *Diasporic Narratives of Sexuality: Identity Formation among Iranian-Swedish women*, Stockholm: Acta Universitatis Stockholmiensis.

Hadadzadeh-Nayeri, M. (2008) 'Mafhum-e onf va ekrah dar maadey-e 82 ghanun-e mojazat-e eslami', www.vekalat.org/public. php?cat=2&newsnum=975520

Haeri, S. (1989) *Law of Desire: Temporary Marriage in Shi'i Iran*, Syracuse: Syracuse University Press.

Iran Official (2003) 'Unemployment rampant among youth women', 1 July, www.payvand.com/news/03/jul/1001.htmi

ISNA (Iranian Student News Agency) (2007) 'Az ravabete penhan ta eghfal ba vadeh ezdevaj' ('From hidden friendship to deception through fake marriage promises'), http://isna.ir/ISNA/NewsView. aspx?ID=News-890209_

ISNA (2008) 'Farmande-ye Naja: amar-e sabt-e parvandehay-e tajavoz be onf rub eh afzayesh ast' ('Head of Naja police: the number of reported rape crime is on the increase'), http://isna.ir/ISNA/ NewsView.aspx?ID=Newa-1145645

ISNA (2009a) 'Rais-e divan-e ali-e keshvar: parvandehay-e tajavoz-e beh onf, aadamrobaie and shararat bayad kharj az nobat residegi shavad' ('The head of the Supreme Court: the rape, kidnapping and insurgence cases should be seen to without having to wait for their turn'), http://isna.ir/ISNA/NewsView.aspx?ID=News-1432456

ISNA (2009b) 'Jorm-e tajavoz-e be mahrem afzayesh nayafteh' ('The number of incest rape has not increased'), http://isna.ir/NewsViews. aspx?ID=News-1440273

Kar, M. (2000) *Pazhoheshi darbareh-ye Khoshunat Alyhe-e Zanan dar Iran (A Research about Violence Against Women in Iran)*, Tehran: Roshangaran and Women's Studies.

Kar, M. (2001) 'Women's strategies in Iran from the 1979 Revolution to 1999', in J.H. Bayes and N. Tohidi (eds) *Globalization, Gender and Religion*, New York, NY: Palgrave.

Khomeini, R. (n.d.) *Towzihol Masael (The Explanation for Problems)*, Tehran: Esteghlal.

Kusha, H. (2002) *The Sacred law of Islam: A Case Study of Women's Treatment in the Islamic Republic of Iran's Criminal Justice System*, Aldershot: Ashgate

Mehran, G. (2003) 'The paradox of tradition and modernity in female education in the Islamic Republic of Iran', *Comparative Education Review*, vol 47, no 3, pp 269-86.

Mir-Hosseini, Z. (2000) *Marriage on Trial: A Study of Islamic Family Law*, London: IB Tauris.

Mir-Hosseini, Z. (2002) 'The conservative–reformist conflict over women's rights in Iran', *International Journal of Politics, Culture and Society*, vol 16, no 1, pp 37-53.

Mohammadinia, A. (1992) *Anche yek zan Bayad Bedanad*, Qom: Centre for Islamic Propaganda Publications.

Moghadam, V. (2003) *Modernizing Women: Gender and Social Change in the Middle East* (2nd edn), London: Lynne Rienner.

Moghissi, H. (1999) *Feminism and Islamic Fundamentalism*, London: Zed Books.

Mojab, S. (2001) 'Theorizing the politics of Islamic feminism', *Feminist Review*, no 69, pp 124-46.

Rajaee, F. (2007) *Islamism and Modernism: The Changing Discourse in Iran*, Austin, TX: University of Texas Press.

Rezaie, S. (2008) 'Banuye Irani, weblog farhangi ejtemai-e banovan-e Iran', http://banooye-irani.blogfa.com/post-5.aspx

Roudi-Fahimi, F. and Moghadam, V. (2006) 'Empowering women, developing society: female education in the Middle East and North Africa', *Al-Ra'idah*, 23 and 24, pp 4-10.

Sadr, S. (2003) 'Women in Iran deem rape laws unfair', www.womensenews.org/story/the-world/031221/women-iran-deem-rape-laws-unfair

Shahidian, H. (2002) *Women in Iran: Gender Politics in the Islamic Republic*, Westport, CT: Greenwood Press.

Shukri, S. and Labriz, S. (1992) 'Tamkin' ('Submission'), *Zanan*, February, pp 58-63.

Tohidi, N. (2009) 'Iran', in S. Kelly and J. Breslin (ed) *Women's Rights in the Middle East and North Africa*, New York: Rowan and Littlefield Publishers.

UNESCO (2007) 'Education in Iran', http://stats.uis.unesco.org/unesco/TableViewer/document.aspx?ReportId=121&IF_Language=eng&BR_Country=3640

Zahedi, H. (2009) 'Qesseh por ghosseh sangsar' *Iran-Emrooz*, 30 March.

EIGHT

Meeting the challenge?
Responding to rape in Scotland

Sandy Brindley and Michele Burman

Introduction

The past decade has seen vigorous activity in Scotland in relation to responses to rape and sexual assault. This has included significant legal, procedural and policy change, as well as support for a hard-hitting public awareness campaign by Rape Crisis Scotland. Yet Scotland continues to have one of the lowest conviction rates for rape in Europe, with recent Scottish government figures showing that only 3% of rapes recorded by the police lead to a conviction (Scottish Government, 2009a). This chapter outlines the Scottish legislative and policy response to rape, discusses some of the problems facing survivors of sexual violence in their search for justice, considers the possible impact of some of the developments in recent years, and suggests some possible future directions.

Prevalence

Unlike other European countries (see Hagemann-White, 2001), there have been no national prevalence studies of rape undertaken in Scotland, despite calls from the United Nations and Council of Europe reiterating the need for baseline measures that establish the scale of the problem (Lovett and Kelly, 2009). While there are plans to introduce a sexual violence self-completion module into the Scottish Crime and Victimisation Survey, it will be some time before data will be available.

The Scottish government policy context

The Scottish government is acknowledged to be at the international forefront of work to tackle violence against women (Coy et al, 2008; Coy and Kelly, 2009). Scotland's innovative domestic abuse strategy has been in place for over a decade, and has since been broadened to cover all forms of violence against women.

Since its inception following devolution in 1999, the Scottish parliament has also demonstrated a commitment to tackling violence against women, in particular domestic abuse, although significant work had already been undertaken in this area before the parliament was established, by both women's organisations and statutory agencies (see COSLA, 1998). In November 2000, the Scottish Executive published a *National Strategy to Address Domestic Abuse* (Scottish Executive, 2000a), which placed a requirement on local authorities and health boards to establish local partnerships to tackle domestic abuse. The Scottish Executive provided £18 million through the Domestic Abuse Service Development Fund to support the work of the partnerships, and established the National Group on Domestic Abuse to monitor the implementation of the strategy.

In common with other UK jurisdictions, Scotland has developed partnership and inter-agency working protocols with a primary focus on crime prevention and community safety. Violence against women, in particular domestic abuse, is currently situated as a community safety concern, and domestic abuse is included within both national and local community safety initiatives. The recognition of domestic abuse as a community safety concern has resulted in awareness-raising campaigns, improved accessibility to services for those affected by domestic abuse, and the appointment of specialised coordinators to oversee the implementation of local policies.

In November 2002, in what would become an annual event, the Scottish parliament debated the issue of 'violence against women'. The (then) Minister for Social Justice announced that the National Group to Address Domestic Abuse would widen its remit to include all forms of violence against women, and would be renamed the National Group to Address Violence Against Women (Greenan, 2004).

The Scottish government has incepted an integrated, broad and strategic approach to tackling violence against women, and is the only UK jurisdiction to adopt an explicitly gendered approach (Coy et al, 2008). In doing so, it has drawn greatly on the definition of violence against women contained within the 1993 United Nations Declaration on the Elimination of Violence Against Women, which views such violence as a form of gender inequality, taking the form of actions that result in physical, sexual and psychological harm or suffering to women and children, or affront to their human dignity, including threats, coercion or deprivation of liberty, whether occurring in public or private life. A broad definition has been adopted that covers different forms of violence against women – including emotional, psychological, sexual and physical abuse, coercion and constraints – and which makes the links between domestic abuse, rape and sexual assault, child sexual abuse, honour crimes and commercial sexual exploitation.

Violence against women is seen by the Scottish government as having its roots in the inequality between men and women in society. There is a clear acknowledgement that acts of violence and abusive behaviour are perpetrated predominantly by men, and affect women and children disproportionately, and tackling violence against women is stated as a prerequisite to reducing inequality between women and men in Scotland (Scottish Executive, 2000a; Scottish Government, 2009b). The recent publication *Safer Lives, Changed Lives: A Shared Approach to Tackling Violence Against Women* (Scottish Government, 2009b) explicitly recognised that violence against women is not only a consequence of gender inequality, it also perpetuates it. The document (re)states that the protection of women and children from all forms of violence is a governmental high priority, and provides a definition, a set of guiding principles and a focus for multi-agency activities and partnership working with the aim to 'provide a shared understanding and approach which will guide the work of all partners to tackle violence against women in Scotland' (Scottish Government, 2009b).

Developing services for survivors of rape: 'Scotland leads the way'

Rape Crisis Scotland, the national office for the Rape Crisis movement in Scotland, was established towards the end of 2002, with funding from the Scottish Executive. Although Rape Crisis Centres had been in existence in Scotland from 1976, since the establishment of the first centre in Glasgow, this was the first time the Rape Crisis movement in Scotland had a national office to liaise with government and provide a strategic national voice.

In 2004, the creation of two new funding streams was announced – the Rape Crisis Specific Fund (RCSF) and the Violence Against Women Fund (VAWF). The RCSF in particular has made a significant difference to the Rape Crisis movement in Scotland, by allocating funding of £ 50,000 per year for every Rape Crisis Centre, thereby guaranteeing a basic level of capacity. The RCSF also provided funding for the development of new Rape Crisis Centres, in Lanarkshire, Western Isles, Argyll and Bute, and Perth and Kinross. In an article in the *New Statesman* entitled 'Scotland leads the way', the Communities Minister stated that 'one of the most satisfying decisions of my ministerial career was my decision to provide Rape Crisis Scotland with the funding it had been crying out for' (Curran, 2008). Rape Crisis Scotland also received funding from the Scottish Executive to develop and establish a national Rape Crisis helpline, to provide initial and crisis support to anyone affected by sexual violence. This helpline opened in October 2007, and is open from 6pm until midnight every day. The RCSF, funding for the national helpline and funding for Rape Crisis Scotland have all been continued under the new SNP (minority) administration, which came to power after the Scottish parliament elections in 2007.

Research carried out for the End Violence Against Women Coalition found that Scotland is the only area of the UK where the number of Rape Crisis Centres is increasing rather than decreasing (Coy et al, 2008). The number of Rape Crisis Centres in Scotland has increased from eight in 2004 to 12 in 2009, with funding being secured from the Scottish government to establish one further centre in the Scottish Borders. The commitment from the Scottish government to developing a strategic approach to violence against women, and the willingness to develop ring-fenced funding to ensure the provision of services such as Rape Crisis, have been crucial in achieving this (Coy et al, 2007).

The Scottish legal framework

Although part of Britain, Scotland has its own criminal justice system, with distinctive systems of prosecution, criminal procedure and sentencing. Scots criminal law is also different in many respects from the law of England and Wales. Following devolution in 1999, the Scottish parliament was (re)established, along with two justice committees and a Cabinet Secretary for Justice. In the early years following devolution, virtually all aspects of criminal justice were subject to scrutiny in the form of consultation and review, resulting in an intense period of policy, legislative and governance changes affecting the provision of many aspects of criminal justice (see Croall, 2006; McIvor and McNeill, 2007; McAra, 2008). Although reform of the criminal justice response to violence against women pre-dated devolution by some time, nevertheless policy and legislative change in relation to Scotland's response to rape accelerated from this point.

Until the passing of the Sexual Offences (Scotland) Act 2009, rape in Scotland was a common law offence, the definition of which – non-consensual penile penetration of a woman's vagina by the accused, with or without emission of semen - was acknowledged as one of the narrowest in Europe. The common law definition excluded oral and anal penetration, or penetration of the vagina by means other than the penis, as well as male rape.

Marital rape was criminalised over a period of several years during the 1980s, culminating in 1989, with reference to various prominent individual cases. Since 1989, a man can be found guilty of raping his wife, even if they were living together at the time of the offence, if it can be proved that the sexual intercourse took place without her consent (*Stallard v HM Advocate*, High Court of Justiciary, 1989).

It was only in 2001, following an appeal by the then Lord Advocate, that Scots law formally recognised that rape occurs when sexual intercourse takes place without a woman's consent, regardless of whether *force* is used to overcome her will. In the case of *HMA v Edward Watt*, the trial judge dismissed the charge of rape, and referred the ruling to the High Court of Justiciary for clarification of the law. This led to the overturning of the requirement that rape should involve the use of force, and effectively redefined the crime of rape. The subsequent Lord Advocates' Reference (No 1 of 2001)[1] clarified that a man commits rape if he has sexual intercourse with a woman without her consent, and that he knew or 'was reckless to' the fact that there was no consent. However, this resulted in only partial reform of the law of rape. Subsequent appeal cases showed that it left some aspects of the law less clear than before, and the law was subject to much criticism as a result (see, for example, Chalmers, 2002).

A key shortcoming concerned the lack of definition of 'consent' and the difficulties raised by the concept of 'honest or genuine' belief in consent on the part of the accused. The concept of 'honest belief' has long been recognised as deeply problematic (Brown et al, 1993; Temkin, 2002). Described as a 'rapist's charter' because it enables a subjective interpretation to be applied to consent, it allows the accused to maintain that the woman's behaviour amounted to what he believed to be consent – even if that belief was not reasonable. There were concerns about the inherent and significant difficulties faced by the Crown Office and Procurator Fiscal Service (COPFS) in bringing about successful prosecutions for rape, due to the requirement of proving the accused's lack of belief in consent. The issue of subjective interpretation, coupled with the lack of a clear definition of consent (it was up to the jury to decide what interpretation they applied to the case in hand) led to a number of serious problems for women seeking justice in cases of rape and sexual assault. Feminist academics and Rape Crisis Scotland drew attention to the ways in which the lack of clarity around consent led to the use of circumstantial evidence concerning matters such as a woman's clothing, demeanour and lifestyle being brought to bear in the case such that trial proceedings were far more likely to focus on the actions of the complainer than on those of the accused, under no obligation to give evidence himself, while the complainer may be forced to undergo a further ordeal in the form of intrusive cross-examination of a highly personal nature (Jamieson, 2001).

In June 2004, Scotland's First Minister requested the Scottish Law Commission to carry out a comprehensive review of the law of rape and other sexual offences, the terms of which were to 'examine the law relating to rape and other sexual offences, and the evidential requirements for proving such offences, and to make recommendations for reform' (Scottish Law Commission, 2006). Following an extensive period of review and wide public consultation during which oral and written evidence was taken from a wide range of stakeholder groups and individuals, the 2009 Sexual Offences (Scotland) Act (hereafter the '2009 Act') received Royal Assent in July 2009. The 2009 Act has drawn together existing common law and statutory sexual offences into a single statutory framework, creating new statutory offences of rape, sexual assault by penetration, sexual assault, sexual coercion, coercing a person to be present during sexual activity, coercing a person to look at an image of sexual activity, communicating indecently, sexual exposure, voyeurism and administering a substance for a sexual purpose. Most notably, the Act has broadened the definition of rape to include penile penetration of the mouth and anus, enabling male rape victims to be recognised for the first time. These changes mean that rape is no longer gender-specific, and so victims can be of either sex, although the retention of a gendered definition of perpetration – penile penetration – is similar to the law in England and Wales and means that only a man can commit rape.

As well as redefining rape, the 2009 Act also introduces, for the first time in Scotland, a statutory definition of consent, as 'free agreement'. This represents a significant change from the previous position, where a defence of consent required an 'honest belief' by the accused regardless of how reasonable that belief may have been. Consent is central to the definition of sexual offence, and the legislation provided much-needed clarity. The Act also identifies a non-exhaustive list of circumstances in which consent can never be present, and makes clear that consent may be withdrawn at any time. Taken together, the widening of the definition of rape, and the statutory clarification of consent, mark radical and wide-ranging changes to the Scottish legal framework for rape and other sexual offences. At the time of writing, it is far too early to tell what the impact of the 2009 Act will be. Certainly, it is envisaged that the placing of the law of rape and sexual offences on a statutory footing will clarify a complex and often confusing area of legislation, and provide Scotland with a modern and robust legal framework. But legislation alone, no matter how enlightened or well intended, is not a sufficient response to rape and other sexual offending.

Scottish legal process: investigation and prosecution of rape

Since their inception, Rape Crisis Centres in Scotland have played a significant role in raising concerns about the manner in which women are treated when they report a rape or sexual assault to the police. In an oral history publication charting the development of the Rape Crisis movement in Scotland from 1976 to 1991, women were asked about their experiences of the police:

> '... the police, at that time, were appalling in their treatment to women. They asked them if they were on contraceptives, did they have a boyfriend, how much they had to drink that night – they were just up for question, completely.... I remember one particular harrowing thing, and she had her underwear, she'd had the examination, she was sitting with her bag, and she had her pants and everything, and the police sort of picked up her pants, and they were quite frilly, if you like, whatever, and he said "This doesn't look like somebody's not asking for it, to me". And it was quite intimidating, and her head just went down, and it was just an enormous sense of anger, you know? It really was harrowing.' (Jane Dorby, quoted in Maitland, 2009, p 111)

In 1983, Chambers and Miller published a highly critical examination of the police investigation of sexual assault cases that drew on the voices of women, many of whom expressed significant concerns about the way they had been treated by the police (Chambers and Millar, 1983). The debate that followed the publication of this research contributed to a shift in policy in the approach to sexual assault investigations in Scotland. Guidelines to chief constables on responding to women alleging rape were published in 1985 (and remained in place until 2004). The first Female and Child Unit, designed to provide a more sympathetic response to sexual offences complainers, was established in Glasgow in 1987 (Burman and Lloyd, 1993; Greenan, 2004). These units – staffed by specialist officers and providing dedicated space for interviewing sexual assault complainers – were set up across

Scotland and led to marked improvements in police responses to rape (Christianson and Greenan, 2001). However, there continues to be concern about the response women reporting rape receive from the police. Rape Crisis Centres claim that 'old-fashioned and insensitive attitudes to rape victims persist' (Foster, 2006) and there continues to be a lack of access to female forensic medical examiners across Scotland despite significant evidence that most women – and many men – who have experienced sexual assault prefer to be examined by a female doctor (Lovett et al, 2004).

At present, there are eight regionally based police forces in Scotland. Because of a variation in procedures and practice, there is a lack of consistency in how rape is investigated. In most areas, rape and sexual assault are investigated by dedicated specialist units, generally Family Protection Units (established in Scotland between the late 1990s and early 2000s) staffed by officers specially trained in working with those who have been raped or sexually assaulted (known as sexual offences trained officers or sexual offences liaison officers). In other police areas, investigators responsible for interviewing and evidence gathering may have had limited or little specialist training. In 2008, the Association of Chief Police Officers in Scotland (ACPOS) published guidelines on investigating serious sexual crimes that outline standards and good practice and state that the welfare and safety of the victim should take precedence over investigative issues (ACPOS, 2008).

Scotland has an adversarial legal system in which the public prosecution service, COPFS, is responsible for investigating and prosecuting crime. Following a rape report, the police carry out an initial crime investigation and submit a report to the local procurator fiscal (PF). On the basis of the initial police investigation report, the PF makes an initial decision as to whether to move to a formal prosecution process and/or investigate the case further. Following a review of the evidence, the PF reports with recommendations to senior prosecutors (Crown Counsel), who make the final decisions about charging and prosecution. Prosecutorial decisions are based on an evidential and 'public interest' test, and in Scots law the evidential test requires corroborative evidence, that is, there must be more than a single evidential source (COPFS, 2006). One of the fundamental rules of Scots law is that the essential elements of the charge must be corroborated before anyone can be prosecuted or convicted. Although the need for corroborated evidence is not peculiar to rape, it does make successful prosecution of such cases more difficult than other crimes. In rape, corroborating evidence is often hard to find. The forensic process attempts to secure evidence to corroborate the woman's version of the events but this is sometimes weak or lacking (Ferguson, 2000). Rape is a crime that is commonly committed in private; there are rarely 'ear' or' eye' witnesses to corroborate what happened; many of those subjected to rape offer no physical resistance and may not suffer serious physical injury (Du Mont and White, 2007) and may delay reporting, often for significant periods (Clay-Warner and Burt, 2005). As has been well documented, the lack of physical and/or forensic evidence in rape cases means that there is a contestation between the word of the woman (see, for example, Brown et al, 1993; Jordan, 2004) and that of the accused. Despite the removal of the requirement of force in the definition of rape, corroboration difficulties persist.

Victims are the chief witnesses for the prosecution and currently do not have the right to separate legal representation in Scotland. Rape Crisis Scotland has recently begun exploring the feasibility of introducing independent legal representation for sexual offence complainers within the Scottish adversarial system (Raitt, 2009). Rape cases are always prosecuted in the High Court presided over by a judge with a 15-person lay jury. Other serious sexual offences are prosecuted either in the High Court, or the Sheriff Court before a sheriff and a 15-person jury. In addition to a finding of guilt, Scottish jurors have the possibility of finding a case 'not proven' as well as 'not guilty', both of which result in an acquittal with no possibility of retrial. A decision can be unanimous (all the jury members agree) or by majority (at least eight of the jury agree). The High Court can sentence up to life imprisonment, whereas a Sheriff Court can sentence up to a maximum of five years, but may refer the case to the High Court if it considers that the sentence should be longer.

Specialist sexual assault services

In 2006, the Scottish Executive provided funding for a three-year pilot Sexual Assault Referral Centre (SARC). In 2007 the first (and currently the only) SARC, known as Archway, opened in Glasgow. Funding for this initiative, totalling £1.6 million, was for the period 1 April 2006 to 31 March 2009. The funding was split between ministerial portfolios – justice, communities and health – reflecting the cross-cutting nature of the issue of sexual violence. In November 2008, local funders – NHS Greater Glasgow and Clyde, Strathclyde Police and Glasgow City Council – agreed funding for Archway Glasgow after the trial period.

Archway Glasgow provides forensic medical examinations, sexual health screening, follow-up support and counselling to victims of recent serious sexual assault. Recent assault is defined as an assault that has occurred within the last seven days. The service is for adults and adolescents aged 13 and above. Service users are guaranteed access to a female doctor – the forensic aspect of the service is staffed exclusively by specialist sexual offence examiners, who are all female. The service is provided 24 hours a day, seven days a week, with access outside of office hours being provided through an on-call service. However, SARC facilities are only currently available in one region in Scotland. Archway Glasgow is currently being externally evaluated, and the evaluation report is imminent. It is not yet clear what steps, if any, the Scottish government will take to encourage the development of similar services across the rest of Scotland.

The Scottish trial process

The ordeal of giving evidence in the witness box is one of a set of ongoing and inter-related concerns about the criminal justice response to rape. The 2004 Vulnerable Witnesses (Scotland) Act introduced several procedural changes, including the introduction of special measures (for example, screens, supporter, a live television link from either another room within the court building or from outside the court in a remote site, evidence by a commissioner and use of a prior statement) to assist child witnesses and those defined as vulnerable adult witnesses in giving their evidence in all cases, including sexual offences cases, although there is as yet no clear evidence that the introduction of these measures has made a material difference to the ordeal of giving evidence in rape trials (Richards et al, 2008).

Much of the concern about women's experience of giving evidence in court relates to the use of questioning and evidence about her sexual history and sexual character, and this has been a concern in Scotland for some time (see, for example, Chambers and Millar, 1986; Brown et al, 1993; Jamieson, 2001). Indeed, Scotland has made two legislative attempts at restricting the use of sexual evidence, although both are seen as limited in effectiveness (Brown et al, 1993; Burman et al, 2005, 2007). Scotland first enacted rape shield legislation in 1986[2], which placed restrictions on the use of sexual history and sexual character evidence of complainers in trials for a wide range of sexual offences. As in other jurisdictions, the prosecution (known as the Crown in Scotland) was exempt from these restrictions. Applications to introduce restricted evidence were made verbally by the defence during the course of the trial (usually after the complainer's examination in chief).

Yet research found that despite the shield legislation, restricted evidence was still being introduced in the Scottish courts (Brown et al,

1992, 1993; Burman et al, 2005). Key problems were that there was no consideration by the court of the relevance of the evidence sought to the charges libelled and the guilt of the accused, and opposition from the prosecution to the introduction of the evidence or questioning was very rare (Burman et al, 2005, 2007).

Throughout the 1990s, there was growing disquiet with the criminal justice response to rape. Against a background of criticism of the conviction rate compared with the number of complaints made to the police, the treatment of complainers in sexual offence trials became an increasing cause for concern. Critical attention focused on the perceived inadequacy of the existing legislation, in particular in relation to the relevance and admissibility of sexual history and sexual character evidence.

In November 2000, the Scottish Executive issued a pre-legislative consultation document entitled Redressing the Balance: Cross-Examination in Rape and Sexual Offence Trials (Scottish Executive, 2000b) seeking views on proposals to change the law of evidence in sexual offence trials in order to:

- prevent the accused in such cases from personally cross-examining the complainer; and
- strengthen the restrictions on the use of evidence about the sexual history and sexual character of the complainer.

The proposals sparked controversy because the legal profession and the judiciary thought the existing system largely satisfactory, and saw no need for reform. This was in stark contrast to Rape Crisis Centres and other support groups, as well as legal academics who had been campaigning for reform for some time.

The first proposal addressed concerns about accused persons seeking to personally cross-examine the complainer. It aimed to prevent complainers from being humiliated, embarrassed, intimidated or inhibited in giving their evidence as a result of having to be questioned by the accused. The second proposal, to widen and strengthen the existing restrictions on sexual history and character evidence, and to sharpen the focus on relevance, were a clear attempt to address the perceived deficiencies of the earlier legislation (Jamieson and Burman, 2001).

Following a lengthy consultation, the Scottish parliament published the Sexual Offences (Procedure and Evidence) (Scotland) Bill in June 2001, which proposed the strengthening of the existing prohibitions and exceptions (s 274 and s 275). The 2002 Sexual Offences (Procedure and Evidence) (Scotland) Act followed, replacing the earlier legislation, which had been in operation for the previous 16 years, and introducing entirely new evidential and procedural provisions. As well as preventing the accused from personally cross-examining the complainer, the use of sexual history and general character are both restricted, and the Act requires that closer attention is paid to the relevance of any evidence or questioning sought to be introduced. Further, it requires that decisions about allowing such evidence must include taking account of a complainer's dignity and privacy. Uniquely, the prohibition now applies to the Crown as well as the defence, and both are required to make a *written* application in order to introduce the evidence, in *advance* of the trial. Written applications must state the nature and relevance of proposed questioning, and the inferences that the court should draw from it. The court is also required to set out the reasons for its decisions. Also, where a defence application is allowed, the Crown is required to disclose any previous analogous convictions that the accused may have. The policy intention here is that the threat of previous convictions being disclosed would deter the defence from seeking to attack the character of the complainer (Scottish Executive, 2000b, p 10). The accused is also required to give prior written notice if his defence is to include a plea of consent.

Yet research commissioned to monitor the use of the legislation found that the volume of sexual history and character evidence introduced in sexual offence trials has substantially increased (Burman et al, 2007). Whereas, under the 1995 Act, just over a fifth (21%) of trials involved an application to introduce prohibited evidence (Burman et al, 2005), applications are now made in almost three quarters (72%) of sexual offence trials heard in the High Court – a three-and-a-half-fold increase (Burman et al, 2007; Burman, 2009). Moreover, applications are almost always successful in that the evidence sought is either fully or partially allowed. The high success rate is similar to the situation in England and Wales (Kelly et al, 2006). It is also important to note that, although applications to introduce sexual history and character evidence are made in most trials, prohibited evidence also continues to be introduced in the absence of any application. The research found that most applications sought to introduce more than one type of questioning or evidence and, in most cases, all of the evidence cited in applications is pursued during the trial, resulting in lengthy cross-examinations (Burman et al, 2007).

Given the significant increase in numbers of applications, and their very high rate of success, as well as the continued introduction of prohibited evidence in the absence of any application, there has been a substantial increase in the amount of sexual history and character evidence elicited and admitted. Moreover, the proportion of cases involving multiple applications directed at the same complainer has more than doubled, with successive applications made both pre-trial and at the trial itself, such that seven out of 10 complainers in serious sexual offence trials are now virtually guaranteed to be questioned on intimate sexual matters (Burman et al, 2007). Submission of an application to introduce sexual history and/or character evidence is now a routine aspect of defence case preparation. The requirement that the application be made in advance and in writing has combined with other changes in procedure, including a greater emphasis on early preparation of cases; more extensive and earlier disclosure by the prosecution of material and evidence that may be pertinent to the decision of whether or not to lodge an application; and the effect of influential appeal court decisions on cases that have involved applications to heighten early consideration of the possibility of an application (Burman, 2009). Despite well-intentioned reform, legal practice can weaken reform intent such that the criminal justice system continues to fail to provide women with the support, safety and justice they need, and the court room remains a site of secondary victimisation.

Concern about conviction rates

Although the criminal justice response to rape is an area characterised by change and reform, the rate of convictions for rape and other sexual offences remains very low, and women continue to feel that they are not being taken seriously when they report rape (Maitland, 2009). Over the 30-year period from 1977 to 2007, Scottish official recorded crime data show that there was an increase of 451% in the number of rapes reported to the police (Scottish Government, 2009a). In marked contrast to reporting, however, there has been virtually no change in the number of prosecutions for rape over the same period. The number of prosecutions grew by just 15% (from 60 to 69), representing a fall in the proportion of reported cases prosecuted from 34% in 1977 to 7% in 2006. What is more, conviction rates have actually decreased over the same period in a manner not dissimilar to England and Wales. Using the national statistical data, Scotland currently has the lowest conviction rate for rape in Europe, at under 4% (Burman et al, 2009; Lovett and Kelly, 2009).

In a European study of attrition of rape cases, which involved the tracking of 100 rape cases from point of report to the police, and which sought to explore in detail the factors involved in attrition and the points at which it occurs (Lovett and Kelly, 2009), it was found that the Scottish arrest and custody rates were the highest of all countries in the study (Lovett and Kelly, 2009), and almost six in 10 suspects (59%) were charged. Attrition in Scottish cases takes place across the legal process, albeit much more of the decision making takes place at a relatively late stage (often just before court) and is made by prosecutors (Lovett and Kelly, 2009). The study identified a conviction rate of 16%, which is mid-range for the study, but considerably higher than that indicated by the national official statistics (3% in 2006 and 5% in 2004-05) (Lovett and Kelly, 2009).

Recent reforms in investigation and prosecution policy and practice

In October 2004, the (then) Solicitor General, Elish Angiolini QC, instructed a wide-ranging review of the investigation and prosecution of rape and serious sexual offences. ACPOS subsequently announced that it would be undertaking a parallel review of its own procedures.

While no report has been made public, ACPOS has released the key recommendations from the review, relating to a variety of aspects of the investigation process, including the updating of the guidance manual for police officers on the investigation of sexual assault; the establishment of a Scotland wide 'Moorov database' (to assist in the gathering of intelligence of cases that are similar enough to have the potential of corroborating each other); and agreeing a standard reporting protocol with COPFS. The review also recommended the commission of a study of closed rape cases categorised as 'insufficient evidence', 'dubious crimes' and 'false allegations' to establish where and how the attrition rate could be improved, along with a review of the current structure and remit of specialist units across Scotland to identify the best approach. The recommendations also identified the need to develop a national training course for officers investigating sexual assault.

An ACPOS Sexual Crime Working Group was established to take forward the recommendations. A national training programme on the investigation of sexual assault has now been developed, to which Rape Crisis Scotland and local Rape Crisis Centres contribute. ACPOS has also developed a training DVD for those who might provide a first response to someone reporting a sexual crime, and published the *Scottish Investigators' Guide to Serious Sexual Offences* (ACPOS, 2008), which, as well as providing detailed guidance on interviewing planning and forensic issues, attempts to dispel myths around how someone who has been raped may react.

Far more is known about the COPFS review of the investigation and prosecution of sexual offence cases in Scotland. COPFS established an advisory group for the review, comprised of a range of representatives from statutory and voluntary organisations, including Rape Crisis Scotland, the Women's Support Project, Scottish Women's Aid, Victim Support and two lesbian, gay, bisexual and transgender organisations. The COPFS report made 50 recommendations for change, which by June 2009 had been implemented in full (COPFS, 2006). These include the production of comprehensive guidance for those investigating and prosecuting serious sexual offences; the development of a comprehensive system of specialised sexual offences training within COPFS, and a system of certification for all COPFS staff working with sexual offences; the establishment of a Standing Group on Forensic and Medical Evidence to represent the interests of the police, COPFS and medical and forensic practitioners and to permit communication about policy and practice around advances in medical and forensic evidence; the establishment of a working group to examine the merits of the use of expert evidence; the publication of a comprehensive information pack for those who have been raped or sexually assaulted (Scottish Government, 2008a); and the provision of better information to the complainers throughout the prosecution process, including advising complainers of any defence application to lead sexual history or character evidence, and notifying them of the outcome of any such applications. With these developments, COPFS has introduced radical changes to the way rape and other sexual offences are prosecuted in Scotland, with a shift towards specialisation in the prosecution of sexual crime. In June 2009, the creation of a new specialist National Sexual Crimes Unit was announced, comprised of Crown Counsel (QCs) with a remit for close involvement in the investigation and prosecution of sexual crimes. Comments from the head of the new unit in a national tabloid on the day of the announcement provide some encouragement as to the approach likely to be taken by the unit:

> 'We will not let difficult cases go. We will investigate until we are sure it is right to give up. We will treat a rape the way we would approach a murder, looking at the whole picture. Does that picture present a story of consent or lack of consent .... If you are a rapist picking on a woman, are you going to pick a woman who is alert or will you hang around a nightclub and spot the woman is stumbling about, who is drunk? It's not just putting that suggestion in the jury speech but also looking at CCTV evidence, tracing

the taxi driver who picked up an accused and complainant, finding the barman and asking how much she drank. What weight is she? What height? What impact will alcohol have on her?' (Head of National Sexual Crimes Unit, quoted in Brown, 2009)

While there is little doubt that criminal justice bodies in Scotland have continued to make advances at the strategic policy level and at the legislative level, there remains a worrying gap in terms of the effective implementation of policy into practice. The provision of special measures, interpretation and support for women during the court process is inconsistent (Burman et al, 2007).

Challenging attitudes towards rape

Recent studies in England and Wales have shown that a significant minority of the population blames women for rape in certain circumstances (see, for example, ICM, 2005). Scotland is not dissimilar, in terms of the prevalence of unenlightened social attitudes about sexual assault and those who experience it. Women who allege sexual assault continue to be regarded as culpable for their sexual victimisation (TNS System 3, 2007). Recent research undertaken for the Scottish government found that 27% of respondents thought a woman can be at least partly responsible if she is drunk at the time of a sexual assault; 27% thought that a woman bore responsibility if she wore revealing clothing; 32% said that there should be some burden of responsibility for rape if the women is flirting; and 18% believed that rape can be the woman's fault if she is known to have had several sexual partners (TNS System 3, 2007).

Rape Crisis Scotland has major concerns about the impact that problematic attitudes towards women who have been raped may have on the criminal justice system. The need for improved public awareness of the nature and reality of sexual offences was identified as a key issue in the COPFS review of the investigation and prosecution of rape and serious sexual offences:

> The high attrition in such cases can be tackled effectively only by concerted efforts throughout the criminal justice system and the wider community in Scotland to raise public awareness and understanding of the nature of sexual offending and its impact upon victims. (COPFS, 2006)

The potentially prejudicial impact of societal attitudes towards rape on the ability of women to access justice has also been recognised within COPFS, and the Lord Advocate has been outspoken on the need to change outdated attitudes to rape if reform of the law is to be successful.

In 2007, Rape Crisis Scotland received funding from the Scottish government to develop and test a public awareness campaign on rape. The campaign was based on one that ran in America in the 1990s called This is Not an Invitation to Rape Me, which featured a series of images of women in scenarios where they might commonly be blamed for rape. The central purpose of the campaign was to challenge women-blaming attitudes to rape by stimulating public debate. The campaign confronts directly the following myths about women and rape:

- A woman is responsible for rape if she is dressed provocatively.
- A woman is responsible for rape if she engages in some level of sexual activity.
- A woman is responsible for rape if she has been drinking.
- Rape is a crime committed by strangers; women cannot be raped by their partners or husbands.

The Rape Crisis Scotland campaign was launched in October 2008, and took the form of a poster campaign displayed on billboards and bus stops across Scotland, as well as adverts in local newspapers. The campaign also has a dedicated interactive website[3,] which contains over a thousand comments on the campaign, suggesting that the campaign objective of creating discussion has been successful. An external evaluation of the campaign (Progressive, 2009) found that it had been successful in generating public discussion on rape, with 98% of people interviewed agreeing that the campaign tackled an important issue, 65% stating that it would encourage them to talk about the subject with their friends and family and 61% saying that it would make them consider their own attitudes towards rape (Progressive, 2009).

Conclusion

Organisations such as Rape Crisis Scotland have welcomed the recent developments in how rape is investigated and prosecuted in Scotland. What remains to be seen is what difference it will make to women's experiences of the justice system, and ultimately to the appalling conviction rate for rape in Scotland. Early indications are positive – in June 2009, figures released by the Scottish government showed that rape convictions as a proportion of recorded rape had increased, from 2.9%

to 3.7%. The figures are still very low and the increase slight. However, on an optimistic reading it could be a sign that recent initiatives are starting to have an impact. Until conviction rates are available for future years, it is impossible to know whether or not the recent increase is a statistical blip, or a sign of a real and sustained improvement to how the Scottish justice system responds to complaints of rape.

Despite significant developments in recent years, questions remain as to how effectively rape can be prosecuted within an adversarial legal system without unacceptable trauma being caused to the complainer. As previously stated, COPFS prosecutes in the 'public interest', which cannot necessarily be assumed to always coincide with the complainer's interest. The potential conflict inherent within COPFS's role is particularly apparent in relation to the issue of sexual history evidence, and use of complainers' medical records. The passivity of the prosecution's response to defence applications to introduce sexual history and character evidence has already been noted. This experience makes it difficult to feel confident that a robust approach will be taken to complainer's privacy rights in respect of their medical records. In a recent briefing commissioned by Rape Crisis Scotland on the issue of disclosure of medical records, the concern was articulated that:

> The Crown may well have an irreconcilable conflict between serving the public interest and representing the complainer's quite proper desire for non-disclosure. They cannot both serve the public interest and adequately shield the complainer from disclosure applications. There are too many conflicts of interest involved. (Raitt, 2009)

This concern has led to Rape Crisis Scotland actively campaigning for the introduction of independent legal representation for complainers of sexual offences. This is a right that complainers of sexual offences have been granted – to varying degrees – in other countries both across Europe and in Canada. It is a development that may give Scottish complainers the sense that there is someone in the criminal justice system directly representing their interests.

Notes
[1] 2002 SLT 466; 2002 SCCR 435

[2] The 1975 Criminal Procedure (Scotland) Act, ss 141A, 141B, 346A and 346B (as inserted by the 1985 Law Reform (Miscellaneous Provisions) (Scotland) Act, s 36).

[3] www.thisisnotaninviationtorapeme.co.uk

Further reading
Burman, M., Jamieson, L., Nicholson, J. and Brooks, O. (2007) *Impact of Aspects of the Law of Evidence in Sexual Offence Trials: An Evaluation Study*, Edinburgh: Scottish Executive.
Christianson, A. and Greenan, L. (2001) 'Rape Crisis movement in Scotland, 1977-2000', in E. Breitenbach and F. Mackay (eds) *Women and Contemporary Scottish Politics: An Anthology*, Edinburgh: Polygon.
Crown Office (2006) *Review of Investigation and Prosecution of Sexual Offences in Scotland*, Edinburgh: COPFS, www.crownoffice.gov.uk/ Resource/Doc/9/0000174.pdf
This Is Not An Invitation To Rape Me website, www.thisisnotaninvi tationtorapeme.co.uk

References
Association of Chief Police Officers Scotland (ACPOS) (2008) *Scottish Investigators' Guide to Serious Sexual Offences*, Glasgow: ACPOS.
Brown, A. (2009) 'New sex crime chief's warning for perverts – we're after you', *Daily Record*, 25 June,
www.dailyrecord.co.uk/news/scottish-news/2009/06/25/new-sex-crime-chief-s-warning-for-perverts-we-re-after-you-86908-21469620
Brown, B., Burman, M. and Jamieson, L. (1992) *Sexual History and Sexual Character Evidence in Scottish Sexual Offence Trials*, Edinburgh: Scottish Office Central Research Unit.
Brown B., Burman, M. and Jamieson, L. (1993) *Sex Crimes on Trial: The Use of Sexual Evidence in Scottish Courts*, Edinburgh: Edinburgh University Press.
Burman, M. (2009) 'Evidencing sexual assault: women in the witness box', *Probation Journal*, vol 56, no 4, pp 1-20.
Burman, M., Jamieson, L. and Nicholson, J. (with Cartmel, F.) (2005) *The Law of Evidence in Sexual Offence Trials: A Baseline Study*, www. scotland.gov.uk/Publications/2005/09/13144738/47390

Burman, M., Jamieson, L., Nicholson, J. and Brooks, O. (2007) *Impact of Aspects of the Law of Evidence in Sexual Offence Trials: An Evaluation Study*, Edinburgh: Scottish Executive.

Burman, M. and Lloyd, S. (1993) *Police Specialist Units and the Investigation of Crimes of Violence Against Women and Children*, Scottish Office Central Research Unit: Edinburgh: Scottish Office.

Chalmers, J. (2002) 'How (not) to reform the law of rape', *Edinburgh Law Review*, vol 6, no 3, pp 388-96.

Chambers, G. and Millar, A. (1983) *Investigating Sexual Assault*, Scottish Office Social Research Study, Edinburgh: Scottish Office.

Chambers, G. and Millar, A. (1986) *Prosecuting Sexual Assault*, Scottish Office Social Research Study, Edinburgh: Scottish Office.

Christianson, A. and Greenan, L. (2001) 'Rape crisis movement in Scotland, 1977-2000', in E. Breitenbach and F. Mackay (eds) *Women and Contemporary Scottish Politics: An Anthology*, Edinburgh: Polygon.

Clay-Warner, J. and Burt, C. (2005) 'Rape reporting after reforms: have times really changed?', *Violence Against Women*, vol 11, no 2, pp 150-76.

COSLA (Convention of Scottish Local Authorities) (1998) *Guidance on Developing Multi-Agency Partnerships to Tackle Violence Against Women*, Edinburgh: COLSA.

Coy, M. and Kelly, L. (2009) *Map of Gaps 2: The Postcode Lottery of Violence Against Women Support Services in Britain*, London: End Violence Against Women Coalition/Equalities and Human Rights Commission.

Coy, M., Kelly, L. and Foord, J. (2007) *Map of Gaps: The Postcode Lottery of Violence Against Women Support Services*, London: End Violence Against Women Coalition.

Coy, M., Lovett, J. and Kelly, L. (2008) *Realising Rights, Fulfilling Obligations: A Template for an Integrated Strategy on Violence Against Women for the UK*, London: End Violence Against Women, www.endviolenceagainstwomen.org.uk/data/files/realising_rights_summary.pdf

Croall, H. (2006) 'Criminal justice in post devolutionary Scotland', *Critical Social Policy*, vol 26, no 3, pp 587-607.

Crown Office & Procurator Fiscal Service (COPFS) (2006) 'Review of the investigation & prosecution of sexual offences in Scotland', www.copfs.gov.uk/sites/default/files/Publications/Resource/Doc/13928/0000566.pdf

Curran, M. (2008) 'Scotland leads the way', *New Statesman*, 18 March, www.newstatesman.com/uk-politics/2008/03/rape-crisis-funding-scotland

Du Mont, J. and White, D. (2007) *The Uses and Impacts of Medico-Legal Evidence in Sexual Assault Cases: A Global Review*, Geneva: World Health Organization.

Ferguson, P. (2000) 'Corroboration and sexual assaults in Scots law'. in M. Childs and L. Ellison (eds) *Feminist Perspectives on Evidence*, London: Cavendish Publishing.

Foster, K. (2006) 'True extent of unreported rapes revealed', *Scotland on Sunday*, 26 November, http://scotlandonsunday.scotsman.com/rapeandthelegalsystem/True-extent-of-unreported-rapes.2830132.jp

Greenan, L. (2004) *Violence Against Women: A Literature Review*, Edinburgh: Scottish Executive.

Hagemann-White, C. (2001) 'European research into the prevalence of violence against women', *Violence Against Women*, vol 7, no 7, pp 732-59.

ICM (2005) *Sexual Assault Research: Summary Report*, Amnesty International, www.amnesty.org.uk/uploads/documents/doc_16619.doc

Jamieson, L. (2001) 'The treatment of women reporting sexual assault by the Scottish criminal justice system', *Scottish Journal of Criminal Justice Studies*, vol 7, no 1, pp 70-86.

Jamieson, L. and Burman, M. (2001) 'Sharpening the focus on relevance?', *SCOLAG Legal Journal*, vol 287, September.

Jordan, J. (2004) *The Word of a Woman: Police, Rape and Belief*, Basingstoke: Palgrave Macmillan.

Kelly, L., Temkin, J. and Griffiths, S. (2006) *Section 41: An Evaluation of New Legislation Limiting Sexual History Evidence in Rape Trials*, Home Office Online Report 20/06, London: Home Office.

Lovett, J. and Kelly, L. (2009) *Different Systems, Similar Outcomes? Tracking Attrition in Reported Cases across Europe*, London: Child and Woman Abuse Studies Unit, London Metropolitan University.

Lovett, J., Reagan, L. and Kelly, L. (2004) *Sexual Assault Referral Centres: Developing Good Practice and Maximising Potentials*, Home Office Research Study, London: Home Office.

Maitland, E. (2009) (ed) *Woman to Woman: An Oral History of Rape Crisis in Scotland 1976-1991,* Glasgow: Rape Crisis Scotland.

McAra, L. (2008) 'Crime, criminology and criminal justice in Scotland', *European Journal of Criminology*, vol 5, no 4, pp 481-504.

McIvor, G. and McNeill, F. (2007) 'Developments in probation in Scotland', in G. McIvor, and P. Raynor (eds) *Developments in Social Work with Offenders: Research Highlights in Social Work 48*, London: Jessica Kingsley.

Progressive (2009) 'This is not an invitation to rape me: Campaign Evaluation, Edinburgh, www.rapecrisisscotland.org.uk/workspace/publications/TINAITRM-final-evaluation.pdf

Raitt, F. (2009) *Disclosure of Personal Records of Complainers of Sexual Assaults: A Briefing Paper for Rape Crisis Scotland*, Glasgow: Rape Crisis Scotland.

Richards, P., Morris, S. and Richards, E. (2008) *Turning up the Volume: The Vulnerable Witnesses Act 2004*, Edinburgh: Scottish Government, www.scotland.gov.uk/Publications/2008/07/25160344/0.

Scottish Executive (2000a) *A National Strategy to Address Domestic Abuse*, Edinburgh: Scottish Executive.

Scottish Executive (2000b) *Redressing the Balance: Cross-Examination in Rape and Sexual Offence Trials*, Edinburgh: Scottish Executive, www.scotland.gov.uk/consultations/justice/rtb-00.asp

Scottish Government (2008a) *Information Pack for Women and Men (Over 16) who have been Raped or Sexually Assaulted*, Edinburgh: Scottish Government, www.scotland.gov.uk/Publications/2008/04/16112631/0

Scottish Government (2008b) *Criminal Proceedings in the Scottish Courts 2007-08*, Edinburgh: Scottish Government.

Scottish Government (2009a) *Recorded Crime in Scotland, 2008-2009*, Statistical Bulletin Crime and Justice Series, Edinburgh: Scottish Government.

Scottish Government (2009b) *Safer Lives, Changed Lives: A Shared Approach to Tackling Violence Against Women*, Edinburgh: Scottish Government, www.scotland.gov.uk/Publications/2009/06/02153519/0

Scottish Law Commission (2006) *Discussion Paper 131: Rape and other Sexual Offences*, Edinburgh: The Stationery Office.

Temkin, J. (2002) *Rape and the Legal Process* (2nd edn), Oxford: Oxford University Press.

TNS System 3 (2007) *Findings from the Wave 10 Post-campaign Evaluation of the Domestic Abuse Campaign 2006/07*, Edinburgh: Scottish Government, www.scotland.gov.uk/Publications/2007/08/01142941/0

NINE

Paradox and policy: addressing rape in post-apartheid South Africa

Lisa Vetten

Introduction

The rate of reported rape in South Africa is considered to be among the highest in the world. As a consequence, the country is better known for its alarming statistics and more sensational manifestations of sexual violence (such as 'baby rape' and the 'corrective rape' of lesbians) than its policy interventions. Yet precisely because of the extent of the problem, a range of measures intended both to combat the incidence of rape, as well as improve the treatment of rape survivors, has been rapidly introduced over the years, making South Africa something of a policy laboratory in this area.

Many of these innovations were made possible by the unprecedented opportunities offered by South Africa's transition to democracy and the space it opened for engagement with the state around the problem of sexual violence. However, this political responsiveness must be set within the broader context of present-day South Africa and the imperative to address its highly unequal nature, often via dysfunctional state structures that are also understaffed and underskilled. In addition, the high rate of crime generally has placed severe pressure on criminal justice system structures and further exacerbated the strain on the state. The result is a situation where, more often than not, policy intent is only rarely realised in the implementation.

The national context in relation to rape

In 1994, following 46 years of apartheid rule, the African National Congress (ANC) became South Africa's first democratically elected government. No small set of challenges had been bequeathed to them by the previous National Party government. In terms of policing, for instance, the new government was required to transform a militarised force dedicated to the violent imposition of racist policies into a service that could be trusted by the very same black[1] communities it had previously brutalised. Further, it was required to integrate 11 separate police forces into one police service, and finally, ensure the equitable redistribution of policing resources. In 1994, 74% of South Africa's police stations were located in areas formerly reserved for 'whites' (Department of Safety and Security, 1998).

These challenges were further heightened by South Africa's high levels of crime. In 2004, spending on the criminal justice system consumed 3.1% of South Africa's gross domestic product (GDP), in contrast to the 1% spent by many other countries around the world (Altbeker, 2005). But while South Africa may spend more on its criminal justice system, it does not necessarily have more human resources at its disposal. According to Altbeker (2005), the South African Police Service (SAPS) employs 234 police officers per 100,000 citizens, compared with the 380 employed in countries for which data is available, while the justice department employs six prosecutors compared with the seven employed elsewhere in the world. This inefficient translation of expenditure into person power, he argues, is a consequence of the government paying criminal justice personnel more than their equivalents in other countries, relative to GDP per capita[2].

South Africa's high crime rate also affects the availability of criminal justice personnel. With seven police officers per murder versus 158, and 0.14 prosecutors per murder versus 2.6 in comparator countries around the world, South African criminal justice officials have higher workloads than those in most other countries for which data are available (Altbeker, 2005).

The extent of reported rape in South Africa

Information on the extent of reported rape pre-1994 is incomplete due to the fact that figures for the 'independent' homelands were not included within South Africa's national rape statistics. Nonetheless, available information points to the fact that South Africa's rape statistics have been rising since at least 1955, increasing by 132% between 1955 and 1990 (Glanz, 1993). The upward trajectory in the rate of reported rape post-1994 therefore continues this historical trend.

Between April 1994 and March 1995, 44,751 rapes were reported to the police. By 2006/07, this number had risen to 52,617 during the same 12-month period (SAPS, 2007) – a prevalence rate of 222 per 100,000 of the female population, which is almost three times the rate for the United States (US Department of Justice, 2007). An even more disturbing picture emerges from a two-province, community-based survey of adult men where 27.6% of those interviewed admitted to having raped at least once in the course of their lifetimes (Jewkes et al, 2009).

The politics of rape statistics

Over the years, the public alarm generated by these astonishing figures has resulted in both defensiveness and the politicisation of the crime statistics. These debates were complicated by the fact that until 2002 no reliable research data were available on the extent of the under-reporting of rape. Up until this time, albeit there was no basis for these figures (let alone a source), estimates on the frequency of rape in South Africa varied from one every 26 seconds to one every 83 seconds. Still other estimates suggested that only one woman in 20 – or else one in 36 – reported being raped to the police. But while effective in drawing attention to the extent of the problem, the unsubstantiated nature of these numbers proved to be their downfall and laid the ground for disputes that continue to this day.

In 1999, the then president Thabo Mbeki challenged the claim that only one in 36 rapes was reported, saying these figures could not be substantiated 'in any way' (*Cape Argus*, 2000). In the same year, South African-born actress Charlize Theron made an advertisement on behalf of Rape Crisis Cape Town Trust (RCCTT). Looking directly at the camera (and viewer), she said: "Many people ask me what South African men are like" and followed this with a recital of South Africa's estimated rape statistics. The Advertising Standards Authority withdrew the advertisement in October 1999 following a complaint by 28 men and one woman that it discriminated against men. Following an appeal against the ban by RCCTT (joined by the Commission for Gender Equality), the advertisement was reinstated (Vetten, 2000, p 111).

The following year, the then ministers of the Department of Justice and Constitutional Development (DJCD) and the Department of Safety and Security told reporters from the US CBS television news programme 60 Minutes that: "We've been standing here for 26 seconds and nobody has been raped" (*Cape Argus*, 2000). The debate turned both vitriolic and personal in 2004 when President Mbeki launched a public attack on journalist and rape survivor[3] Charlene Smith. This was triggered by a newspaper article in which she highlighted the substandard treatment of rape survivors by the healthcare system (among others) and argued that this neglect was driving HIV infection among women and children (Smith, 2004). Her article also cited a number of statistics that, among other things, included the claim that South Africa has the highest rate of rape in the world. In a scathing response, President Mbeki wrote that many South Africans appeared incapable of acknowledging the police's success in combating crime, and that their willingness to turn good news into bad was a symptom of racism (*ANC Today*, 2004a, 2004b).

Nonetheless, public concern was such that in 2004 the government's Justice, Crime Prevention and Security (JCPS) cluster set the SAPS the goal of reducing serious and violent crimes like rape by 7-10 % annually. This policy decision not only introduced a perverse incentive into the system, but also fundamentally misunderstood a key policy challenge: the low rate of reported rape.

Like elsewhere in the world, rape is extensively under-reported in South Africa. Drawing on data collected for the 1997 national South African Demographic and Health Survey, researchers calculated that only one in nine women who had been raped and had also had physical force used against them had subsequently reported the attack to the police (Jewkes and Abrahams, 2002). Unfortunately, police practice further contributes to under-reporting, it having been observed that the nature of the relationship between the victim and the accused plays a role in police officers' willingness both to accept and investigate rapes reported by women against their former boyfriends (Francis, 2000).

Newspaper reports suggest other, performance-related reasons for the police dissuading women from laying charges (*The Star*, 2006, 2007). These include the victim's inability to recognise or identify the suspect(s) (thus reducing the arrest rate), the perception that the victim's case is weak and pressure to decrease rape statistics ahead of the 2010 football World Cup (The Star, 2006). Indeed, in 2009, evidence emerged that police stations in three provinces were failing to register rape cases on their Crime Administration System, as well as dumping or destroying police dockets in an effort to reduce the number of rapes (among other crimes) reported to their stations (*Sunday Times*, 2009).

Legal framework

The role of gender inequality and discrimination in perpetuating sexual violence is recognised at a variety of levels. Policy such as the 1996 National Crime Prevention Strategy and *South Africa's National Policy Framework for Women's Empowerment and Gender Equality* (Office on the Status of Women, 2000) both link all forms of violence against women with gender inequality. The 2000 Promotion of Equality and

Prevention of Unfair Discrimination Act contains a prohibition against unfair discrimination by the state or any person and lists gender-based violence as an instance of such unfair gender-based discrimination. In addition to other measures, the Act requires the state to promote and achieve equality. But the most important recognition of rape as a form of gender inequality resides in the Constitution and key legal decisions derived therefrom.

Bill of Rights

All South African law must conform to the Bill of Rights contained in the Constitution. Sections relevant to rape include s 12(1)(c), which states that every person has the right to be free from all forms of violence from either public or private sources; s 9, the equality clause; s 12, which recognises that everyone possesses an inherent dignity that must be respected and protected; and s 14, the right to privacy.

Section 7(2) obliges the state to 'respect, protect, promote and fulfil' the rights in the Bill of Rights. In key decisions such as *S v Baloyi* (2000 (1) BCLR 86 (CC)) and *Omar v Government of South Africa* (2006 (2) SA 289 (CC)), the Constitutional Court has held that one of the ways in which the South African government should protect women's right to freedom from violence is to put appropriate legislation in place to address gender-based violence. The nature of state obligations was developed further in *Carmichele v Minister of Safety and Security* (2001 (4) SA 938 (CC)). The court held that the constitutional guarantee of the rights to life, dignity and freedom and security of the person imposes a duty on the state (and all its organs) to refrain from infringing on these rights. In certain circumstances, this guarantee also involves a positive duty to provide appropriate protection to everyone through the laws and structures designed to afford such protection. The court remarked that in addressing the constitutional obligations resting on the state, 'few things can be more important to women than freedom from the threat of sexual violence'.

The approach taken in the Carmichele matter was confirmed by the Supreme Court of Appeal in *Van Eeden v Minister of Safety and Security* (2002 (4) AllSA 346 (SCA)). The court also confirmed the role of the Constitution as an overarching normative value system in determining the duties of the police to protect the applicant from potential violence. In *K v Minister of Safety and Security* (2005 (9) BCLR 835 (CC)), the Constitutional Court similarly applied this normative constitutional framework in evaluating the common law principles of vicarious liability.

2007 Sexual Offences Act

Little legislative attention was paid to rape pre-1994. In late 1993, this neglect began to be addressed with the enactment of the Prevention of Family Violence Act, which allowed for husbands to be charged and convicted for the rape of their wives. In 1997, a project committee was appointed by the South African Law Commission (SALC) to investigate sexual offences against children and its remit was later extended to include adults. The Criminal Law (Sexual Offences and Related Matters) Amendment Act (the 2007 Sexual Offences Act) was finally enacted in 2007 and is now the main body of legislation dealing with sexual violence against both adults and children.

According to the new Act, 'Any person (A) who unlawfully and intentionally commits an act of sexual penetration with a complainant (B) without B's consent is guilty of the crime of rape'. 'Sexual penetration' is widely defined to include penetration of the genital organs and/or anus by another person's genital organs or any other body part or object. Penetration with an animal's genital organs also constitutes rape, as does penetration of the mouth with another person's genital organs.

The Act also codifies other existing common law and statutory offences and enacts a number of new offences (such as compelled rape[4]). Two chapters deal with sexual offences against children and persons with mental disabilities respectively. Rape survivors are now entitled, by law, to post-exposure prophylaxis (PEP) to prevent HIV infection and also permitted to apply for court orders instructing the alleged rapist to undergo testing to determine his HIV status. The Act also includes interim provisions on trafficking in persons for sexual purposes.

The Act repeals or amends certain rules of evidence pertaining to sexual offences, including that no negative inference may be drawn from there being a delay between the commission of a sexual offence and its reporting. The Act also allows for defences to certain charges and institutes a national register for offenders aimed at ensuring that persons who have been convicted of sexual offences against children or persons with mental disabilities are prohibited from certain types of employment. Further, any person knowing of a sexual offence committed against a child must report such knowledge to a police official. Their failure to do so constitutes an offence that can result in up to five years' imprisonment. Likewise, knowledge, or a reasonable belief, or suspicion, that a sexual offence has been committed against a person with a mental disability must also be reported. The same sanctions apply as in failing to report a sexual offence against a child.

(A separate law, the 2006 Older Persons Act, makes it obligatory to report sexual abuse perpetrated against older persons.)

Importantly, the Act introduces a supportive structure aimed at ensuring effective implementation: the Inter-Sectoral Committee for the Management of Sexual Offences. The committee is to consist of the most senior officials in the DJCD, the SAPS, the Department of Correctional Services (DCS), the Department of Social Development, and the Department of Health (DH) and the National Director of Public Prosecutions. The committee has the initial responsibility of developing a National Policy Framework (NPF), while each department represented on the committee is required to submit a report to parliament annually detailing its efforts to implement the Act. Finally, national instructions, directives and training courses dealing with sexual offences must be developed for police officials, prosecutors and medical practitioners.

The 2007 Sexual Offences Act is also supported by other legislation. The 1977 Criminal Procedure Act contains rules dealing with (among others) trials *in camera*, young witnesses giving evidence through an intermediary, the admissibility of evidence relating to a complainant's previous sexual history, the competence and compellability of witnesses and the determination of bail. The latter was subsequently amended to the effect that in some circumstances, the accused must first prove that 'exceptional circumstances' exist in the interests of justice that warrant his release on bail[5].

Partly in response to increases in particular crimes and as a crime control measure, minimum sentences for rape, murder and robbery were introduced through the 1997 Criminal Law Amendment Act (made permanent in December 2007 via the Criminal Law (Sentencing) Amendment Act). Minimum sentences for rape have been set at 10 years, 15 years, 20 years and life and are determined with reference to an accused's previous convictions and/or selected characteristics of the particular rape[6].

Finally, in terms of the 1977 Criminal Procedure Act, read with the 1998 Correctional Services Act, courts must inform rape survivors that they have a right (subject to directives issued by the Commissioner of Correctional Services) to make representations when the prisoner's placement on parole, day parole or correctional supervision is considered.

Policy interventions

Policy responses to sexual offences are found both in documents with general applicability and those specific to sexual offences. However, the development of these responses across departments has been uneven and fragmented. In addition, the urgent need to respond to the problem has resulted in particular interventions being introduced that were not explicit policy but have become, by virtue of their establishment, *de facto* policy. Policy addressing rape has also been developed by departments outside of the criminal justice system, such as the Department of Provincial and Local Government. This complex state of affairs is recognised in the preamble to the 2007 Sexual Offences Act, which notes that a uniform and consistent approach to implementing laws and providing services in relation to sexual offences is not evident across government departments.

Policy applicable to crime victims in general

The 2004 Service Charter for Victims of Crime ('the Victim's Charter') addresses itself to victims generally and aims to eliminate secondary victimisation by the criminal justice process and ensure that victims remain central to this process. A number of other documents have been issued in support of the Victim's Charter, including one on minimum standards of services for victims of crime. However, the standards proposed are better described as conditional expectations – what victims may expect from the system, circumstances permitting. There is no undertaking on the part of the state to expand existing services.

Rape and other forms of sexual violence are also singled out for particular attention in the *Victim Empowerment Programme Policy Guidelines* (Department of Social Development, 1998) and the *Strategic Plan for the SA Police Service 2005-2010* (SAPS, 2005), although neither document provides much guidance around what such prioritisation means in practical terms.

Policy specific to rape

In 1998, the DJCD released a set of uniform national guidelines for all role players handling rape and other sexual offence cases. These *National Policy Guidelines for Victims of Sexual Offences* (DJCD, 1998) represented government's first attempt at developing policy specific to sexual offences and were applicable to the DJCD, the DH, the SAPS, the Department of Welfare (as it was then called), the DCS and appropriate non-governmental organisations (NGOs). Those applicable to the police have been subsequently superseded by National Instructions and those for the DH by the National Sexual Assault Policy. Directives issued by the National Prosecuting Authority (NPA) have also largely replaced those applicable to the DJCD. It is only those applicable to the Department of Welfare and DCS that do not appear to have been updated. Further, the relationship between the DCS guidelines and the legislation dealing with the release of prisoners is unclear[7].

Psycho-social services for rape survivors

The 1998 guidelines for welfare largely confine themselves to describing how to support or accompany a victim through the reporting procedure. There is no reference to principles guiding the provision of services. The policy guidelines do make some attempt to identify the training and competencies required of social workers attending to sexual offences: it is 'desirable' for social workers to have had some training around trauma counselling that provides them with medico-legal knowledge, and to have the confidence to testify in court and the knowledge and skills to work with survivors of sexual abuse. While the guidelines acknowledge the need to develop separate guidelines for those victims whose experience of sexual assault is historical rather than recent, such guidelines have never been forthcoming.

To a limited extent, these guidelines were added to in 2005 when the Sexual Offences and Community Affairs (SOCA) unit of the NPA issued the Uniform Protocol for the Management of Victims, Survivors and Witnesses of Domestic Violence and Sexual Offences. The protocol is intended to regulate the services provided by civil society organisations, traditional leaders, private individuals and volunteers to victims of sexual offences, as well as those who witness these crimes. The protocol is justified on three grounds. First, it is said to provide a regulatory framework that is absent from the Victim's Charter. Second, it is intended to prevent service providers' interventions from having a negative effect on the preservation of evidence and the integrity of witnesses and survivors. Finally, the Protocol notes a lack of uniformity and consistency in the provision of services (although it does not propose a comprehensive approach to dealing with this problem).

Specialist facilities

In 1992, outrage over the handling of two rape cases in the Western Cape province led the then Acting Attorney-General Frank Kahn to establish a Task Group on Rape consisting of both government and

NGO representatives. A pilot specialist sexual offences court staffed by two trained regional court prosecutors was then established in Wynberg to meet the following three broad objectives:

- the reduction or elimination of inappropriate and insensitive treatment (or secondary victimisation) of sexual offence complainants;
- the development of a coordinated and integrated approach to the processing and management of sexual offence cases by criminal justice agencies; and
- the improvement of the reporting, prosecution and conviction rate for sexual offences.

Seven years later, in its 1999 Gender Policy Statement, the DJCD committed itself to establishing further specialist sexual offences courts modelled on the Wynberg example. In terms of the blueprint subsequently developed to guide the functioning of these courts, each court required two dedicated sexual offences prosecutors, a dedicated magistrate, closed circuit television and victim assistance services among other things.

In 2003, the NPA and the DJCD agreed on a national strategy to roll out specialised sexual offences courts dealing with both adult and child victims. However, in 2005, the Minister of Justice and Constitutional Development called for a moratorium on the establishment of all dedicated courts (including sexual offences courts) on the basis that dedicated courts placed too great a demand on resources and forced magistrates to specialise. A National Project Oversight Committee was established to decide on the establishment of future dedicated courts and a set of criteria to guide the setting-up of further courts. Not unsurprisingly, the number of specialist courts has been dwindling ever since.

The SAPS also established what it describes as 'victim-friendly' facilities that promote the right to privacy, particularly for victims of sexual offences. Only Gauteng Province would appear to have issued guidelines and standards on the establishment of victim empowerment services in police stations. These guidelines have not been formally adopted. Such generic victim empowerment services must also be distinguished from the specialist one-stop centres established by the Department of Safety and Security and the Thuthuzela Care Centres (TCC) established by the NPA. The TCCs are described as 'victim-centred' in that they locate health, policing and counselling services within a victim-friendly centre based at a hospital. Intended to provide comprehensive rape care management, they give follow-up medical treatment, counselling and information to the victim regarding the progress of the case. Ten TCCs currently exist nationally, with plans afoot to establish more through donor funding.

Specialised services and personnel

SAPS policy in relation to sexual offences is dealt with through its National Instructions and Standing Orders. National Instruction 3/2008 Sexual Offences consists in 23 sections that address the testing of suspects for HIV; various aspects of the investigation and gathering of evidence; the roles and responsibilities of investigating officers and station commissioners; discontinuing investigations; and support and assistance to victims of sexual offences at all stages of the criminal justice process. Up until 2006, when the SAPS announced that it would devolve specialist detective units, these instructions would have chiefly applied to the Family Violence, Child Protection and Sexual Offence (FCS) units.

The origins of the FCS units lie in the Child Protection Units established in 1986. In 1995, the investigative mandate of these units was broadened and they became FCS units. These units were often located in separate victim-friendly offices that served police stations within a particular area. Where the distance between police stations was great, FCS detectives were based at local police stations instead. However, many areas had no access to FCS detectives, with the result that rape cases were investigated by general detectives. This unevenness of access to FCS services was one of the reasons given for the units' restructuring in 2006, which was intended to relocate resources and expertise from area level to station level and so improve service provision. The consequences of this decision are discussed later in the chapter.

Responsibility for the prosecution of sexual offences lies with two units in the NPA: the National Prosecutions Service (NPS) and the SOCA unit. The former is responsible for the actual prosecution of cases, while the latter is more concerned with determining and implementing policy.

National policy directives issued in 1999 to all prosecutors prescribed that all matters of rape, indecent assault (where the victim is under the age of 16) and statutory rape where the victim is under the age of 16, as well as all matters involving child abuse in contravention of s 50 of the 1983 Child Care Act, were to be prosecuted in the regional courts. This was to ensure that more experienced prosecutors would handle such matters. The directives called for a victim-centred approach that took into account the physical, emotional and psychological well-being of the victim. The directives also advised that:

- a single specialist prosecutor deal with the matter from beginning to end;
- privacy and confidentiality be protected and delays in proceedings be avoided;
- separate waiting areas be made available;
- special measures to protect survivors during trial processes be requested and expert evidence introduced where appropriate; and
- special vigilance be required to protect victims from intrusive cross-examination.

Finally, all matters involving child victims 12 years and younger were to receive absolute prioritisation on the court roll.

Court preparation services were introduced by the NPA at a number of courts. Described as the process of familiarising witnesses with trial procedures, they are intended to allay victims' fears and concerns about testifying in court, reduce secondary victimisation and improve victims' ability and willingness to remember and relate their experiences in court. (Previously these services had been provided by NGOs.)

The DH issued the National Sexual Assault Policy ('the policy') and National Management Guidelines for Sexual Assault Care in 2005. The policy sets as its goal the improvement of healthcare after sexual assault for women, children and men in South Africa. Importantly, the policy states that services for sexual assault patients should be seen as specialist services and that they should also be provided by specialists – both doctors and nurses who have completed the required training.

These documents were supplemented in 2008 with directives mandated by the 2007 Sexual Offences Act. The directives address the testing of rape accused for HIV; the reporting of sexual offences at health facilities; and how health workers are to assist with the investigation and prosecution of sexual offences. Significantly, the directives recognise that the full range of health services must also be offered to all those who do not wish to report the incident to the police, including the medico-legal examination (in the event that some victims decide later to lay a charge with the police).

Key issues faced

The challenges of policing and prosecuting rape may be grouped broadly under three, inter-linked headings: the attrition of cases through the criminal justice system; the administration of the criminal justice system (referring to its resourcing and management); and the prejudiced, discriminatory treatment meted out to victims of sexual crimes.

Attrition of rape cases in South Africa's criminal justice system

The conviction rate for rape in South Africa is low, with many cases filtered out of the criminal justice system long before the trial stage is reached. In one study[8], 68% of rape cases involving adult victims and 58% of those involving children did not progress beyond the police investigation (SALC, 2000). Another, covering the province of Gauteng, found that 45% of rape cases failed to proceed beyond being reported to the police (Vetten et al, 2008). In both studies, failure to identify a suspect was the most common reason why cases did not proceed to court. In Gauteng, a sizeable proportion of victims (37%) also opted out of criminal justice system processes, with 14% of victims withdrawing their cases for various reasons and some one in five victims (22.9%) becoming untraceable (Vetten et al, 2008). Overall, the latter study, which tracked a random, representative sample of 2 068 reported rape cases, found 50.5% of reported rapes to have resulted in arrests, 17.3% to have resulted in a trial and a scant 4.1% to have led to a conviction for rape. Adult women fared worst at the hands of the criminal justice system relative to girls and teenagers. Those who raped young girls were twice as likely to be convicted of any crime (10.1%) as those who perpetrated their crimes against adults (4.7%) (Vetten et al, 2008).

Differential case outcomes on the basis of age have been found elsewhere. In one study, 9.1% of children's cases resulted in convictions, as opposed to 5.0% of adults' cases, (SALC, 2000), while data for the year 2000 identified 8.9% of children's cases and 6.8% of adults' cases to have led to convictions. This rate varied across provinces (Interdepartmental Management Team, 2002)[9].

Weaknesses in the collection and handling of forensic evidence also reduce the likelihood of a conviction in some instances. In Gauteng, a sexual assault evidence collection kit was completed in 67% of cases but only 51% of kits sent to the police forensic science laboratory. Because the suspect's blood was taken in only 16.4% of cases, DNA evidence was rendered largely irrelevant to almost all victims' cases (Vetten et al, 2008).

Administering and managing criminal justice system procedures

Poor police record keeping and statement taking contribute to the loss of evidence and witnesses. Victims' residential and work addresses, as well as the address of the crime scene, may not be captured, nor statements from other witnesses taken. Because arrests are not always promptly effected as instructed by commanding officers, suspects are given time to disappear.

The victim's statement is central to the investigation and prosecution of her matter. According to SAPS National Instructions, the 'victim's statement must be comprehensive. (Rather write too much, than too little)'. To underline this point, the instructions provide a checklist of 77 details that should be included in the victim's statement[10]. But as a number of studies report, even this level of prescriptiveness does not ensure the quality of the statements (Stanton et al, 1997; SALC, 2002; Artz et al, 2004; Vetten et al, 2008). Lack of proficiency in particular languages has also been noted as contributing to the indifferent quality of statements.

Difficulties in locating victims and other witnesses are exacerbated by the lack of telephones or work contact details for victims and witnesses; difficulties in locating temporary addresses; a shortage of working vehicles; and difficulties in accessing areas without streets or lighting, particularly after dark. This is particularly true of survivors who live in informal settlements with no street names and numbers and where the layout constantly changes as people pick up and move their shacks (Artz et al, 2004). Corruption also contributes to the loss of cases, with 37% of police officers interviewed for one study claiming that one or more of their rape cases had been mishandled due to corruption (Andersson et al, 1998).

Ideally, 20 is the maximum number of dockets any detective should be investigating at any one time, according to a 1996 SAPS evaluation (Stanton et al, 1997). In 2004, research conducted at three police stations found detectives carrying anything between 27 and 300 dockets for all types of crimes, with anything between 1% and 100% of these dockets being rape investigations (one detective was responsible for 178 rape investigations alone) (Artz et al, 2004). This state of affairs led one researcher to observe that detectives appeared to be caught up in 'perpetual crisis management, responding to whoever yells the loudest.... The women who get their cases attended to are the ones who show up at the station and demand it' (Artz et al, 2004, p 72).

Police capacity to respond to rape was further decimated by the decision to restructure the specialist FCS units in 2006. While in some areas that had previously had no access to FCS detectives were now benefiting from their skills, this was at the expense of other areas that had lost such services and in the context of a decline in the quality of services. The restructuring of FCS units resulted in new, inexperienced personnel being brought in to undertake investigations for which they had not been adequately trained. Such personnel had not been screened beforehand to assess their suitability to FCS work and nor had they necessarily chosen to provide FCS services. In some instances, they did not have the necessary basic requirements to undertake this work (such as a driving licence).

Many FCS personnel now fell under station managers generally, who had limited, if any, understanding of the intricacies of rape investigations and the management and care of rape victims. They could thus only offer limited guidance to new, inexperienced FCS detectives. FCS staff could not focus on their mandates but were obliged to take up other investigations too, thus limiting their ability to focus on rape investigations. FCS units no longer had their own identifiable budgets and it was unclear how resources to enable their investigations were to be funded at station level. In some instances, FCS officers no longer had access to private, victim-friendly facilities (Frank et al, 2008).

Coordination between investigating officers and prosecutors has also been noted as lacking, with the question of who should guide the investigation sometimes becoming a further source of tension leading to a less than harmonious relationship between prosecutors and detectives (Artz et al, 2004).

As with the police, a high caseload limits the amount of time available to prosecutors to consult with witnesses and prepare for trial – in its 2006/07 annual report, for example, the NPA reported a 24% vacancy rate. The high caseload, combined with a court backlog and pressure to secure conviction, can unfortunately create a perverse incentive to withdraw all but the strongest cases.

Cases are also withdrawn due to a high number of postponements, either because there is a need for further investigation; the docket has been lost or not brought to court; the accused needs to obtain legal representation; witnesses fail to appear at court; the SAP 69 form (which details previous convictions) is not available on time; the accused's attorney fails to appear or requests further time to prepare for trial; or because there is a need to obtain expert evidence (van Vuuren and van Rooyen, 1994; Vetten and Motelow, 2004). Multiple postponements may also ultimately lead to witnesses not coming to court or becoming untraceable (Vetten and Motelow, 2004).

Instances have also been recorded of both magistrates and prosecutors failing to adhere to the rules of evidence and procedure applicable to rape during the course of a trial (Bronstein, 1994;Vetten and Motelow, 2004). Whether these are isolated lapses or illustrations of a more widespread systemic failure by the courts has yet to be determined.

Secondary victimisation of rape survivors

The preamble to the 2007 Sexual Offences Act acknowledges that government, in too many instances, has 'fail[ed] to provide adequate and effective protection to the victims of sexual offences' and thus worsened their situation through secondary victimisation. Steyn and Steyn's (2008) interviews with rape survivors found that a number of victims considered the police to have been unsympathetic towards them and stated that they would not seek assistance from the SAPS in future.

Healthcare workers are not free of discriminatory attitudes either. A survey carried out at 31 health facilities around the country that treat rape survivors recorded one in three (32.6%) health practitioners as saying they did not consider rape to be a serious medical condition (Christofides et al, 2005). Two different studies of medico-legal services in Gauteng also found health workers to demonstrate unsympathetic, judgemental and impatient attitudes towards rape survivors (Suffla et al, 2001;Vetten and Haffejee, 2005).

The law too has been complicit in the discriminatory treatment of rape survivors. Common law, for example, elevated many stereotypes to the status of legal fact through the application of the cautionary rule to the testimony of sexual offences victims. This rule obliged judicial officers to treat rape complainants' evidence with caution and invited them to speculate about possible reasons for the falsity of rape allegations[11], thus ensuring that survivors of rape were the only crime victims to have been treated as inherently deceitful. The last remnants of this particular cautionary rule were abolished by the 2007 Sexual Offences Act.

Health sector response to rape

In 2002, the government took the decision to make anti-retroviral drugs, or PEP, available to rape survivors to prevent transmission of HIV. Later, via the 2007 Sexual Offences Act, this policy decision was elevated to the status of law, illustrating the extent to which HIV has come to overshadow all other health consequences of rape. Indeed, an earlier effort to legislate, at state expense, for the provision of medical care, treatment and counselling for all survivors who sustained physical, psychological or other injuries as a result of the rape was dismissed by legislators on the basis of being too costly (Vetten and Watson, 2009). Health services have thus inadvertently become PEP services. At the same time, the failure to embed PEP within comprehensive counselling and support services contributes to the low completion rate of PEP (Vetten and Haffejee, 2005).

Other aspects of inadequate healthcare services include:

• lengthy waits for medico-legal examinations (Human Rights Watch, 1997; Christofides et al, 2003; Vetten and Haffejee, 2005);
• delays in the provision of PEP (Schleifer, 2004; Vetten and Haffejee, 2005);
• lack of privacy and confidentiality during the medico-legal examination (Christofides et al, 2003; Vetten and Haffejee, 2005);
• the absence of referral systems, as well as counselling services (Suffla et al, 2001); and
• inadequate record keeping and documentation (Smythe et al, 2008; Vetten et al, 2008).

Analysis of policies and interventions

Two distinctions may be drawn between the various policies outlined in this chapter: that between formal and informal policy, and that between a policy decision and a policy. Formal policy refers to that which is written down, available in the public domain and formally recognised or authorised. Informal policy, by contrast, must typically be inferred from practice because there is generally no documentation defining and setting out the parameters of the particular practice. In addition, it has not been formally authorised or officially adopted. A policy decision is essentially a specific choice among alternatives and not to be conflated with policy, which generally unfolds over time to flesh out and substantiate the particular choice.

The specialist sexual offences courts offer a clear example of these distinctions. When the first such court was piloted in 1993, there was no national, official policy in support of such measures. Sexual offences courts were therefore an example of local-level, informal policy. But with the release of the DJCD's Gender Policy Statement and its stated commitment to establishing such courts nationally, it is clear that a decision was taken to create sexual offences courts as a matter of national policy. The policy itself, however, has not materialised and so the thinking around these courts remains confined to documents whose status is uncertain, such as the blueprint document for sexual offences courts. These documents are not necessarily binding and may not even enjoy much official recognition. As a consequence, the acceptance and implementation of such measures is likely to be weak for a number of reasons. First, many of these responses are ad hoc, rather than the consequence of thought-out strategy. Accordingly, their implementation is inconsistent and open to multiple interpretations. Because they are not planned, they are inadequately resourced and highly vulnerable to the personal preferences and whims of decision makers. This is particularly true of NPA interventions. While it is to their credit that they have introduced so many measures intended to improve the treatment of rape victims, none of these responses is firmly anchored within a comprehensive, overarching policy framework (which also reflects the failure of the DJCD, at the time of writing, to comply with its statutory obligation to develop the NPF).

The NPA's prominent role has also ensured that responses to rape are often driven by the interests and concerns of the prosecution services. The Uniform Protocol, for example, sees the NPA attempting to determine therapeutic services on the grounds that such services should not be allowed to interfere with the preservation of evidence. This highlights how the interests of the criminal justice system may take precedence over individual survivors' interests. By contrast, the DH policy notes that the healthcare needs of the patient take precedence over criminal justice system demands and challenges sexual assault care providers to think beyond the medico-legal evidentiary needs of the criminal justice system alone. These two approaches illustrate a paradoxical understanding of what qualifies as 'victim-centred' policy.

There is also no consistent understanding of, or support for, specialised responses to rape across departments. Indeed, only the DH's policy provides some concrete detail around the meaning of specialist services in practical terms. This ambivalence finds further expression in the near silence, in policy terms, on specialised psycho-social services to rape survivors.

Conclusion

South Africa's policy response to rape derives from two different sources: its commitment to gender equality and the pressure to be seen to be curbing crime. The latter has seen a drive to reduce the number of reported rapes, as well as the introduction of a harsh system of minimum sentencing. While there are many dimensions to the problem of rape (including its prevention), responses thus far have chiefly been confined to the criminal justice system, due in no small way to the rapid introduction of a variety of prosecutor-led responses to rape. However, the effects of many of these interventions have been lessened due to the fact that they are not located within a comprehensive and formalised policy framework, but fragmented across a range of documents of uncertain status. The approach of the NPA has therefore inadvertently reinforced the underdeveloped, under-resourced and barely enforceable nature of measures to support victims of sexual offences. Finally, policy is largely silent on how to respond to the majority of rape survivors – those who do not report the violation done to them. Indeed, current official approaches to reducing sexual violence in South Africa can only continue to silence rape survivors and thus undermine more positive policy responses.

Notes

[1] Apartheid categorised people into four different racial groups: white, coloured, Indian and African. In this chapter, the term black refers to all those disenfranchised on the basis of their skin colour, that is, those classified as coloured, Indian or African.

[2] Altbeker (2005 p 19) suggests that this is largely a function of South Africa's high rates of unemployment, which drag down the country's GDP per capita and so raise the ratio of average salaries to that figure.

[3] The terms 'victim' and 'survivor' are used interchangeably in this chapter. Some writers prefer to refer to those who have been raped as 'survivors' rather than 'victims' to emphasise the inherent strength needed to recover from rape. Others recommend using both terms but in a manner that differentiates between the stages of recovery from rape, with 'victim' more applicable to someone recently assaulted and 'survivor' more appropriate to someone increasingly able to cope with the effects of rape. Both terms are used to recognise that a violent crime has been inflicted on someone and to acknowledge the long-term work required to cope with rape (Campbell, 2001, p 2).

[4] This allows for the prosecution of third parties who force two unwilling parties into having sex.

[5] This is in terms of the 1997 Criminal Procedure Second Amendment Act.

[6] Life imprisonment is mandatory for those convicted of two or more offences of rape, but who have not yet been sentenced in respect of such convictions.

It should also be applied when the victim is younger than 16, or is physically disabled and rendered particularly vulnerable to victimisation due to her disability or is mentally ill. In circumstances where the rape is accompanied by the infliction of grievous bodily harm to the victim, where the victim was raped more than once, whether by the accused or by any co-perpetrator or accomplice, or where the victim was raped by more than one person, where such person acted in the execution or furtherance of a common purpose or conspiracy, life imprisonment should again result. Finally, if the accused knew that he had HIV/AIDS at the time of the rape, life imprisonment should also be imposed as the mandatory sentence. Deviation from any of these minima is only permissible when 'substantial and compelling circumstances' are found to exist.

[7] The guidelines for the Department of Correctional Services are addressed to institution committees and parole boards, as well as the heads of prisons and community corrections. They focus on the conditional and unconditional release of sex offenders, as well as the factors parole boards should take into account when considering the possible release of a sex offender. Procedures guiding institution committees' selection of programmes and interventions for sex offenders are also set out.

[8] This was conducted in the eight police areas of Western Metropole and Boland in the Western Cape; Port Elizabeth and Cradock in the Eastern Cape; Durban and Midlands in KwaZulu-Natal; and Johannesburg and East Rand in Gauteng.

[9] Mpumalanga, the worst-performing province, recorded a 3.1% conviction rate for cases involving children and a 4.1% rate for cases involving adults. Gauteng was the third worst-performing province, recording a 7% conviction rate for cases of child rape and 4.9% for adult rape. The best-performing province was the Northern Cape, which recorded a 16.8% conviction rate overall.

[10] Apart from the obvious details of the crime, the checklist also includes how the suspect approached and maintained control of the victim; the exact words spoken; a description of anything touched by the perpetrator; a continual description of the victim's state of mind during the whole incident; whether the suspect was circumcised or not; whether the suspect took steps to avoid leaving fingerprints; a full description of the suspect from head to toe; and the inclusion of the fact that the victim did not give consent, even if this is obvious.

[11] See for example *S v Balhuber* 1987 (1) PH H22 (A); *R v Rautenbach* 1949 (1) SA 135 (A); *R v M* 1947 (4) SA 489 (N); and Hoffman and Zeffert, 1998, pp 579-80.

Further reading

Artz, L. and Smythe, D. (2008) *Should we consent? Rape Law Reform in South Africa*, Cape Town: Juta and Co Ltd.

Vetten, L., Jewkes R., Fuller R., Christofides N., Loots, L. and Dunseith, O. (2008) *Tracking Justice: The Attrition of Rape Cases through the Criminal Justice System in Gauteng*, Johannesburg: Tshwaranang Legal Advocacy Centre, South African Medical Research Council and the Centre for the Study of Violence and Reconciliation.

References

Altbeker, A. (2005) *Paying for Crime: South African Spending on Criminal Justice,*. Pretoria: Institute for Security Studies.

ANC Today (2004a) vol 4, no 39, 7 October.

ANC Today (2004b) vol 4, no 42, 22-28 October.

Andersson, N., Mhatre, S., Mqotsi, N. and Penderis, M. (1998) *Prevention of Sexual Violence: A Social Audit of the Role of the Police in the Jurisdiction of Johannesburg's Southern Metropolitan Local Council*, Johannesburg: CIETafrica in collaboration with the Southern Metropolitan Local Council.

Artz, L., Smythe, D. and Leggett, T. (2004) *Reflections on Integrated Rape Case Management*, Cape Town: University of Cape Town.

Bronstein, V. (1994) 'The rape complainant in court: an analysis of legal discourse', in C. Murray (ed) *Gender and the New South African Legal Order*, Kenwyn: Juta and Co Ltd.

Campbell, R. (2001) 'Mental health services for rape survivors: current issues in therapeutic practice', www.mincava.umn.edu/documents/commissioned/campbell/campbell.html

Cape Argus (2000) 'Anger at ministers' rape remark on US TV', 4 February.

Christofides, C., Jewkes, R., Webster, N., Penn-Kekana, L., Abrahams, N. and Martin, L. (2005) '"Other patients are really in need of medical attention" – the quality of health services for rape survivors in South Africa', *Bulletin of the World Health Organization*, vol 83, no 7, pp 495-502.

Christofides, C., Webster, N., Jewkes, R., Penn-Kekana, L., Martin, L.J., Abrahams, N. and Kim, J. (2003) 'The state of sexual assault services: findings from a situation analysis of services in South Africa', www.mrc.ac.za/gender/sexualassault.pdf

Department of Safety and Security (1998) *In Service of Safety 1999-2004*, Government White Paper on Safety and Security.

Department of Social Development (1998) *Victim Empowerment Programme Policy Guidelines*, Pretoria: Department of Social Development.

DJCD (Department of Justice and Constitutional Development) (1998) *National Policy Guidelines for Victims of Sexual Offences*, Pretoria: DJCD.

Francis, V. (2000) *A Rape Investigation in the Western Cape*, Cape Town: Bureau of Justice.

Frank, C., Waterhouse, S., Griggs, R. and Rontsch, R. (2008) *Raising the Bar: A Review of the Restructuring of the SAPS Family Violence, Child Protection and Sexual Offences Units*, Cape Town: Resources Aimed at the Prevention of Child Abuse and Neglect.

Glanz, L. (1993) 'Crime in South Africa: incidence, trends and projections', in L. Glanz (ed) *Managing Crime in the New South Africa: Selected Readings*, Pretoria: Human Sciences Research Council.

Hoffman, L.H. and Zeffert, D.T (1998) *The South African Law of Evidence*, (4th edn) Johannesburg: Butterworth Publishers (Pty) Ltd.

Human Rights Watch (1997) 'Violence against women and the medico-legal system', *Human Rights Watch*, vol 9, no 4(A), www.hrw.org/reports/1997/safrica

Interdepartmental Management Team (2002) *Towards Developing an Anti-Rape Strategy: Report of the Interdepartmental Management Team*, Report by National Directorate of Public Prosecutions, South African Police Service, Department of Health, Department of Social Development and Monitor Group.

Jewkes, R. and Abrahams, N. (2002) 'The epidemiology of rape and sexual coercion in South Africa: an overview', *Social Science and Medicine*, vol 55, no 7, pp 1231-44.

Jewkes, R., Sikweyiya, Y., Morrell, R. and Dunkle, K. (2009) *Understanding Men's Health and Use of Violence: Interface of Rrape and HIV in South Africa*, Pretoria: Medical Research Council.

Office on the Status of Women (2000) *South Africa's National Policy Framework for Women's Empowerment and Gender Equality*, Pretoria: Office on the Status of Women.

SALC (South African Law Commission) (2000) *Conviction Rates and Other Outcomes of Crimes Reported in Eight South African Police Areas*, Research Paper 18, Project 82, Pretoria: SALC.

SALC (2002) *Sexual Offences: Process and Procedure*, Research Paper 102, Project 107, Pretoria: SALC.

SAPS (South African Police Service) (2005) *Strategic Plan for the SA Police Service 2005-2010*, Pretoria: SAPS.

SAPS (2007) *Crime in the RSA for April to March 2001/02-2006/07*, www.saps.gov.za/statistics/reports/crimestats/2007/_pdf/rsa_total. pdf

Schleifer R. (2004) 'Deadly delay: South Africa's efforts to prevent HIV in survivors of sexual violence', *Human Rights Watch*, vol 16, no 3(A), www.hrw.org/reports/2004/southafrica0304/southafrica0304.pdf

Smythe, D., Artz, L., Combrinck, H., Doolan, K. and Martin, L.J. (2008) 'Caught between policy and practice: health and justice responses to gender-based violence', in A. van Niekerk, S. Suffla and M. Seedat (eds) *Crime, Violence and Injury Prevention in South Africa: Data to Action*, Tygerberg: Medical Research Council, University of South Africa Crime Violence and Injury Lead Programme.

Stanton, S., Lochrenberg, M. and Mukasa, V. (1997) *Improved Justice for Survivors of Sexual Violence? Rape Crisis (Cape Town)*, African Gender Institute (University of the Western Cape), Human Rights Commission.

Steyn, E. and Steyn, J. (2008) 'Revictimisation of rape victims by the South African police service', *Acta Criminologica: CRIMSA Conference Special Edition 1*, pp 41-60.

Suffla, S., Seedat, M. and Nascimento, A. (2001) *Evaluation of Medico-legal Services in Gauteng: Implications for the Development of Best Practices in the After-care of Rape Survivors*, Johannesburg: UNISA Institute for Social and Health Sciences and Centre for Peace Action and MRC-Unisa Crime, Violence and Injury Lead Programme.

Sunday Independent (2004) 'Rape has become a sickening way of life in our land', 26 September.

Sunday Times (2009) 'How cops fiddle crime statistics', 4 July.

The Star (2006) 'Police in rape shame', 18 September.

The Star (2007) 'Rape statistics are skewed – experts', 7 July.

US Department of Justice (2007) *Crime in the United States 2007*, www.fbi.gov/ucr/cius2007/data/table_01.html

van Vuuren, R. and van Rooyen, J.H. (1994) 'Postponement in criminal cases in Pretoria magistrates' courts: a cost-effectiveness study', *South African Criminal Justice*, vol 1, pp 1-35.

Vetten, L. (2000) 'Paper promises, protests and petitions: South African state and civil society responses to violence against women' in Y.J Park and J. Fedler (eds) *Reclaiming Women's Spaces: New Perspectives on Violence Against Women and Sheltering in South Africa*, Johannesburg: Nisaa Institute for Women's Development.

Vetten, L. and Haffejee, S. (2005) 'Factors affecting adherence to post-exposure prophylaxis in the aftermath of sexual assault: key findings from seven sites in Gauteng Province', Report prepared for the Gauteng Department of Health, www.csvr.org.za/docs/gender/factorsaffectingadherence.pdf

Vetten, L., and Motelow, D. (2004) 'Creating state accountability to rape survivors: a case study of the Boksburg Regional Court', *Agenda*, vol 62, no 2,1, pp 45-52.

Vetten, L. and Watson, J. (2009) *Engendering the Parliamentary Agenda: Strategic Opportunity or Waste of Feminist Energy?*, Cape Town: Gender Advocacy Project and Tshwaranang Legal Advocacy Centre.

Vetten, L., Jewkes, R., Fuller, R., Christofides, N., Loots, L. and Dunseith, O. (2008) *Tracking Justice: The Attrition of Rape Cases through the Criminal Justice System in Gauteng*, Johannesburg: Tshwaranang Legal Advocacy Centre, South African Medical Research Council and the Centre for the Study of Violence and Reconciliation.

TEN

'Impressive progress alongside persistent problems': rape law, policy and practice in the United States

Lynn Hecht Schafran and Jillian Weinberger

Introduction

Between 1982 and 1999, in response to judicial education programmes exploring gender bias in the courts initiated by the National Judicial Education Program to Promote Equality for Women and Men in the Courts (a project of Legal Momentum in cooperation with the National Association of Women Judges, known as NJEP), almost all the state supreme courts across the United States established high-level task forces to investigate gender bias in their own state court systems and recommend reforms[1]. With respect to rape, the task forces concurred that these cases are often viewed from the wrong end of the telescope, with the complainant rather than the defendant being put on trial. The conflicting stereotypes about women's sexuality – either purity incarnate or seductive temptress – led to the victim's clothing, demeanour, conduct, associations and lifestyle rather than the accused's threats and use of force becoming the focus. Although there was evidence that courts were treating stranger rape cases with greater seriousness and sensitivity than in the past, non-stranger rapes, which constitute the vast majority of rape crimes, were still minimised and trivialised. Minnesota Supreme Court Justice Rosalie Wahl, chair of her state's task force, stated:'Judicial procedures for handling "acquaintance rape" promises to be one of the major upcoming issues with which the legal system must learn to deal effectively and with fairness to the victim' (quoted in Schafran, 1990, p 30; NJEP).

Many states then established standing court committees charged with implementing the task forces' recommendations. 'Impressive progress alongside persistent problems' was the phrase coined by New York

State's Chief Judge, Judith Kaye, to capture the impact of the New York Committee on Women in the Courts on its 20th anniversary, and it is the perfect phrase for summarising rape law, policy and practice in the United States.

Since the US women's movement initiated a major rape reform movement in the 1970s, there have been significant law reforms, such as elimination of the resistance requirement and the marital rape exemption. In 1994, Congress passed the 1994 Violence Against Women Act, since reauthorised twice, which enacted law reforms such as barring polygraphs for rape victims and sent $4 billion to individual states to improve every aspect of preventing and responding to all forms of violence against women. Services for rape victims improved with the advent of specialised victim advocates, medical personnel, psychological counselling and organisations focused on victims' needs. Research with offenders yielded insights into who they are, how they operate and how the law should deal with them. Education about the myths and realities of rape for police, prosecutors, judges and probation officers improved the criminal justice system's response. Despite this impressive progress, problems persist. Many justice system professionals, members of the media and the public and victims themselves adhere to myths and stereotypes about rape that undermine the effectiveness of these improvements and reforms. This chapter discusses the successes of the rape law reform movement, as well as the cultural and other barriers that continue to prevent fair treatment of rape cases.

United States context: victims, offenders and convictions

Victims

Accurate data are essential to every aspect of rape and sexual assault: prevention, victim services, concerns of specific populations, media reporting, public education and the justice system's response. In the US, the gold standard for studies of female victims is research from the Crime Victims Research and Treatment Center at the Medical University of South Carolina, *Rape in America* (Crime Victims Research and Treatment Center, 1992) and *Drug-facilitated, Incapacitated, and Forcible Rape: A National Study* (Kilpatrick et al, 2007). According to the latter study, in 2006, approximately 800,000 women were subjected to forcible rape, 300,000 women were subjected to drug-facilitated rape involving drugs or alcohol deliberately administered by the perpetrator, and 300,000 women were victims of incapacitated rape, that is, rape committed when they had voluntarily ingested drugs or alcohol and were too high to consent. According to this study, 18% of US women have been raped at least once in their lifetime and only 16% of victims reported to law enforcement. After analysing data from methodologically comparable studies conducted in 1991, 1995 and 2006, the researchers concluded: 'There is no evidence that rape in America is a smaller problem than it was 15 years ago, and there is no evidence that women are more willing to report rape cases today than they were 15 years ago' (Kilpatrick et al, 2007, pp 2, 62).

The US government collects and publishes national rape statistics through the Department of Justice Bureau of Justice Statistics (BJS), but its data are highly problematic. BJS uses flawed methodologies to collect data on rape and sexual assault, sharply underestimating the number of victims and overestimating the rate at which victims report. This is of great concern because BJS enjoys particular credibility and the statistics are used by the media (Kilpatrick and MacCauley, 2009; Schafran and Weinberger, 2009).

There is less research on male and same-sex victims, but it is believed that male victims are even less likely than female victims to report because of the even greater stigma for victimised men. According to the most current data available, 97,748 men were raped in 1995, and 2.8 million US men (3%) have been forcibly raped at some point in their lives (Tjaden and Thoennes, 2006).

Offenders

National data document that the most rape victims are women and most perpetrators are men (Tjaden and Thoennes, 1998). Researchers have often wondered at the large number of rape victims compared with the small number of men reported for committing these assaults. Since studies document that few victims report, researchers have begun to examine the phenomenon of 'undetected rapists' – offenders who commit rapes that are never reported. By asking behaviourally-based questions that do not label the offender's conduct (for example, *not* 'Have you ever raped a woman?', but rather, 'Have you ever obtained sexual intercourse with a woman by deliberately getting her too drunk to resist?' (Lisak and Roth, 1988, Appendix)), several studies have found that men freely describe acts that meet the legal definition of rape or attempted rape for which they were never reported. For example, in a study of 1,882 men at a north-east 'commuter' university whose students are diverse in age and ethnicity, 6.4% of these men self-reported acts met the legal definition of these crimes. In most of these 120 cases, the men concerned (63%) committed multiple assaults, with an average of 5.8 rapes per repeat offender. These 120 men committed a total of 483 rapes and attempted rapes and 49 sexual assaults, none of which were ever reported (Lisak and Miller, 2002). This offender research documents that a small number of men are committing a large number of rapes without legal consequences.

Conviction rates

The BJS method for determining US conviction rates – as a percentage of reported rapes or cases in which there was an arrest – presents a highly distorted picture of the degree to which US sex offenders are held accountable. In 1999, the National Center for Policy Analysis reported that *if* the crime is reported to police, the offender has a:

- 50.8% chance of being arrested;
- of these, 80% will be prosecuted;
- of these, 58% will be convicted of a felony;
- of these, 69% will go to prison;
- overall, a sex offender has a 16.3% chance of going to prison *if* the case is reported. (National Center for Policy Analysis, 1999, p 9)

According to government statistics, in 2004, 62% of those arrested for rape were convicted (BJS, 2008). However, given the small percentage of rapes that are reported – according to Kilpatrick (2007), only 18% of forcible rapes and 10% of drug-facilitated and incapacitated rapes are reported – and the fact that only half of reported cases result in arrest, the real picture emerges only when convictions are presented in comparison with victimisation data.

The US Senate Judiciary Committee reported in 1993 that only 1.9% of female victim sexual assaults resulted in prison for the offender (Majority Staff of the Senate Judiciary Committee, 1993). A 2005 study by a prominent U.S. researcher using the same methodology found that only 0.35% of female victim rape cases resulted in offenders' imprisonment – a significant decrease over time (Koss, 2006).

A boon to conviction rates in recent years is the advent of sexual assault forensic examiners (SAFEs) and sexual assault nurse examiners (SANEs). These are medical personnel specially trained to examine rape victims to determine their medical needs and collect any physical evidence in a 'rape kit' to be tested if the victim decides to report to law enforcement. If the case goes to trial, the SAFE or SANE is available to testify about how they collected the evidence and what they found, such as DNA and external and internal bruising. The Boston, Massachusetts Sexual Assault Nurse Examiner Program reported that since 1998 there has been a conviction rate of over 90% in the adult and child rape cases in which a SANE collected evidence and testified in court (WCVB TV Boston, 2009).

Legal framework

US law is a combination of statutes enacted by a legislature and the interpretation and application of these statutes by individual trial judges and appellate judges who sit in panels. Each state and the federal system have its own rape laws and case precedents. The New York State statute is typical:

> 'A person is guilty of rape in the first degree when he or she engages in sexual intercourse with another person:
> 1. By forcible compulsion; or
> 2. Who is incapable of consent by reason of being physically helpless; or
> 3. Who is less than eleven years old; or
> 4. Who is less than thirteen years old and the actor is eighteen years or more.'

Other parts of the statute address oral, anal, digital and foreign object rape; victims' inability to consent because of mental disability or mental incapacitation including drug-facilitated rape; and statutory rape (New York Penal Law, s 130).

Of the few rapes that are prosecuted, the majority are prosecuted in state systems. A rape defendant can plead guilty to the charge, plea bargain to a lesser charge and shorter sentence, or plead not guilty and go to trial. Defendants are sometimes eager to plead to a lesser charge for a non-sexual offence (for example, plead to assault instead of sexual assault), so they do not risk having to register as sex offenders if they are found guilty at trial. Most rape cases that go to trial are heard by a jury, although the defendant may request to have the case tried by a judge.

A US criminal defendant is presumed innocent until proven guilty beyond a reasonable doubt. This is an established, apparently unremarkable legal principle, but it creates unique problems for rape victims. Rape is the only crime for which consent is a defence. Assault victims do not have to prove that they did not consent to be punched. Robbery victims do not have to prove that they did not consent to hand over their cash. But in rape cases, even though officially it is the defendant on trial, in practice it is the victim who must prove that she did not consent. Some countries place the burden of proving consent in a rape case on the defendant and some start from a neutral position. But conceptually, US law presumes that every woman says yes to every man every time he wants sex, unless she can prove beyond a reasonable doubt that she refused. A few states ameliorate this anomaly by defining physical force as any act against the victim's free and affirmatively given permission, making the issue not what the victim did to show non-agreement, but what she did to actually show agreement to the act. Even with this modification, securing a conviction in any rape case is a steep uphill climb.

To understand the evolution of US rape law, it is essential to understand the myths and stereotypes about rape that still pervade society. Rape myths are 'beliefs that are generally false but widely and persistently held, and that serve to deny and justify male sexual aggression against women' (Lonsway and Fitzgerald, 1994, p 134). They include the belief that 'real rape' involves a stranger jumping out of the bushes with a weapon; that 'real victims' sustain serious, visible injuries and immediately report to the police; that women routinely lie about rape; that women who have been drinking, taking drugs, wearing revealing clothing or walking alone at night 'deserve' to be raped; that victims will show just the right amount of emotion on the witness stand, neither stoic nor 'hysterical'; and that rapists are so deviant in their appearance and behaviour that they can readily be distinguished from the ordinary man.

Historically, US rape law derived from British common law and like its progenitor was a quagmire of sexist stereotypes and acute fear of false accusations. Statutes and case law made it all but impossible for a victim without serious physical injuries even to have her case indicted, much less to secure a conviction. The rape law reform movement initiated in the 1970s has had considerable success and is still ongoing.

Before the law reform movement

Limited definitions of rape, rape victims and offenders

Before reform, rape was ubiquitously defined as an act forcibly committed by a male against a female not his wife, and the act was sexual intercourse (that is, penile/vaginal penetration) only. Neither men nor wives could be victims. Women could not be offenders. Anal, oral, digital and object penetration were not perceived as 'rape'.

Victims' sexual history on trial

Courts assumed that a woman who had said 'yes' to any man other than her husband after their marriage would say 'yes' to any man at any time. Thus it was appropriate to cross-examine an alleged rape victim about her entire sexual history. As the Georgia Supreme Court held in 1955:

> In prosecutions for rape, the defense may introduce evidence tending to prove the previous unchaste character of the female; this evidence is admissible for two purposes: one, to discredit her as a witness, and the other to disprove the charge that the intercourse was forcible and against her consent. (*Frady v State*, 1955)

Lord Hale Jury Instruction

In 1736, British Chief Justice Sir Matthew Hale wrote that rape is 'an accusation easily to be made, hard to be proved, and harder to be defended by the party accused, notwithstanding his innocence' (Hale, 2003 [1736], p 635). US courts adopted this statement, known as the 'Lord Hale Jury Instruction', and until the 1980s and 1990s, US judges gave juries the instruction in every sexual assault case. A typical instruction read:

> A charge such as that made against the defendant in this case is one which is easily made and once made difficult to defend against even if you think that person is innocent. Therefore, the law requires that you examine the testimony of the female person named in the Information with caution. (Schafran, 1985, p 48)

In no other category of crime were juries specially cautioned to be sceptical of the alleged victim.

Resistance and corroboration requirements

The resistance and corroboration requirements similarly reflected mistrust of women and fear of false accusations. Rape statutes codified this mistrust by defining the crime as penetration 'by force and against her will' (Spohn, 1999, p 123). The victim had to fear death or serious physical injury and demonstrate her lack of consent by resisting. Some states required 'earnest resistance' and some demanded 'utmost resistance'; either way, women's testimony alone was not sufficient. Prosecutors had to have corroborative evidence – injuries, torn clothing, witnesses – to prove that there was a rape and that the victim had done everything in her power to resist (Anderson, 2004a). Given that rape typically happens without witnesses and, contrary to myth, rarely results in visible physical injuries, it is no surprise that the corroboration and resistance requirements meant few convictions.

Marital rape exemption

Before law reform, prosecuting rape of a spouse was legally impossible because every state had a complete marital rape exemption (Schafran et al, 2008). Cultural assumptions regarding rape in marriage abounded, as exemplified by California State Senator Bob Wilson's remark to advocates who sought to abolish the marital rape exemption in his state: 'If you can't rape your wife, who can you rape?' (quoted in Eskow, 1996, p 689).

Women were considered their husbands' property and their legal existence was incorporated into their husbands'. Charging a man with raping his wife would be equivalent to charging him with raping himself, a conceptual absurdity. The most enduring rationale for the marital rape exemption was the ongoing consent theory, first articulated by Sir Matthew Hale.

The marriage contract guaranteed ongoing consensual sexual relations between husbands and wives. No matter what the circumstances, a wife could never say 'no' (Hale, 2003 [1736]).

Reform and the limits of law reform

Over the past 40 years, US rape laws have been significantly reformed. These reforms have increased reporting, prosecutions and convictions, but they have not eliminated rape myths from being a barrier to fairness at every stage of the criminal justice process.

Rape shield laws

Rape shield laws bar questioning complainants about their sexual history apart from limited exceptions. Many legal scholars consider these laws the most important success of the rape law reform movement. Advocates argued that publicly detailing a complainant's sexual history deterred victims from reporting. Sociological evidence demonstrated that 'character assassinations' of victims who did report contributed to the high acquittal rate (Anderson, 2004a). Furthermore, advocates charged, the complainant's sexual history had no probative value. In most rape cases the issue is whether the complainant consented to sex with a specific person or persons on a specific occasion. Whether she consented before is irrelevant. These arguments proved persuasive: all 50 states and the federal system now have rape shield statutes (Galvin, 1986; National Center for Victims of Crime, 'Rape shield laws').

All rape shield laws allow judges discretion to admit aspects of a complainant's sexual history under certain limited circumstances after the defendant has made an offer of proof explaining why this evidence is necessary to a fair trial and the prosecutor has had an opportunity to object. Unfortunately, the exceptions sometimes swallow the rule.

The 2003-04 case of basketball player Kobe Bryant, accused of raping a woman in his Colorado hotel room, demonstrates judicial mishandling of a shield law exception. Colorado judges may admit sexual history evidence to prove that someone other than the defendant is the source of semen, or caused the victim's pregnancy, injury or sexually transmitted infection (Anderson, 2004b). The Bryant case complainant had internal and external injuries that she claimed Bryant inflicted during the rape. The defence claimed that another sexual partner caused her injuries and requested a pre-trial hearing to show cause why it should be allowed to have this evidence admitted at trial. The judge properly held the hearing, but he allowed Bryant's attorneys to subpoena the victim to ask her questions about her sexual history up to *one year prior* to the assault, and to present a parade of witnesses (NSVRC, 2004; Murphy, 2007). This is an absurd inquiry with respect to injury evidence, which should be limited to the few days prior to the alleged assault. Unsurprisingly, the complainant dropped her criminal charges against Bryant rather than endure a trial in which her sexual history would be rehearsed in front of a courtroom and, due to the extensive media coverage of the case, the world. She settled her case for a monetary award in a civil suit, a growing avenue of redress for US rape victims.

Corroboration, resistance and consent

The last state to eliminate the requirement that every element of the crime be corroborated was New York in 1974. Legislators substantiated their case for reform by citing crime statistics from 1969, a year in which there were 1,085 rape indictments and only 18 convictions (Andrias, 1992). Today, only three states continue to require corroboration for some sexual offences (Anderson, 2004a). Most states have either struck the resistance requirement from their rape statutes or explicitly state that consent must be 'freely given' (Spohn, 1999). Recent cases have held that a rape has been perpetrated if a woman initially consents to intercourse, then withdraws her consent after penetration, and the man does not desist. Despite reforms, juries and criminal justice professionals often continue to want rape charges 'corroborated' by physical injury. They consider injuries the essential signifier of resistance, which they equate to non-consent (discussed below).

Lord Hale Jury Instruction

Most states have eliminated the Lord Hale Jury Instruction from formal law and more than half now actively prohibit it (Anderson, 2004a). For example, after a judicial education programme about the under-reporting and under-prosecution of rape, the Oregon Supreme Court eliminated the instruction in 1983, stating: '[W]e find no reason to continue the institutional assumption that alleged rape victims are less trustworthy than other victims of crime' (*Oregon v Bashaw*, 1983, p 50).

Terminology

Because 'rape' is such a loaded word, rape reform advocates debated whether using different terminology would put focus on the fact that rape is about violence and power, not an irresistible sexual urge prompted by a mini skirt. With the hope that the former would prevail, several states changed their statutes to eliminate the word 'rape', substituting 'sexual assault', 'sexual battery' and 'criminal sexual conduct' (American Prosecutors Research Institute, 2006). These changes do not appear to have had any impact. Some argue that the substituted terms trivialise the crime and devalue the victim by blurring the fact that rape is not just a physical assault but also a uniquely horrific crime often called 'soul murder' (Giacopassi and Wilkinson, 1985).

Expert witness testimony

US rules of evidence provide that either party to a case may call an expert witness when there is subject matter beyond the ordinary understanding of the jury or judge. As research with rape victims expanded, advocates and prosecutors realised that it would be possible to help juries understand frozen fright, dissociation, absence of visible physical injuries, delayed reporting, post-rape contact with the offender, flat affect (absence of emotion) on the witness stand and other seemingly counter-intuitive victim behaviours through testimony by expert witnesses involved in or familiar with this research. Experts may not testify that they believe there was a rape. They may testify that a particular behaviour or lack of injury is consistent with there having been a rape, based on the research showing commonalities of victims' behaviours and injuries (National District Attorneys Association, 2007a, 2007b).

The judge may not call an expert but does decide whether the expert called will be allowed to testify. This depends on whether the individual's education and experience actually qualifies him or her as an expert on the issue in question, and on the judge's perception of the need for an expert.

Today, in all but two states, calling an expert in rape cases is an accepted practice that has proven very helpful to jurors. For example, psychologist Dr Janine D'Anniballe, Director of Access, Emergency, and Community Services at a Rape Crisis centre in Colorado, has been an expert witness in more than 40 criminal rape trials. Colorado jurors are allowed to question witnesses, and even after Dr D'Anniballe testifies, there are often repeated questions from jurors grappling with the fact that her explanation does not match their expectation of how a 'real' rape victim would behave. Colorado also permits post-trial jury questioning in which the attorneys and/or judge question the jurors about matters such as what evidence persuaded them and what evidence they felt was missing[2]. Jurors in Dr D'Anniballe's cases have said that the expert testimony was extremely helpful and that they would never have understood why they should convict without it. She has even had jurors contact her personally after trial to tell her how she helped them understand the case and thank her.

However, sometimes counsel fails to call an expert and judges refuse to allow expert testimony. For example, after an acquittal in a Wisconsin rape trial in which the victim showed little emotion during her testimony, the judge, a former sex crimes prosecutor, asked jurors whether it would have helped them to have an expert to explain why a rape survivor would display such a flat affect. They said that indeed it would.

Confidentiality of mental health records

Recent law reforms concern the confidentiality of rape victims' mental health records. A major advance in helping rape survivors was the 1970s research by Ann Burgess and Lynda Holmstrom (1977) that developed the concept of rape trauma syndrome. Subsequent research showed similarities between the psychological states of many rape survivors and Vietnam veterans, resulting in the diagnosis now called post-traumatic stress disorder.

The good news is that rape survivors can now turn to Rape Crisis counsellors and mental health professionals specially trained to help them heal. The bad news is that defence counsel regularly seeks access to victims' mental health records, claiming the need to review them for exculpatory evidence. Victims who want counselling and also want to report the crime often feel they must choose between their privacy and accessing the criminal justice system.

Privilege is a legal concept that protects designated information from disclosure (for example, attorney/client communications are privileged and thus completely confidential). The US Supreme Court first recognised the importance of protecting mental health records in the 1987 case *Ritchie v Pennsylvania* and by 1996 every state and the federal system protected communications between patients and their psychologist, psychiatrist, or psychiatric social worker (*Jaffee v Redmond*, 1996; Fishman, 2007).

These reforms have had a limited impact. State case law regarding privilege varies greatly. In six states, a complainant who asserts absolute privilege is barred from testifying. While some state courts have ruled that a complainant may testify even if she does assert absolute privilege, other states' intermediate appellate courts are divided on the issue (Fishman, 2007). Some state statutes grant privilege to victim communications with crisis counsellors who have 40 hours of training (such as Rape Crisis hotline volunteers). In other states, counsellors must be licensed by the state to maintain privilege (American Bar Association, Commission on Domestic Violence, 2007).

Defence counsel's demands for these records are a constant source of litigation. Some prosecutors fail to assert the victim's right to privilege. Some judges turn the records over to the defence without reviewing them, even when by statute the judge is supposed to determine whether there is any exculpatory material and turn over only that.

Private attorneys in criminal rape cases

Under US criminal law, the prosecutor represents the government, not the victim. Prosecutors sometimes fail to vigorously protect victims' rights, for example, failing to protect victims from defendants' efforts to improperly breach the rape shield law or obtain the victims' privileged mental health records. Sometimes courts rule that because prosecutors do not represent the victim, they lack standing to assert the victim's rights. Victims can retain private attorneys to represent their interest in the criminal trial. There are two US organisations specialising in this type of representation, the Victims Rights Law Center (www. victimrights.org) and the National Crime Victim Law Institute (www. ncvli.org), which specialises in rape cases. Both groups have had significant success in matters such as maintaining the confidentiality of victims' mental health records and private life and the right of a victim to be present at trial.

Marital rape exemption

Eliminating the marital rape exemption was a major goal of the first wave of the US women's movement that began in 1848. As the decades of struggle rolled on, the movement's focus turned to securing the right to vote in the mistaken belief that once women could vote a wide range of reforms would quickly follow. In reality, US women did not obtain the vote until 1920, and it was not until 1976 that any state eliminated its marital rape exemption. Thanks to another decades-long effort, by 2005 rape reform advocates had eliminated the complete marital rape exemption under all state, federal and military laws (Schafran et al, 2008).

But this reform is far from complete. In 26 states, certain rape crimes cannot be prosecuted if the victim and perpetrator are married, including rapes committed when the victim is incapacitated because of mental illness or intoxication. Four states allow lesser penalties for marital rape or judicial discretion in sentencing if the victim and defendant are married. Eleven states impose extra requirements to prosecute marital rape, including that the couple must be separated or divorced at the time of the rape, uniquely short time limits in which to report the rape, and additional corroborative requirements to demonstrate force or violence. Shockingly, four states have extended the exemptions in their marital rape statutes to unmarried intimate partners or cohabiting persons (Schafran et al, 2008).

Marital rape remains largely unreported. This is of particular concern because research documents that women subjected to forced sex in addition to physical violence are seven times more likely to be killed than women subjected to physical violence alone (Campbell et al, 2003; NJEP, 'Intimate partner sexual abuse', module IV, 2008).

Prior bad acts evidence

US defendants must be convicted on the evidence respecting the particular crime with which they are charged, not their propensity to commit this type of crime as evidenced by their criminal history. Thus, the circumstances under which defendants' 'prior bad acts' may be admitted are extremely limited. Recognising that despite law reform rape complainants are still viewed with unique scepticism, making it difficult to secure a conviction on the testimony of one victim alone, Congress, as part of the 1994 Violence Against Women Act, amended the Federal Rules of Evidence to provide that 'In a criminal case in which the defendant is accused of an offense of sexual assault, evidence of the defendant's commission of another offense or offenses of sexual assault is admissible and may be considered for its bearing on any matter to which it is relevant' (FRE 413). The Federal Rules of Evidence are often a model for state evidence rules, and many states have become more open to admitting evidence of prior sexual assaults, whether or not the victim reported to the police, if the judge is satisfied that the claims are credible and admitting the evidence would be 'more probative than prejudicial'.

The critical difference prior bad acts evidence can make is seen in a 1991 case in which the late Senator Ted Kennedy's nephew, William Kennedy Smith, was charged with 'sexual battery' – Florida's statutory term for rape. After Smith was acquitted, one of the most prominent US writers on high-profile criminal cases wrote 'The verdict ... [was] a surprise to no one. From the moment on the first day of the trial when Judge Mary Lupo disallowed, without comment, the testimony of the three other women – a doctor, a medical student, and a law student ... who claimed they were sexually assaulted by Smith between 1983 and 1988, the die was cast' (Dunne, 1992).

Barriers to progress

Adherence to rape myths: a persistent problem

Despite law reform, belief in rape myths persists. Judges, juries, police, prosecutors, the media, and victims themselves are not exempt from the cultural stereotypes that the sexual assault legal framework expressed for so long:

> [T]he reality is that everyone in our society is exposed to the same cultural messages about sexual assault, and they inevitably influence how we think about it. Because these are societal stereotypes, they impact not only jurors but also other professionals involved in sexual assault response (e.g., law enforcement professionals, forensic examiners, victim

advocates, prosecutors, and other professionals). (Lonsway et al, 2009, p 3)

The myth of rampant false allegations

Despite publication of rigorous research documenting a minimal false allegation rate (Lisak et al, 2010), the most influential myth about sexual violence that continues to infect the US justice system is the belief that women routinely lie about being raped. Police and prosecutors frequently want to polygraph rape complainants, a practice rejected by every credible agency that works on rape cases. The 2005 Violence Against Women Act provides that jurisdictions that polygraph rape victims will be ineligible for particular government grants (Lisak, 2007). If a police officer or prosecutor threatens to polygraph a rape victim, that victim may feel that her allegations are not believed and recant in order to end her involvement with the criminal justice system.

Police adherence to rape myths

Because police are the criminal justice system's 'gatekeepers', their response to rape victims is highly consequential. Unfortunately, many still trivialise the crime and subscribe to rape myths that completely undermine their investigations and interactions with victims.

A major US concern is police devaluation of rape and rape cases, especially where the victims are women from low-income or ethnic minority backgrounds. In 1999, *The Philadelphia Inquirer*, Pennsylvania's leading newspaper, reported that for nearly 15 years the Philadelphia police department's sex crimes unit deliberately miscoded thousands of rape cases so as not to be bothered investigating them. A former rape squad supervisor noted that many of these victims were low-income women from dangerous neighbourhoods and told one reporter: 'If it was from a shady part of the city, who's going to complain? These people are from the inner city' (quoted in Fazollah et al, 1999).

A current nationwide US police scandal is the enormous backlog of untested rape kits. Whether or not they want to report immediately to law enforcement, US rape victims can go to a hospital emergency room for a forensic sexual assault examination to gather physical evidence from their body and clothing. This evidence is collected and secured in a rape kit that is submitted to the police for testing if the victim decides to report. These kits are crucial for obtaining the DNA of the accused and can prove there was sexual contact when the defendant denies it. In a stranger case, DNA can prove the identity of the rapist.

However, because of the pervasive influence of television shows such as CSI: Crime Scene Investigation, juries expect to see DNA even in non-stranger, consent defence rape cases where the DNA proves nothing. A recent survey of 1,000 prospective jurors intended to test the 'CSI effect' found a uniquely high demand for scientific evidence in rape cases and that 'only 14 percent of respondents said that they would find a defendant guilty in a rape case if the victim's testimony was presented without any scientific evidence' (Shelton, 2008).

The rape kit examination is long and harrowing for the already traumatised victim, who endures it with the expectation that the kit will be tested and will provide vital evidence if she prosecutes. A recent investigation of 24 US cities found 20,000 untested rape kits and massive disparities in the time it takes to have a kit tested. Victims are horrified when they learn that their kits have never been tested. There are also cases where rapists who could have been detected have gone on to rape again because the rape kit taken from their first victim was not tested until years later when the rapist's name came up in a subsequent case. The difference prompt testing of every kit can make is seen in New York City where this practice has resulted in a 70% arrest rate for reported rapes, three times the national average (Keteyian and Strickler, 2009).

One reason few rape victims report is fear of police mistreatment. Media reports about rape cases in which police begin their investigation by asking the victim what she was wearing persuade women that if they are victimised, the police will not be supportive. Whether a victim pursues a case through the criminal justice system is affected by how the police treat her (see the discussion above on polygraphs and recantation). The quality of police reports and investigations has a critical impact on the prosecution of rape cases. Too often police reports are sloppy or sketchy, with the result that the victim's trial testimony appears inconsistent with the police report. The police often fail to investigate the defendant, missing opportunities to identify other victims to testify at trial and enhance the initial victim's credibility. For example, in the William Kennedy Smith case referenced earlier, although investigators found three women other than the victim willing to testify to Smith's assault on them, many other victims were identified subsequent to trial (Dunne, 1992).

Studies document that in reported rape cases in which the victim identifies the offender, police are more likely to refer stranger cases to a prosecutor than non-stranger cases, a strong indication that police believe stranger cases are more credible (Campbell and Johnson, 1997). Police are more likely to question suspects when they are strangers to the victim, when the victim has physical injuries, when there is a witness to the rape, and when the victim has suffered penile/vaginal penetration (Frazier and Haney, 1996). Given that most rapes are committed by someone known to the victim, that victims rarely have observable physical injuries, that even more rarely are there witnesses to the crime and that, legally, rape now includes anal, oral, digital and object penetration, this police mindset is completely counter to what it should be.

At the time of writing, police adherence to rape myths is literally on trial in a case pending before a federal appeals court in which a young woman was raped and robbed at gunpoint in the convenience store where she worked. She promptly reported to the police and underwent a forensic exam. Despite the fact that a nearly identical crime was perpetrated within a few miles shortly thereafter, the detective assigned to the case was so certain the victim was lying that he had her indicted for the robbery and false reporting. She spent five days in jail before her assailant was arrested in the midst of a third rape and confessed to the crime. The victim sued the detective and his police department for unlawful search, unlawful seizure, false imprisonment and malicious prosecution. The federal district court judge, as wedded to rape myths as the police detective, ruled against her, holding that there was enough inculpatory evidence for the detective to reasonably believe that she was lying about the rape. The 'inculpatory evidence' included the fact that while the rapist was holding a gun to her head, the victim 'failed' to press an alarm button that was within her reach (*Reedy v Evanson*, 2009).

Prosecutors

A US prosecutor must prove every element of the crime charged and proof must be 'beyond a reasonable doubt'. Before legal reform, the elements of rape statutes were so out of touch with the way rapes are typically perpetrated that most cases could not even be indicted. As described in the 'Legal framework' section above, statutes required that victims strenuously resist and that there be corroboration of every aspect of their account. Thus, for example, the typical victim who froze with fright or decided not to resist in order to survive could not even access the justice system.

Law reform has enabled prosecutors to indict and prosecute offenders at a much higher rate. Thanks to funding from the 1994 Violence Against Women Act and its 2000 and 2005 reauthorisations, there are excellent training programmes available to sex crimes prosecutors from entities such as AEquitas and the National Center for the Prosecution of Violence against Women (NCPVAW)[3]. Many prosecutors participate in these trainings with significant positive effects on their ability to try these cases (discussed below). Well-trained prosecutors have been able to secure convictions even for what have been called 'unworthy victims', for example, drug addicts, homeless people and prostitutes.

The problem is that myths and stereotypes still shape many prosecutors' handling of rape cases in two ways: prosecutors' own adherence to rape myths, and their belief that jurors in their community are so wedded to these myths that they will not convict in a case that runs counter to them. Some prosecutors concur with the head of the Queens, New York Sex Crimes Unit, Marjory Fisher, who says that if a sex crimes prosecutor has a great win/loss record, she is not trying the hard cases and educating her community. Others are more likely to agree with the Kentucky prosecutor who told the investigative reporter covering the backlog of untested rape kits discussed earlier that he did not bother testing the kit of a woman who claimed she was drugged and raped because his office made a 'judgement call' that the case was unwinnable because there were issues with the victim's memory and alcohol was involved. Given that most non-stranger rape cases involve alcohol, refusing to try a case because the victim drank is an untenable position for a prosecutor (Keteyian and Strickler, 2009).

Research documents that if a sexual assault victim is not considered credible because she does not fulfil certain stereotypes, it is unlikely that the prosecutor will proceed with the case (Frohman, 1991). Prosecutors are more likely to try the case if the victim sustains visible physical injuries (Frazier and Haney, 1996) and promptly reports to the police (Frohman, 1991). Given that most rapists inflict no physical injuries other than the rape itself and that of the small percentage of victims who do report, few do so immediately, even the number of cases a prosecutor may consider pursuing is unfairly restricted.

As with some policemen, some prosecutors devalue rape and allow defendants to plea bargain to minor crimes, with very serious repercussions. For example, in 1993 a Nebraska prosecutor allowed an 18-year-old charged with first-degree rape after a vicious four-hour assault on his 14-year-old date to plead to a misdemeanour and be sentenced to one year of probation. The defendant went on to sexually assault two women at his university – which, as is unfortunately often the case with US universities, did nothing about it – and another 14-year-old girl. Again he was indicted for a first-degree felony, and again he was allowed to plead down to a third-degree misdemeanour, sexual assault. The 1996 prosecutor later acknowledged that he did not bother to thoroughly read the defendant's file because even though the police reports detailed the 1993 victim's allegations of being raped repeatedly, he noted that it was a date rape allegation and assumed it had been prosecuted as a misdemeanour with no felony charge ever filed (Schafran, 2000).

Juries

Of the US rape cases that go to trial, most are tried before a jury of 12 individuals who must unanimously agree on the verdict. US juries are selected through a process in which they are questioned by the prosecutor, defence attorney and judge about matters such as whether they know the parties involved and whether they or someone close to them have been victims of a crime similar to that alleged in the current case. They are also asked questions relating to the case at bar. For example, in a marital rape case, a juror who does not believe a husband can rape his wife would be excused for cause.

The US jury system rests on the belief that judges and attorneys can select jurors who do not have – or can put aside – their biases, listen open-mindedly to the evidence, and follow the law as the judge instructs. However, research with rape case jurors shows that these cases are often decided on extra-legal factors relating to rape myths and jurors' psychological needs (Schafran, 2005). In the first of these studies, the researchers concluded that 'the jury chooses to redefine the crime of rape in terms of its notions of assumptions of risk' (Kalven and Zeisel, 1966, p 254). If the victim went to a bar, went to the defendant's home, or accepted a ride from him, she assumed the risk of rape.

In the 1980s, a team of social scientists conducted in-depth, 90-minute interviews with 331 men and women who had sat on rape case juries in Indianapolis. The researchers found that jurors made their decisions based on victims' 'character' and lifestyle, even where there was proof of use of a weapon or victim injury. Jurors were less likely to believe in the defendant's guilt when the victim reportedly drank or used drugs, was acquainted with the defendant, or engaged in sex outside marriage. Jurors disregarded the evidence and decided cases on the basis of their personal values. Despite the elimination of utmost resistance laws, 32% of these jurors believed that a woman's resistance to her attacker was a critical factor in determining the rapist's culpability and 59% believed a woman should do everything she can to repel her attacker (LaFree, 1989).

A particular difficulty is identifying the male juror who has engaged in conduct that meets the legal definition of rape, but has never viewed his behaviour as criminal. Such a juror may come to understand the true nature of his conduct during the trial and realise, consciously or subconsciously, that if he votes to convict the defendant he is convicting himself. Or he may identify with the behaviour and not think the defendant did anything wrong. In either case, he is likely to vote to acquit, no matter what the evidence (Schafran, 2005).

Seating an unbiased jury in a sexual assault case is a serious challenge. Untrained prosecutors do not know how to conduct the selection process. Some judges do not allow the time or the types of question necessary to uncover jurors' biases. Thus, despite law reform, rape myths and other extra-legal factors continue to be decisive in the outcome of rape cases.

Judges' attitudes toward rape cases

Many US judges are deeply committed to conducting rape trials that minimise retraumatisation of victims without undermining defendants' rights. These judges participate in judicial education about sexual violence, bring this information to their colleagues and the public, and provide leadership on these issues in the criminal justice system and the community. Their evidentiary rulings, opinions, sentences and interactions with victims in the courtroom reflect an understanding of matters such as frozen fright, the extreme difficulty of testifying about rape, and the profound victim impact of this crime in all its stranger and non-stranger configurations. But not every judge is immune to the myths and stereotypes about rape that pervade society.

In 1996, a federal appeals court decision exemplified judicial belief in the myth that rape is less harmful than other physical assault. A woman was raped at gunpoint in the course of a carjacking. The federal carjacking statute provides for an additional sentence if a carjacking victim sustains 'serious bodily harm', and the trial court imposed the extra sentence. The appeals court held that the rape was not 'serious bodily injury' warranting the extra sentence because the victim had no visible physical injuries (*US v Rivera*, 1996).

The myth that 'real rape' involves force or the use of a weapon shaped the Pennsylvania Supreme Court's decision in a 1994 case involving a female college student raped by a man she considered a friend in his college dorm room. Although the defendant acknowledged that she repeatedly said 'no', the court reversed his first-degree rape conviction, holding that the assault was not rape because the defendant did not use enough force to meet the statutory standard for forcible compulsion

(*People v Berkowitz*, 1994). Both of these cases prompted a legislative response (discussed later).

Sentencing

In the past, judges' sentencing decisions often did not reflect the serious trauma rape victims suffer. In 1993, the US Senate Judiciary Committee reported that nearly half of convicted rapists were sentenced to less than one year (Senate Judiciary Committee, 1993). At the other end of the spectrum were cases involving a white female victim and an African-American male defendant that resulted in the death penalty. The US Supreme Court has since ruled capital punishment for rape unconstitutional for adult and child victim rape (*Coker v Georgia*, 1977; *Kennedy v Louisiana*, 2008).

In the 1994 Violence Against Women Act, Congress increased the federal penalty for rape, which had been less than that for property crimes. This disparity prevailed in many states and has been rectified in recent years as states developed sentencing guidelines to ensure proportionality between the crime and the sentence, and that a defendant's sentence did not depend on the predilections of a particular judge. Of continuing concern, however, are prosecutors and judges who allow pleas and minimal sentences for rapists, or set probation conditions that fail to impose tight restrictions and allow offenders to attend sex offender treatment offered by unqualified providers.

Judges may also require restitution, ordering offenders to pay victims' costs, such as new locks and therapy. Victims may also seek reimbursement from their state crime victims' compensation board.

Analysis of policies and interventions

While rape myths and stereotypes remain pervasive, there have also been an extraordinary number of recent initiatives to prevent rape; to improve rape law, the justice system's response and services for victims; and to educate the public. This is why 'impressive progress alongside persistent problems' is the perfect phrase to summarise rape law, policy and practice in the US.

1994 Violence Against Women Act

In recognition of the severity of the crimes associated with domestic violence, sexual assault and stalking, Congress passed the 1994 Violence Against Women Act (VAWA) as part of the 1994 Violent Crime

Control and Law Enforcement Act. The protections and provisions afforded by this legislation were expanded and improved in the 2000 Violence Against Women Act and the 2005 Violence Against Women and Department of Justice Reauthorization Act.

The 1994 Bill, the brainchild of then Senator, now Vice President, Joe Biden, was a watershed, marking the first comprehensive federal legislative package designed to end violence against women. It was also a triumph for women's groups that lobbied hard to persuade Congress to legislate for federal protections for women on the grounds that states were failing in their efforts to address such violence. Since 1994, the Office on Violence Against Women – the US Department of Justice division that awards VAWA grant funds – has awarded nearly $4 billion to state, tribal and local governments, non-profit organisations and universities focused on ending violence against women (Office on Violence Against Women, 'The facts about the violence against women act').

Many VAWA provisions focus on rape. Community activism against rape began with the second wave of the feminist movement that started in the early 1970s[4]. Women organised speak-outs against rape, Take Back the Night marches, and the first US Rape Crisis centres in Berkeley, California and Washington, DC (Collins, 2009). For their first 20 years in existence, Rape Crisis centres faced a severe lack of funding, staff and other resources. VAWA fundamentally changed the treatment of US rape victims by providing consistent funding to Rape Crisis centres and hotlines, enabling these organisations to maintain and expand staff and resources, and investigate new ways of helping victims. For instance, VAWA funded Rape, Abuse, Incest National Network (RAINN), a national Rape Crisis organisation that maintains a toll-free Rape Crisis hotline routing calls from victims across the country to their local Rape Crisis centres and an online hotline to serve victims through online instant messaging. RAINN has served over a million callers since it began in 1994 (RAINN, 2009; RAINN, 'About us').

VAWA funds professional education for victim advocates, forensic sexual assault examiners, law enforcement, prosecutors, judges, court personnel and probation officers. There are now excellent police training programmes about sexual assault available from entities such as Ending Violence Against Women (EVAW) and the International Association of Chiefs of Police (IACP)[5]. Police officers from a wide variety of law enforcement agencies have used these programmes and successfully applied their lessons (Schafran, 2009).

VAWA funds have also vastly improved prosecutor education on sexual violence. The coordinator for all violence against women prosecutor education in Michigan recently recounted that VAWA funds enabled his office to train over 1,100 professionals in 2008. He wrote:

> I think what VAWA money has meant to Michigan prosecutors is that we have highly trained prosecutors who have access to the best practices, and who should see the value of working collaboratively in their communities. If we didn't have VAWA money, we would return to the days where prosecutors existed more or less on an island. I remember those days, and they weren't a lot of fun. (Violence against women prosecutor education coordinator, quoted in Schafran, 2009)

VAWA also funds judicial education about sexual assault. In the mid-1990s, Legal Momentum's NJEP, the organisation at which the authors of this chapter work, created a two-day curriculum titled 'Understanding sexual violence: the judicial response to stranger and nonstranger rape and sexual assault'. It provides current research on how different victims react during and after the assault, the neurobiology of trauma, sex offenders, sex offender treatment and sentencing, jurors' attitudes toward rape and the implications of all these issues for judicial responsibilities in a rape trial. VAWA funding enabled NJEP to present this curriculum in over 25 states and create a four-hour DVD version (NJEP, 2005), with most welcome results. For instance, after our 2009 'Understanding sexual violence' programme in Louisiana, three members of the state probation department who monitor sex offenders and attended the programme wrote to tell us that almost immediately afterwards, probation officers in their unit noticed a difference in sentencing and the treatment of victims on the part of judges who came to the programme (Schafran, 2000, 2009).

Responding to judges' need for distance learning, NJEP created an online resource entitled 'Intimate partner sexual abuse: adjudicating this hidden dimension of domestic violence cases' (available at www. njep-ipsacourse.org; the resource is free and open to all). This has been extremely well received, with two Wisconsin judges even developing a short in-person version that they presented at district court judges meetings through the state, highlighting the critical implications of forced sex in this context for risk assessment (Schafran, 2010).

Corrective legislation

Legislators have responded to court decisions based on rape myths by passing corrective legislation. After the Pennsylvania Supreme Court's decision in *People v Berkowitz*, discussed above, and in response to community outrage, the Pennsylvania legislature created a new offence of 'sexual assault', known as the 'no means no' law (*Definition of Offenses, Sexual Assault, Pennsylvania*).

The US Congress responded similarly to the First Circuit Court of Appeal's decision in *US v Rivera*, which held that rape is not 'serious bodily injury'. Congressman John Conyers quickly introduced the 1996 Carjacking Corrections Act, which amended the carjacking statute to make clear that rape in and of itself is serious bodily injury. Congressman Conyers noted the First Circuit's reliance on rape myths, stating: 'This legislation will correct a dangerous precedent that trivialised the brutal crime of rape. Any judge who can argue that rape is not a serious bodily injury needs to spend more time with rape victims' (quoted in McKim, 1996).

Congress is now trying to address the backlog of untested rape kits described above with a bipartisan Bill that would provide funding to police departments to test the kits. However, given that Congress appropriated funds for this purpose in 2004 and still the backlog persists, we would query whether new funds alone will be the cure.

Collaboration with advocates

The Philadelphia Inquirer's 1999 investigation of the city police department's systematic 'unfounding' of rape cases spurred an intense response from the Philadelphia women's rights community. Responding to their pressure, the police commissioner took action. In 2000, he reached out to several Philadelphia women's advocacy groups to form a committee to review all of the unfounded rape cases from the previous year. The Women's Law Project, Women Organized Against Rape and the University of Pennsylvania Women's Center, among others, joined this unprecedented collaboration between advocates and the police, which continues to this day (Fazollah, 2001). Carol Tracy, Executive Director of the Women's Law Project, recently reflected on the Philadelphia Police Department's remarkable turnaround 10 years after the *Inquirer's* original investigation, noting that the 'the greatest advance is in the way Philadelphia police treat those who report attacks' (Rubin, 2009).

Addressing rape in prison

US prison inmates, male and female, suffer high rates of sexual violence committed by other inmates and guards (Human Rights Watch, 2001; Amnesty International, 2006; Buchanan, 2007; Rothstein and Stannow, 2009). In 2003, Congress passed the Prison Rape Elimination Act, designed to develop national standards, gather statistics and establish the National Prison Rape Elimination Commission, a review panel charged with holding public hearings (Rothstein and Stannow, 2009). In 2009, the commission released a voluminous report with myriad recommendations including zero tolerance policies, strict guidelines concerning cross-gender supervision and searches, and external monitors and review boards. The commission also recommended that Congress amend the 1996 Prison Litigation Reform Act to change the requirements that prisoners exhaust all administrative remedies within the prison system before bringing a case to court, and that inmate victims must prove physical injuries to receive compensatory damages. The US Attorney General has one year from the time the commission released its report in June 2009 to establish national standards regarding prison rape (National Prison Rape Elimination Commission, 2009).

Sex offender treatment

Sex offender treatment is highly specialised, rigorous and long. Effective treatment programmes are usually based on a cognitive-behavioral model that teaches offenders how to recognise their own offence patterns to avoid relapse. Even though participation may reduce a sentence, many offenders avoid it because it is too emotionally painful.

Sex offender treatment is not consistently made available to incarcerated offenders. As of 2000, only 12 states have mandated that convicted sex offenders undergo treatment while in prison or on probation. In a number of jurisdictions where treatment is not mandatory, however, parole consideration and the earning of good time are contingent on treatment, and parole boards are significantly influenced by participation in programmes, triggering higher participation rates (West, 2000). A great deal of sex offender treatment is conducted with offenders on probation. A concern is treatment providers who are unqualified and judges and probation officers who approve individual psychotherapy as a condition of probation.

The first question always asked about sex offender treatment is, 'Does it work?' Early studies concluded that treatment programmes did not appear to reduce recidivism. More recent studies evaluating newer treatment methods indicate that programmes can lead to lower recidivism rates for motivated participants. The effectiveness of treatment depends on the attitude of the offender. Treatment is unlikely to change an offender's behaviour if he has a history of violence or other sexual assaults and if he displays elements of psychopathology (National Judicial Education Program, *Intimate Partner Sexual Abuse*, Module XII).

Sex offender management

Judges usually sentence sex offenders to a period of probation after their incarceration. Sometimes the sentence is probation only, with conditions of release. Sometimes after incarceration, probation lasts a lifetime. All released sex offenders must register with their local law enforcement agency and regularly report on where they are living and working. Some states require sex offenders to register for life, while others require registration for a few years. Sex offender management laws vary according to jurisdiction. Restrictions may include no contact with victims and/or minors, limited internet access, no alcohol and drug use, and restrictions on where offenders can live, work, and travel (Center for Sex Offender Management, *Frequently Asked Questions*).

In the US today, anyone can go online and learn from their state sex offender registry where sex offenders are living. These registries create a false sense of security because they focus on 'stranger danger' when most sexual assaults are committed by someone the victim knows.

Sex offender residency restrictions are particularly strict in some jurisdictions. Many cities in Florida, for example, bar registrants from living within 2,500 feet of schools, parks and playgrounds. Critics argue that this legislation limits where sex offenders can live to the point that many are now homeless. In 2009, investigations by the media revealed that Florida's severe residency restrictions forced a colony of homeless offenders to seek refuge under a bridge in Miami. Homeless offenders are difficult to treat and nearly impossible to track: when Iowa passed sex offender residency restrictions, the number of offenders who absconded doubled in six months. Researchers conclude that there is little evidence that residency restrictions help protect citizens from sexual predators (Skipp and Campo-Flores, 2009, pp 48, 50).

Beginning in the 1990s, states enacted civil 'sexual predator laws' to continue the confinement of offenders considered too sexually violent to be allowed back into the community. Civil commitment programmes in 19 states now allow the criminal justice system to involuntarily confine sex offenders beyond their prison sentences. Offenders are screened for commitment at the end of their sentence and most stand trial before a judge or jury who decide whether to commit them. The US Supreme Court's 1997 decision in *Kansas v Hendricks* upheld the constitutionality of these programmes, but their effectiveness is uncertain and their price is high: these programmes cost taxpayers approximately $450 million per year. Even though the commitment is for purposes of treatment, offenders are not required to participate in treatment during their stay – in fact, most offenders' attorneys tell their clients not to participate, for fear that they will disclose additional sex crimes previously unreported to law enforcement. Since 1990, out of nearly 3,000 offenders, only 50 have successfully completed treatment and been released (Davey and Goodnough, 2007).

Specialised sex offence courts

A few states have specialised sex offence courts modelled on the specialised domestic violence courts popular across the US. In New York State, which has five sex offence courts, the court's presiding judge meets periodically with all the stakeholders: the district attorney's office, the public defender, victim advocates, sex offender treatment providers, probation officers, the mental health agency that deals with civil commitment and others. The focus is not on individual sex offence cases, which would violate the code of judicial conduct, but on process and best practice for handling every aspect and phase of these cases. The Office on Violence Against Women has a new grant programme, created by the 2005 Violence Against Women Act reauthorisation, which provides funding and technical assistance to state courts to encourage them to establish these specialised sex offence courts.

Pursuing justice in civil court

In addition to, or instead of, a criminal case, US rape victims can bring a completely separate civil suit to seek monetary damages from the offender and/or a third party whose actions facilitated the rape. Offenders can be sued on grounds such as battery and intentional infliction of emotional distress. Suits against third parties involve situations such as a shopping mall failing to light its parking lot at night or a motel failing to provide effective locks on its doors.

In the federal system, Title VII of the 1964 Civil Rights Act bars sex discrimination in employment. Under this US law, sexual harassment is considered sex discrimination and rape is considered sexual harassment. Thus, someone raped by her supervisor or co-worker may sue her employer in the civil courts.

US schools, colleges and universities are subject to Title IX of the Education Amendments of 1972, which bars sex discrimination in federally aided educational institutions. Here, too, sexual harassment is considered sex discrimination and rape is considered sexual harassment. Many students have brought Title IX suits against universities for their failure to respond to complaints of rape by fellow students. US universities are notorious for failing to take action, especially when the student rapist is a prominent school athlete. For example, the University of Georgia (UGA) recruited and admitted a student athlete who then participated in the gang rape of an undergraduate. It was later revealed that UGA knew that this student had been expelled from one college for sexually assaulting two women with whom he worked and dismissed from the basketball team at another college for incidents involving sexual harassment (*Williams v Board of Regents of the University System of Georgia*, 2007).

An exhaustive new study by the Center for Public Integrity reveals the failure of higher education institutions to deal properly with sexual assault. Students who report to school disciplinary panels are often forced to sign confidentiality agreements, barring them from pursuing the case in the criminal or civil courts. Students are often forced into mediation sessions with school officials that supposedly serve to counsel and settle 'conflicts' between the victim and the offender. Higher education's inadequate response to sexual assault is of particular concern because fewer than 5% of college victims report the crime and most transfer schools or drop out altogether (Fisher et al, 2000; Lombardi, 2009).

Conclusion

Forty years into the US rape law reform movement, the laws on the books have been vastly improved. The federal 1994 Violence Against Women Act and its 2000 and 2005 reauthorisations have made a striking difference in every aspect of the US response to sexual assault. Excellent educational materials on the dynamics of sexual assault and how best to investigate, prosecute, adjudicate and sentence these crimes are available in every component of the justice system. There have been significant successes, but adherence to rape myths and stereotypes is still the controlling factor in these cases. Comparing the data on victimisation and convictions, it is clear that still today only a tiny percentage of rapists are being held accountable – hence the title of this chapter, 'Impressive progress alongside persistent problems'.

Notes

[1] Learn more about NJEP at www.legalmomentum.org/our-work/njep

[2] For more information, see 'Colorado Jury Instructions, Chapter 1. General instructions prior to or during trial and upon discharge of jury, C. Discharge of fury, 1:16 Mandatory instruction upon discharge', www.loegalbears.com/cojury/papers/001.pdf

[3] Learn more about AEquitas at www.aequitasresource.org and NCPVAW at www.ndaa.org/ncpvaw-home.html

[4] The 'first wave' of the US women's movement in the late 19th and early 20th centuries began with a focus on marital rape reform, but soon changed its focus to political inclusion and voting rights for women. Women of colour have a long history of activism against rape in the US. At the turn of the 20th century, African-American women like Ida B. Wells organised against the lynching of black men (falsely) accused of raping white women by highlighting the rampant phenomenon of black women raped by white men (see, for example, Bevacqua, 2000).

[5] Learn more about EVAW at www.evawintl.org and the IACP at www.theiacp.org/PublicationsGuides/Projects/LeadershipInstituteonViolenceAgainstWomen/tabid/306/Default.aspx

Further reading

Andrias, R. (1992) 'Rape myths: a persistent problem in defining and prosecuting rape', *Criminal Justice*, vol 7, no 2, pp 2-7, 51-3.

Kilpatrick, D. et al (2007) *Drug-facilitated, Incapacitated, and Forcible Rape: A National Study*, Washington, DC: National Institute of Justice, www.ncjrs.gov/pdffiles1/nij/grants/219181.pdf

NJEP (National Judicial Education Program) 'Intimate partner sexual abuse: adjudicating this hidden dimension of domestic violence cases' (web resource), www.njep-ipsacourse.org

Schafran, L (1993) 'Writing and reading about rape: a primer', *St. John's Law Review*, vol 66, no 4, pp 979-1045.

References

American Bar Association, Commission on Domestic Violence (2007) 'Summary of domestic violence/sexual assault advocacy laws', www.abanet.org/domviol/docs/AdvocateConfidentialityChart.pdf

American Prosecutors Research Institute (2006) 'State rape statutes', www.ndaa.org/pdf/vaw_rape_statute.pdf

Amnesty International (2006) 'Abuse of women in custody: sexual misconduct and the shackling of pregnant women', www.amnestyusa.org/violence-against-women/abuse-of-women-in-custody/page.do?id=1108288

Anderson, M. (2004a) 'The legacy of the prompt complaint requirement, corroboration requirement, and cautionary instructions on campus sexual assault', *Boston University Law Review*, vol 84, pp 945-1022.

Anderson, M. (2004b) 'Time to reform rape shield laws: Kobe Bryant case highlights holes in the armor', *Criminal Justice*, vol 19, part 2, pp 14-19.

Andrias, R. (1992) 'Rape myths: a persistent problem in defining and prosecuting rape', *Criminal Justice*, vol 7, no 2, pp 2-7, 51-3.

Bevacqua, M. (2000) *Rape on the Public Agenda*, Boston, MA: Northeastern University Press.

Buchanan, K. (2007) 'Impunity: sexual abuse in women's prisons', *Harvard Civil Rights Civil Liberties Law Review*, vol 42, pp 45-87.

BJS (Bureau of Justice Statistics) (2008) 'Felony defendants in large urban counties, 2004 – statistical tables', Washington DC: US Department of Justice.

Burgess, A. and Holmstrom, L. (1977) 'Rape trauma syndrome', in D. Ness (ed) *The Rape Victim*, Dubuque, Iowa: Kendall/Hunt.

Campbell, J. et al (2003) 'Risk factors for femicide in abusive relationships: results from a multisite case control study', *American Journal of Public Health*, vol 93, no 7, pp 1089-97.

Campbell, R. and Johnson, C. (1997) 'Police officers' perceptions of rape: is there consistency between state law and individual beliefs?', *Journal of Interpersonal Violence*, vol 12, no 2, pp 255-75.

Center for Sex Offender Management, 'Frequently asked questions', www.csom.org/ref/ref.html#managing

Coker v Georgia 433 US 584 (1977).

Collins, G. (2009) *When Everything Changed: The Amazing Journey of American Women from the 1960s to the Present*, Boston, MA: Little, Brown.

Crime Victims Research and Treatment Center (1992) *Rape in America: a report to the nation*, http://academicdepartments.musc.edu/ncvc/resources_prof/rape_in_america.pdf.

Davey, M. and Goodnough, A. (2007) 'Doubts rise as states hold sex offenders after prison', *The New York Times*, 4 March, www.nytimes.com/2007/03/04/us/04civil.html

Definition of Offenses: Sexual Assault, Pennsylvania (18 Pa.C.S. § 3124.1).

Dunne, D. (1992) 'The verdict', *Vanity Fair*, March, www.vanityfair. com/magazine/archive/1992/03/dunne199203.

Eskow, L. (1996) 'The ultimate weapon? Demythologizing spousal rape and reconceptualizing its prosecution', *Stanford Law Review*, vol 48, pp 677-709.

Fazollah, M. (2001) 'Women activists monitor Philadelphia rape squad', *Women's E-News*, 19 February, www.womensenews.org/story/ rape/010219/women-activists-monitor-philadelphia-rape-squad

Fazlollah, M., Matza, M., McCoy, C.R. and Benson, C. (1999) 'Women victimized twice in police game of numbers', *The Philadelphia Inquirer*, 17 October, http://inquirer.philly.com/packages/crime/html/ sch101799.asp

Fisher, B., Cullen, F. and Turner, M. (2000) 'The sexual victimization of college women', National Institute of Justice, www.ncjrs.gov/ pdffiles1/nij/182369.pdf

Fishman, C. (2007) 'Defense access to a prosecution witness's psychotherapy or counseling records', *Oregon Law Review*, vol 86, pp 1-63.

Frady v State 90 SE2d 664, 665 (Ga 1955).

Frazier, P. and Haney, B. (1996) 'Sexual assault cases in the legal system: police, prosecutor, and victim perspectives', *Law and Behavior*, vol 20, no 6, pp 607-28.

Frohman, L. (1991) 'Discrediting victims' allegations of sexual assault: prosecutorial accounts of case rejections', *Social Problems*, vol 38, no 2, pp 213-26.

Galvin, H. (1986) 'Shielding rape victims in state and federal courts: a proposal for the second decade', *Minnesota Law Review*, vol 70, pp 763-913.

Giacopassi, D. and Wilkinson, K. (1985) 'Rape and the devalued victim', *Law and Human Behavior*, vol 9, no 4, pp 367-83.

Hale, M. (2003 [1736]) *Historia Placitorum Coronae: The History of the Pleas of the Crown*, Clark, NJ: The Lawbook Exchange Ltd.

Human Rights Watch (2001) 'No escape: male rape in US prisons', www.hrw.org/legacy/reports/2001/prison

Jaffee v Redmond, 518 US 1 (1996).

Kalven, H. and Zeisel, H. (1966) *The American Jury*, Boston, MA: Little, Brown.

Kennedy v Louisiana 554 US (2008).

Keteyian, A. and Strickler, L. (2009) 'Rape in America: justice denied', CBS News, 9 November, www.cbsnews.com/stories/2009/11/09/ cbsnews_investigates/main5590118.shtml

Kilpatrick, D. and MacCauley, J. (2009) 'Understanding rape statistics', *VAWnet*, http://new.vawnet.org/Assoc_Files_VAWnet/AR_RapeStatistics.pdf.

Kilpatrick, D.G., Resnick, H.S., Ruggiero, K.J., Conoscenti, M.A. and McCauley, J. (2007) 'Drug-facilitated, incapacitated, and forcible rape: a national study', National Institute of Justice, www.ncjrs.gov/pdffiles1/nij/grants/219181.pdf

Koss, M. (2006) 'Restoring rape survivors: justice, advocacy, and a call to action', *Annals of the New York Academy of Sciences*, vol 1087, pp 206-34.

LaFree, G. (1989) *Rape and Criminal Justice: The Social Construction of Sexual Assault*, Belmont, CA: Wadsworth Publishing Company.

Lisak, D. (2007) 'False allegations of rape: a critique of Kanin', *Sexual Assault Report*, vol 11, no 1, pp 1-2, 6, 9.

Lisak, D. and Miller, P. (2002) 'Repeat rape and multiple offending among undetected rapists', *Violence and Victims*, vol 17, no 1, pp 73-84.

Lisak, D. and Roth, S. (1988) 'Motivational factors in nonincarcerated sexually aggressive men', *Journal of Personality and Social Psychology*, vol 55, no 5, pp 795-802.

Lisak, D., Gardiner, L., Nicksa, S. and Cote, A. (2010) 'False allegations of sexual assault: an analysis of ten years of reported cases', *Violence Against Women*, vol 16, no 12, pp 1318-34.

Lombardi, K. (2009) 'Sexual assault on campus shrouded in secrecy', Center for Public Integrity, 1 December, www.publicintegrity.org/investigations/campus_assault/articles/entry/1838

Lonsway, K. and Fitzgerald, F. (1994) 'Rape myths in review', *Psychology of Women Quarterly*, vol 18, no 2, pp 133-64.

Lonsway, K., Archambault, J. and Lisak, D. (2009), 'False reports: moving beyond the issue to successfully investigate and prosecute nonstranger sexual assault', *The Voice*, vol 3, no 1, pp 1-12, www.ndaa.org/publications/newsletters/the_voice_vol_3_no_1_2009.pdf

Majority Staff of the Senate Judiciary Committee (1993) *The Response to Rape: Detours on the Road to Equal Justice*, Report prepared for the use of the Committee on the Judiciary, United States Senate, 103rd Congress, First Session, US Government Printing Office.

McKim, J. (1996) 'Congress bill reverses US court on rape case', *The Boston Globe*, 25 September.

Murphy, W. (2007) *And Justice for Some*, New York, NY: Penguin Group.

National Center for Policy Analysis (1999) 'Crime and punishment in America: 1999', Report prepared by M. Reynolds, www.ncpa.org/pdfs/st229.pdf

NCVC (National Center for Victims of Crime) (2010) 'Rape shield laws', www.ncvc.org/ncvc/main.aspx?dbID=DB_FAQ:RapeShieldLaws927

National District Attorneys Association (2007a) *Victim Responses to Sexual Assault: Counterintuitive or Simply Adaptive?*, American Prosecutors Research Institute, Special Topics Series, Alexandria: VA.

National District Attorneys Association (2007b) *Introducing Expert Testimony to Explain Victim Behavior in Sexual and Domestic Violence Prosecutions*, American Prosecutors Research Institute, Special Topics Series, Alexandria: VA.

National Judicial Education Program 'Intimate partner sexual abuse: adjudicating this hidden dimension of domestic violence', Web resource, www.njep-ipsacourse.org

National Judicial Education Program (2005) 'Understanding sexual violence: the judicial response to stranger and nonstranger rape and sexual assault', www.legalmomentu,m.org/our-work/njep/njep-sexual-assault.html

National Judicial Education Program, 'Task Forces on Gender Bias in the Courts', www.legalmomentum.org/our-work/njep/njep-task-forces.html

National Prison Rape Elimination Commission (2009) 'National Prison Rape Elimination Commission report', www.cybercemetery.unt.edu/archive/nprec/20090820155502/http://nprec.us/files/pdfs/NPREC_FinalReport.PDF, pp 3-24.

NSVRC (National Sexual Violence Resource Center) (2004) 'Recent rule in Kobe Bryant case assaults Colorado's rape shield and jeopardizes fair judicial process', Press Release, 18 March, www.nsvrc.org/news/press-releases/299

Office on Violence Against Women 'The facts about the violence against women act', www.ovw.usdoj.gov/ovw-fs.htm#fs-act

Oregon v Bashaw 296 Or. 50, 54, 672 Po. 2d 48, 50 (1983).

People v Berkowitz 415 Pa.Super. 505, 609 A.2d 1330 (1994).

RAINN (Rape, Abuse, Incest National Network) (2009) *Newsletter*, October. For more information, see http://apps.rainn.org/ohl-bridge

RAINN 'About us', http://rainn.org/about-rainn

Ritchie v Pennsylvania 480 US 39 (1987).

Rothstein, M. and Stannow, L. (2009) 'Improving prison oversight to address sexual violence in detention', American Constitution Society for Law and Policy Issue Brief, www.acslaw.org/files/Rothstein%20Stannow%20Issue%20Brief.pdf

Rubin, D. (2009) 'Philadelphia police upgrade handling of rape cases', *The Philadelphia Inquirer*, 28 September, www.philly.com/philly/news/local/62303547.html

Schafran, L. (1985) 'Eve, Mary, superwoman: how stereotypes about women influence judges', *The Judges Journal*, vol 24, no 1, pp 12-17, 48-52.

Schafran, L. (1990) 'Overwhelming evidence: reports on gender bias in the courts', *Trial*, vol 26, February, pp 28-35.

Schafran, L. (2000) 'Serial sex offenders in the courts', Speech at the American Psychological Association Annual Meeting, Washington, DC, 8 August.

Schafran, L. (2005) 'What the research about rape jurors tells us', Understanding Sexual Violence: The Judicial Response to Stranger and Nonstranger Rape and Sexual Assault, National Judicial Education Program, www.legalmomentum.org/our-work/njep/judicial-response.html

Schafran, L. (2009) Remarks for the panel, 'The impact of VAWA: billions (yes, billions with a "b") for prevention, victim services, law enforcement and the courts, and looking ahead to VAWA IV', Speech at symposium celebrating the 15th anniversary of the Violence Against Women Act, Georgetown Law Center, Washington, DC, 22 April, *Georgetown Journal of Gender and The Law*, vol XI, no II, (2010) pp 584-9.

Schafran, L. (2010) 'Risk assessment and intimate partner sexual abuse: the hidden dimension of domestic violence', *Judicature*, vol 93, no 4, January-February, pp 161-3.

Schafran, L. and Weinberger, J. (2009) 'New US crime reports: flawed methodology sharply underestimates rape rates against women and persons with disabilities', Legal Momentum blog, 26 October, http://legalmomentum.typepad.com/blog/2009/10/new-us-crime-reports-flawed-methodology-sharply-underestimates-rape-rates-against-women-and-persons-.html

Schafran, L., Lopez-Boy, S. and Davis, M. (2008) 'Making marital rape a crime: a long road traveled, a long way to go', *Connections*, vol 10, no 1, pp 15-21, www.wcsap.org/advocacy/PDF/CONNECTIONS_IPSV.pdf

Shelton, D. (2008) 'The "CSI effect": does it really exist?', *NIJ Journal*, no 259, www.ojp.usdoj.gov/nij/journals/259/csi-effect.htm

Skipp, C. and Campo-Flores, A. (2009) 'A bridge too far', *Newsweek*, 3 August, pp 46-51.

Spohn, C. (1999) 'Rape reform movement: the traditional common law and rape law reforms', *Jurimetrics Journal*, vol 39, pp 119-29.

Tjaden, P. and Thoennes, N. (1998) 'Prevalence, incidence, and consequences of violence against women: findings from the National Violence Against Women survey', National Institute of Justice and Center for Disease Control and Prevention, www.ncjrs.gov/pdffiles/172837.pdf

Tjaden, P. and Thoennes, N. (2006) 'Extent, nature, and consequences of rape: findings from the National Violence Against Women survey', National Institute of Justice, www.ncjrs.gov/pdffiles1/nij/210346.pdf

US v Rivera 1996 WL 338379 (1st Cir.).

US Department of Justice (2009) 'The Department of Justice's efforts to prevent staff sexual abuse of federal inmates', www.justice.gov/oig/reports/plus/e0904.pdf

WCVB TV Boston (2009) 'Sexual assault nurse program to be cut', 4 November, www.thebostonchannel.com/politics/21520330/detail.html

West, M., Hromas, C.S. and Wenger, P. (2000) *State Sex Offender Treatment Programs: 50-State Survey*, Colorado Springs, CO: Colorado Department of Corrections.

Williams v Board of Regents of the University System of Georgia 477 F.3d 1282 (11th Cir. 2007).

Index

The letter n following a page number indicates an endnote.